SMALL PROPERTY
PROPERTY
VERSUS
BIG
GOVERNMENT

SMALL PROPERTY
PROPERTY
VERSUS
BIG
GOVERNMENT
SOCIAL ORIGINS OF THE
PROPERTY TAX REVOLT
CLARENCE Y.H. LO

UNIVERSITY OF CALIFORNIA PRESS
Berkeley   Los Angeles   Oxford

University of California Press
Berkeley and Los Angeles, California

University of California Press
Oxford, England

Copyright © 1990 by The Regents of the
University of California

Library of Congress Cataloging-in-Publication Data

Lo, Clarence Y. H.
    Small property versus big government : social
origins of the property tax revolt / Clarence
Y.H. Lo.
        p.   cm.
    Includes bibliographical references.
    ISBN 0-0520-05971-9 (alk. paper)
    1. Property tax—California—Public
opinion—History. 2. Public opinion—
California—History. 3. Tax and expenditure
limitations—California—History. I. Title
HJ4121.C22L6   1990
336.22′09794—dc20   89-20228
                                                CIP

Printed in the United States of America

1 2 3 4 5 6 7 8 9

To my wife Laurie Castro Lo,
who put up with this and everything else

Contents

Preface

This is the story of citizens who were so outraged at their property tax bills that they stormed into city hall to protest. They were so angered when politicians ignored their problems that they gathered a million and a half signatures in California to place a proposal on the ballot cutting out two-thirds of the property tax. These were the taxpayers whose victorious campaign for Proposition 13 in 1978 set into motion political forces that reduced federal taxes and limited the revenues in cities and states throughout America.

Much has been written about the tax revolt, and about Proposition 13 in particular. This book, unlike others, does not focus on the effects of tax limitation on schools or city budgets. It does not particularly probe into the life and work of Howard Jarvis, the media-appointed hero of Proposition 13. Nor does it ask why millions of voters gave "Prop. 13" such a resounding endorsement. Between the exalted hero and the anonymous voter were the activists, who organized the fund raisers and made the speeches that gave the tax revolt its grass-roots strength. In their own communities, they were familiar faces; but to the world outside, they are still unknown.

The activists in the tax protest movement were the stewards of the great American Middle Class. They were proud of being small property owners—unlike the urban poor with no stake in society, and unlike those with great fortunes who surely, they thought, had been corrupted. But within that one, mythic middle class, lived an equally mythic truck driver and an electrical engineer.

Each owned a house on the opposite side of the same hill. The truck driver first saw California as he crossed the Colorado River in his dad's car on the family trek from Arkansas during the Great Depression. Later, he took out a Veterans Administration loan to buy a two-bedroom home on the inland side of the hill. By 1978, the real estate boom in California had driven up the price of that tiny home to $64,000, which yielded a tax bill of $2,000, four times his annual mortgage payments and 40 percent of the social security benefit that he was about to collect.

The engineer first saw California from 35,000 feet at Mach 0.8 as he was relocating, three months after President Kennedy had pledged to land a man on the moon. With his wife working as a part-time nurse, they could afford, so the realtor convinced them, to buy a four-bedroom house on the top of the hill, overlooking the ocean. But in 1978, after a pediatric neurologist bid on and bought the same-style house across the street for a quarter-million dollars, the engineer's tax bill jumped to $6,000 a year.

The engineer and the truck driver had never met before they sat next to each other, shouting the same obscenities at the county assessor during a tax protest rally. Together with the realtor who had sold both of them their houses, they wandered the halls of big government. They met the assessor who claimed he was not responsible for taxing houses, only determining their value. State law, so he said, required houses to be assessed at 25 percent of whatever was the current market price. Go to the city council, the assessor said, the council sets the tax rate; zero percent of a quarter-million is still . . . Meanwhile, the city council cut a few dollars (from projects where the lobbyists had even failed to show for the hearings), congratulated themselves, and then raised tax rates once again.

The truck driver and the engineer emerged from the halls of big government in a mood to kick it all down. After all, they were the people; they were the government; they paid the bills. They could do something about taxes if no politician would. But what was to be done?

How the property tax would change depended upon who joined in the protest and what their interests were. Although the truck driver and the engineer had different backgrounds, educations, and work, both of them were consumers. What they had in common was ownership of a home, the largest consumer purchase they would make in a lifetime. Higher property taxes made this already-expensive possession cost even more, even for those who had settled on a fixed-rate, 4-percent mortgage decades ago.

Throughout the suburbs of California, homeowners associations and other community groups created a property tax revolt—a consumerist movement to reduce housing costs. In middle-income communities, protesters sought to lower the taxes on their own homes, not the taxes on office buildings, stores, or industries. Some activists favored measures that would particularly benefit low-income homeowners who could not afford to pay their tax bills. Others turned their populist fervor against big business as well as big government, arguing that oil companies should be taxed to provide property tax relief for homeowners.

Homeowners did succeed in building a movement that drastically altered tax policy in California. But the program that the homeowners themselves put on the ballot, Proposition 13, reduced property taxes for businesses as well as homeowners. In fact, Prop. 13 gave about two-thirds of the benefits to business owners, and only one-third to home-owners (see chap. 1).

This program of tax reduction, mostly for business with some for the middle class, was the darling of probusiness think-tanks and the hallmark of Ronald Reagan's presidency. But the program triumphed in California not because of Republican politicians or big business lobbyists, who actually opposed Prop. 13 down through the election. Strangely enough, this probusiness program was demanded by legions of homeowning consumers, who had heretofore trusted Ralph Nader to fight for their interests as consumers and rights as citizens. This time, the tax protesters turned to Howard Jarvis, who gained a probusiness program in California and inspired a national tax-limitation movement that the largest businesses could finally applaud.

How are we to explain this redistributive twist, whereby angry and hard-squeezed homeowners gave up their relief to business? After all, taxes before Prop. 13 had been rising the fastest on single-family homes in the suburbs, where eager buyers were bidding up prices to unheard-of levels. Assessments on business properties as a percentage of value had been systematically reduced in California and many other states.

Nor did suburban homeowners willingly subsidize business out of attraction to the probusiness doctrines of the times (see chap. 3). Unlike monetarist economists, homeowners wanted easy credit and lower interest rates to pay for their homes and consumer purchases. Unlike Arthur Laffer, they wanted more spending for consumer goods on the demand side, rather than more saving and investment for the supply side. And unlike Milton Friedman, these homeowners wanted more services and regulations to support the style of consumption they were accustomed to.

California homeowners built a movement with a probusiness program as they waged a decades-long fight against unresponsive big government. At first, the movement had no direction. In the communities hardest hit by tax increases, some activists would lobby while others would march. Some demanded special relief for elderly homeowners on fixed incomes, and others pointed to the plight of the young, first-time home buyer, hopelessly burdened with debt. A few activists, making contact with homeowners groups in other communities, would try to form an ongoing organization.

By the next year, many had given up. But those who were still in the fight would have learned something from their confrontations with big government. For some, experiences in city hall were yet another kick that they had come to expect from institutions that supervised them and ruled them. Others were awakened from their complacent expectations that government had been created to serve the public. These lessons and interpretations of American political life would be discussed in countless living rooms and community meeting halls, as new protesters arrived waving their tax bills.

The tax revolt was not simply composed of individuals getting mad, yelling out a window, and watching the resulting spectacle on network television news. It was a face-to-face social process, and yet a process that had profound impacts on what government did about large fortunes and small property.

The clash between Small Property and Big Government involved political forces and ideologies on a world–historic scale, as chapter 2 will show. But the drama was played out in sleepy suburbs, amid the familiar routines of getting to work and washing the dishes, punctuated by un-glamorous meetings about the town budget in the back rooms of Denny's restaurants. As everyday life streams on, social history must reveal the unforeseen and the yet unseen, amid the commonplace and common sense.

Clarence Y. H. Lo

Westside Los Angeles, California, 1979–1987
Sociology Department, University of Missouri at Columbia, 1989

Acknowledgments

If you're trying to get a job someplace, so everybody's got a big stick to hit you down because you're going to take their job or you're showing you're a little bit better. . . . If you have to go from the bottom up you meet all the resistance. It happens no matter what you're doing, whether its on the job or a new idea or you want to improve yourself. You get a constructive idea for UCLA—if you try to bring it out, you'd have to climb over how many departments to get up to who you want to reach . . . ? Everybody that is in the way is going to have a big stick to knock you down because you're either threatening their position or you got a better idea than they have and how could they use your idea because of the insecurity of people. It's always this way. So you go to public officials and there you've got even a worse problem. . . .

I would like to have seen a guy like Wallace get elected president. . . . Not this guy from the South. I'm talking back way back when [Henry A.] Wallace ran for president. . . . He was a former secretary of agriculture. There was an interesting guy . . . and he didn't even stand a chance.[1]

The tax revolt was made by a multitude that left no annals. The *San Gabriel Valley Tribune,* the *Valley News,* and other newspapers in southern California made available their files of newspaper clippings, which allowed me to chronicle legendary and obscure events. One hundred and twenty activists in the tax protest movement provided documents and, in lengthy interviews, told of their experiences and views. Without their help it would have been impossible to tell the complete story of the tax revolt.

The Academic Senate of the University of California, Los Angeles, provided seven years of funding for my research, which enabled me to hire a succession of talented assistants, including Marianna King, Lynn Spiegel, and Marcia Ellison (who conducted interviews in Massachusetts), and especially Janice Schuler and Gail Schwartz, who conducted and transcribed some of the interviews in the San Fernando Valley, the San Gabriel Valley, and the Palos Verdes peninsula.

The California Council for the Humanities in Public Policy, the National Endowment for the Humanities, and the Seed Fund provided grants for my initial explorations into the social history of American conservatism. Many colleagues provided encouragement and helpful comments on the manuscript, including Michael Ames, Philip Bonacich, G. William Domhoff, Joseph Gusfield, Trevor Leger, Ivan Light, Seymour Martin Lipset, John D. McCarthy, Gary T. Marx, Harvey Molotch, James O'Connor, Michael Rogin, Michael Schwartz, Charles Tilly, Ralph H. Turner, Michael Useem, John Walton, Alan Wolfe, Maurice Zeitlin, and especially J. Kenneth Benson, J. Craig Jenkins, Kristin Luker, Melvin Oliver, and Erik Olin Wright. The manuscript was also strengthened by its encounter with David O. Sears, the coauthor of a competing and methodologically distinctive book on the California tax revolt, who also functioned as our eminent Dean of Social Sciences at UCLA. An anonymous reviewer for Temple University Press provided an exhaustive commentary on an earlier version of the manuscript. The friendly yet realistic words of Stanley Holwitz, my sponsoring editor at the University of California Press, inspired me as I finished the work.

Hopefully, the pages that follow will be worthy of the ideals of my teachers at Harvard in the late 1960s and Berkeley in the 1970s. In order to write convincingly about the mundane life of the American middle class, one must inject a sense of the epochal into matters that most people take for granted or cannot see. I learned and gained a perspective from the life and work of my parents, Dr. Chien-Pen Lo and Lucy Lo, and my aunt, Professor Edith Chu, the pioneering generation of Chinese students who came to the United States during the tumultuous years of World War II to discover professional middle-class life here.

Another sage of the minority perspective, my wife Laurie Castro Lo, gave her sense of the passionate, the aesthetic, and the absurd in life. On a practical level, she moved twice for my career, while her professional income enabled me to at least support illusions of middle-class status and homeownership in southern California. In addition, she maintained the highest standards of authentic ethnic cooking, even as she and we cared for our children, Nigel C. Lo, whose learning and cooperation were super, and Justin C. Lo, from whom much more will be heard.

Introduction

Late one night in June 1978, there was a boisterous party in the Hotel Biltmore, an aging establishment in downtown Los Angeles. Howard Jarvis, Paul Gann, and a devoted band of tax protesters downed Biltmore-label generic Scotch and celebrated a landslide victory, the two-to-one vote in favor of Proposition 13 in California. Television reporters stood in the middle of the bustling festivities, straining as they made the short, proper commentaries on the significance of Jarvis's stunning victory. Property taxes in California would be reduced by about seven billion dollars and would henceforth be limited to 1 percent of assessed value. As correspondents telephoned their stories, one could hear above the murmurs the repeated words, "populist," "mad as hell," and "tax revolt."

This newly created phenomenon, this tax revolt, went on to reshape the political landscape of the United States. Howard Jarvis crisscrossed the country, meeting with governors and senators, thundering against big government in countless media appearances. And the people were with him. In a nationwide poll conducted by *Newsweek*, a majority of 57 percent favored cutting property taxes, with only 30 percent opposed.[1]

By the end of 1978, tax-protest activists in a dozen states had placed measures on the ballot to reduce or limit taxes or government spending. Voters passed five proposals (out of eight) to limit property taxes, including Jarvis-style, 1-percent ceilings in Idaho and Nevada. In addition, voters enacted four (out of six) measures curbing state spending or taxes other than the property tax. Chief among these was the Headlee Amendment in Michigan, which restricted state taxes to 9.5 percent of total personal income in the state, constrained increases in property taxes to the rate of inflation, and required that voters approve tax increases. In 1978, more tax-cutting initiatives appeared on state ballots than during the entire period between 1945 and 1976. During those thirty-one years, there had been only thirteen measures to limit or reduce taxes, of which three had passed.

State legislatures quickly responded to the public outrage at high taxes. During legislative sessions in 1978 and 1979, thirty-seven states passed laws reducing property taxes while another twenty-eight reduced income taxes. Wisconsin passed a $942 million tax cut; Minnesota and Oregon cut over $700 million. Although a few measures aided lower-income citizens, most of the tax cuts benefited the middle-class taxpayer, along with the business interests influential in state politics.

In 1980, although voters defeated Howard Jarvis's initiative to cut the California income tax, the tax revolt continued. Across the nation, five initiatives to limit taxes and spending passed in November 1980. Some were relatively mild measures—tax exemptions, limits to taxes, and tax indexing to correct for inflation. But one measure was as drastic as Proposition 13. In Massachusetts, voters approved Proposition 2½, which reduced property taxes by $1.3 billion, forcing the city of Boston to cut its budget by over 11 percent. In 1982, two more statewide initiatives passed which reduced or limited the property tax, along with three to restrain other taxes or government spending.[2]

From Populists to Limousine Conservatives

The deluge of ballot measures was something new in American politics. In years past, tax policy had been a matter for the head of the manufacturers' association to discuss with the chair of the state legislature's finance committee, in polite company after the table had been cleared for dessert. The ordinary citizen knew nothing of the arcane annals of tax legislation and could barely fill out a tax return. But now the voters had stormed into the dinner party and had turned over the table. Now citizens were protesting by reenacting the Boston Tea Party; they were gathering signatures for initiatives and were running grass-roots campaigns to enact drastic tax cuts. Tax policy was not being made by the politicians, but by a social movement.[3]

Sometimes outsiders totally unfamiliar with politics even had the opportunity to write tax legislation, set into law by voters. For example, Don Chance, a retired insurance salesman, led a successful campaign in Idaho to limit property taxes to 1 percent.

At first, Chance and his Idaho Property Owners Association proposed the simplest of solutions: abolish the property tax. "They didn't take me seriously, of course," says Chance. . . . Finally in early 1978, "a real estate lady told me about Proposition 13." Chance got his lawyer to draft a nearly exact copy, complete with the misspellings and references to provisions that didn't exist in the Idaho constitution.[4]

The drama of the little people versus big government played throughout the United States in the late 1970s. After spending two years traveling to small tax-protest meetings throughout the Chicago suburbs, James L. Tobin had earned his title, president of the National Taxpayers United of Illinois. Taxpayers United had a modest mailing list of three thousand and an annual budget of around ten thousand dollars. After large tax increases in suburban Cook County in 1977, Tobin encouraged the angry homeowners there to join a tax strike. Some sixty thousand refused to pay their property tax bills. At one meeting, two hundred irate homeowners demanded that any tax increases be subject to the voters' approval. That year, voters defeated more than a dozen referenda on tax increases in Cook and Du Page counties.[5]

On the East Coast as well, the ordinary taxpayer confronted the powers of the establishment. In Massachusetts, Barbara Anderson worked as a swimming instructor and then as a volunteer secretary for Citizens for Limited Taxation. She soon became executive director of the group that put over Proposition 2½. Anderson recounted the populist fervor of the times:

> We have a . . . [staff] that's only three people and you've got to compete with organizations like [the] Massachusetts Teachers' [Association] that had their own building. . . . [I]t wasn't so much a taxpayer revolt . . . as it was a populist revolt. It was people who just were tired of being pushed around. The phrase that Howard [Jarvis] was using, that we were using from [the movie] *Network,* you know, "I'm mad as hell" . . . , that applies . . . [to] people who are tired of not having their voices heard at high levels. . . .
>
> It was a matter of going and talking about 2½ . . . and then . . . people would stand up outraged and say why they were supporting it. Mostly I think it was the same thing that made me angry when I first encountered government, which is the arrogance on the part of the state and local officials. They [the officials] just simply didn't care what the tax burden was or what you wanted; they were in charge."[6]

In the great expanses of California's metropolitan areas, county government was issuing higher and higher property tax bills to millions of homeowners. Those who could least afford to pay, the elderly and low-

and moderate-income earners, initially made the loudest protests. Many protesters in California argued that tax relief should be channeled to homeowners, because it was the homeowner, rather than business, who was beset with ridiculously inflated tax bills. Some homeowners went further and wanted their own taxes lowered and the taxes on businesses raised. But the tax-cutting measure that voters finally enacted, Proposition 13, especially benefited the owners of business property, who received twice as many dollars of tax relief compared to homeowners.

Proposition 13 demonstrated that in a single stroke, citizens could fight back against government and gain lower taxes for themselves. Businesses as well could reduce their own tax bills, in California and elsewhere. As a leader of the Proposition 2½ campaign in Massachusetts put it: "We couldn't have done it if California hadn't done it first. Simply because it was an example to point to."[7] The success of Proposition 13 encouraged the formation of other coalitions of citizens and businesses throughout the United States.

Amid the ordinary people who were tired of government ordering them around, and among the angry homeowners who could barely afford to pay their tax bills, there were those whose fortunes were clearly more ascendant. For example, Richard Headlee spearheaded the ballot initiative in Michigan that put limits on property taxes and all state revenues. Headlee, the president of a life insurance company, raised almost a million dollars for the campaign and secured the support of the Michigan Chamber of Commerce, the farm bureau, real estate professionals, and retailers such as the Amway Corporation.

The tax revolt was far from being a unified movement. Sometimes, community leaders denounced the corporate power structure as an oppressive special interest. The campaign for Proposition 2½ brought out differences between citizen activist Barbara Anderson, the heads of local homeowners associations, and business groups such as the Massachusetts High Tech Council.

This book tells the story of how citizens and business leaders fought high taxes. In doing so, they also fought each other. And in fighting each other, both sides learned much about the nature of political power and inequality in the United States.

To the Century Plaza

The tax revolt eventually adopted a program with an upward redistribution tilt, benefiting business and high-income individuals. Ronald Reagan could sense the political opportunity. As governor of California, he had placed his own tax-cutting Proposition 1 on the ballot, which would have gradually reduced state spending. When Howard Jarvis was circulating petitions for Proposition 13, Reagan, then a full-time candidate for president, quietly signed one.

Two and a half years later, reporters gathered to cover another victory celebration, this one at the Century Plaza Hotel, which periodically glittered with gala events. It was here that Ronald Reagan strode from his suite to make his appearance at the election-night festivities in 1980. This time, the short, proper television reports used the words, "mandate," "conservatism," "the economy." A new group of voters, the Reagan Democrats, came into being, and they would haunt the old Democrats in every election thereafter.

Reagan had captivated the middle class with his crusade against high taxes and big government. His denunciations of the economic misery of the Carter years had even enthralled a majority of trade union members. The CBS News/*New York Times* exit poll flashed the election results on the screen. Among Reagan voters, 40 percent ranked inflation and the economy as one of the two most important issues, 21 percent chose jobs and employment, and 26 percent the balancing of the federal budget. Reagan Democrats were as vehement as loyal Republicans in disapproving of President Carter's handling of inflation (92 percent disapproval) and unemployment (89 percent disapproval).[8]

But the populist rhetoric of the campaign was soon dissipated by a program to benefit big business and the affluent. The Economic Recovery Tax Act of 1981, according to the Congressional Budget Office, gave 80 percent of the tax reductions to families making between $20,000 and $80,000 a year. Only 7 percent of the benefits went to families who then earned less than $20,000, but numbered one-half of all families. For example, a family with an income over $40,000 gained about $2,200, whereas a family making less than $10,000 would lose about $160 if cuts in government benefits were included. The Economic Recovery Tax Act also reduced taxes for business investments and depreciation, giving 80 percent of the benefits to the 1,700 largest corporations.[9]

Ronald Reagan's secret was his ability to appeal to blue-collar and middle-class voters on economic issues even as he pursued a program to benefit corporations and upper-income earners. A decade earlier, hidden in the populist rhetoric of the tax revolt, was a similar unforeseen result. The tax revolt began as a movement of homeowners reacting to the skyrocketing costs of owning a home. But then it put forth a program that mainly benefited the owners of business property. This is the secret this book seeks to reveal.

1

Whose Interests? Whose Programs? Redistributing the Property Tax Burden

Occasionally, politics has to settle a great issue of economic redistribution, determining who among us shall benefit, who shall prosper, and who must pay—now, and for future generations. Sometimes, such redistributive moments provoke impassioned public discussions and end with clear decisions. The advocates of the first permanent income tax in the United States were crusaders for a tax on the rich. The Progressives fought the plutocrats as state legislatures debated the ratification of the income tax amendment. The Progressives won the first round. In 1913, the Internal Revenue Service struck it rich, levying only those with taxable incomes over $4,000.[1] At a time when the average annual earnings of a worker were a mere $621, only those with taxable incomes over $500,000 a year had to pay a 7-percent rate. In a country of 92 million, it must have been a great social honor even to be one of the 357,000 who filed an income tax return.

Redistributive moments also occur when there is a large increase in government spending. As the United States drained its treasury to fight World War II, the government for the first time levied income taxes on the middle and working classes, who now had taxes directly withheld from their paychecks.

Not only tax increases but also reductions can pose redistributive issues. The tax revolt made the 1970s a redistributive opportunity with huge stakes. In California, tax protesters campaigned for a $7 billion reduction in property taxes in the first year alone; Kemp and Roth sought a federal tax cut of $120 billion.

Strangely enough, despite the sizable interests involved, the redistributive issues of the property tax revolt were imperceptible at the time, outshone by a fireball of populist rhetoric. Then, it seemed that the conflict was between the people and the politicians—all the taxpayers against big government. But some taxpayers were business owners, some were homeowners, and some renters, with each group having its own plight and interests.

The strains between business owners and homeowners had been developing decades before the passage of Proposition 13. County assessors and reform-minded legislators, while claiming to make property taxes equal for all, actually implemented measures that decreased the assessments on businesses and increased those on homes. As the prices of California houses skyrocketed, state laws requiring that assessments keep up with market values made tax bills double, and then double again for many unfortunate homeowners.

It was no surprise that homeowners revolted. What is surprising is how homeowners began by defending their interests but, somehow, developed a program that advanced a very different package of interests.

Self-interest, Plights, and Programs in Social Movements

Some social movements are inspired by altruism or religious convictions. But ever since the dawn of the modern era, when world trade and profit motives led individuals to seek material gain, many movements have been motivated by self-interest. *Self-interest* is the pursuit of pleasure and the avoidance of pain, what Jeremy Bentham and other utilitarian philosophers and economists saw as the foundation of human behavior. For individuals in the short run, self-interests are often clear. The worker wants higher wages and shorter hours; the farmer wants higher prices for his crops and lower prices for his tools; the taxpayer wants lower taxes and more government services.

A *plight* in this context is the frustration of self-interest—an unpleasant or unfavorable situation, including physical and economic hardships such as pain and poverty. Individuals faced with a common plight, such as low wages, have a group interest in gaining advantages (higher wages) for group members and may form a social movement devoted to that cause.[2]

A social movement elaborates the reforms that it seeks—the desired changes in laws, officials, organization, or values in society. This package of reforms is the movement's *program*. Programs are highly complex affairs; even the program of a single-issue movement needs to specify which groups receive what advantages. For every group that gains, there is some other group that will lose an advantage or could have benefited but will not.

A group of skilled workers can strike for a program of narrow interests, protecting their own relative privileges in a particular shop. Or they can envision their interests in broad terms, reformulating the politics and culture that guide a society, tackling basic issues of how inequalities are created and perpetuated. Workers can consciously pursue a program of class interests—the interests that are shared by all those who own no businesses, supervise no one, and even lack control over their own work. Karl Marx proclaimed a program for revolutionary change, *The Communist Manifesto.* Later, social-democratic parties adopted programs advocating the nationalization of key industries and, in the twentieth century, the use of government spending to stimulate economic growth and promote social welfare.

Thus, a social movement, even one whose members are motivated by immediate self-interests, has the choice of many programs that confer different advantages and disadvantages to groups in a society. Although self-interests can be a spur to quick actions, self-interests are an unreliable guide for selecting programs. A worker's immediate self-interest is a higher standard of living. But does the worker have an interest in a communist program of revolution, a social-democratic program of reform, or even acquiescence to a procapitalist program of business growth? Not even your leftist intellectual knows for sure. Scholars today still debate whether or not acquiescent labor movements have produced higher profits and, therefore, higher wages in the long run.[3]

Changes in tax policy have long been an important part of social movement programs. The *Communist Manifesto* called for steep income taxes. Taxes were needed to finance social-democratic programs and the welfare state. The differences between self-interest, plight, and program are central to understanding not only nineteenth-century workers but suburban homeowners as well. I first examine the plight of California homeowners and then contrast their self-interest to the program that their movement ultimately developed.

The Plight of High Property Taxes

Proposition 13 passed in June 1978 as a tidal wave of resentment against taxes swept over California. The 1950s, though, marked the highest tide of rising property taxes. In Los Angeles County, property tax assessments rose 126 percent between fiscal 1949 and 1958, but only 71 percent in the following ten years and 65 percent in the decade immediately before Proposition 13.

Fiscal year 1958 marked the largest annual increase in L.A. County property tax assessments—14.6 percent—recorded during the three decades prior to Proposition 13. In fiscal 1958, Los Angeles County Assessor John R. Quinn increased the valuations on all buildings by at least 10 percent, and by up to 20 percent for structures constructed the previous year. Hardest hit were the new housing tracts in the San Gabriel Valley, where assessments increased 49 percent in the town of Covina, 37 percent in Glendora, and 31 percent in West Covina.

But the countywide assessment increase of 14.6 percent, by itself, did not necessarily have to generate higher tax bills. The tax bill is the product of the assessment multiplied by the tax rate. If local government budgets had remained the same in fiscal 1958 as in 1957, *tax rates* could have been *reduced* by about 13 percent to compensate for the assessment increase. But instead of reducing rates, governments actually increased them, thereby reaping additional revenues. While the headlines blared, ("Huge Taxes Jeopardize L.A. Home Ownership"), the tax rate in the City of Los Angeles increased 3.7 percent to pay for higher city, county, and school expenditures. As one county supervisor put it, "We're growing in excess of 200,000 new permanent residents a year. . . . We're putting in 15 branch civic centers, increasing our courts, enlarging jails. . . . And city and county charters require us to pay our employees prevailing wages."[4]

The towns of the San Gabriel Valley were also hit with large increases in tax rates, on top of their assessment increases. In West Covina, tax rates went up by 16.1 percent to reach $8.58 per $100 assessed value; in Covina, up 15.5 percent; in Glendora, 6.3 percent. (By contrast, in Beverly Hills, the affluent community west of Los Angeles, the rate was around $4.50 per hundred.) Over half of the property taxes collected in the San Gabriel Valley were being used to fund the schools. County Assessor Quinn sought to explain: "I don't think that they've built a new schoolhouse in Brooklyn in the last 20 years. But we've got to build a new one every week."[5]

"Equalization" as Redistribution

After the protests sparked in 1958 (described in chap. 6) were quickly extinguished, property tax assessments and rates continued their inexorable climb. The next sharp increases, occurring in the mid-1960s, particularly afflicted homeowners but spared industries, shopping centers, and other businesses. Thus began a trend that would continue as property tax bills escalated.

In the Los Angeles of the early 1960s, assessments on businesses had been running at about 45 percent of market value, compared to 21 percent for residences. Businesses began to file lawsuits on equity grounds demanding tax refunds totaling more than one billion dollars. A group of shopping center owners succeeded in winning a refund in court and, in doing so, came into contact with a young, energetic appraiser named Philip E. Watson. The shopping center owners, along with James M. Udall, a prominent real estate investor, backed Watson's successful campaign in 1962 to become assessor of Los Angeles County.[6]

The past practice of assessing property at varying and unannounced rates of up to 50 percent of value, struck Watson as arbitrary and inequitable. Soon after taking office, Watson announced that he would assess all types of property—businesses and homes—at the same standard rate, 25 percent of market value. If he found any areas where the assessments were running below 20 percent or above 30 percent of value, every property in that area would be reappraised.

Watson discovered that some 60 percent of the county's 1.8 million land parcels needed revaluation. Watson began reassessing the areas that deviated most from the 25 percent guideline. In the Malibu–Topanga area, a rustic beach community where actors Ronald Reagan and Bob Hope had bought large holdings, assessments were running at only 4 to 17 percent of current market prices. Malibu assessments were revised upward. In the town of Alhambra, fiscal year 1965 assessments increased 13.8 percent (and tax rates by 4.3 percent), inciting the protests to be described in chapter 4.

After Watson's first round of reappraisals had been completed, he thought that he only had to conduct a small update program, monitoring the real estate market and reassessing only those areas where prices had significantly changed. "Year by year, all will go up or down closely to current market movements."[7] But for homeowners, it was up, up, up, and never down or even standing still.

Los Angeles County assessments increased by 8.9 percent in fiscal 1967 and another 6.7 percent the following year. Appraisals on homes in Malibu again jumped, as aspiring orthodontists tried to follow the movie stars seeking ocean-view homes that might be pictured in *Sunset* magazine. As sea breezes fanned a hot real estate market, assessments went up in the Westside of Los Angeles; tax rates were also up for the entire City of Los Angeles, adding to the tax bills. In fiscal 1967, 17,200 people filed formal appeals of their assessments with the county, an all-time record. But the 1967 and 1968 increases were just a foreshadowing of more to come.

Watson's policy in Los Angeles County to assess all property at 25 percent of market price, enforced through periodic revaluations, shifted property taxes onto homeowners and made them vulnerable to the inflation of home prices, which would automatically trigger higher assessments. In San Francisco, too, the tax burden was shifting from businesses to homeowners. But ironically, the homeowner's greater burden stemmed from the misdirected efforts of progressive reformers, who were trying to make business pay its full share of taxes. The political confusion over who was overtaxed and who would get tax relief would continue, right through the debates over Proposition 13.

A process that shifted property taxes onto homeowners was set in motion during a 1965 scandal involving San Francisco County assessor, Russell Wolden. An accountant provided the *San Francisco Chronicle* with filing cabinets full of documents detailing how corporations contributed money to the assessor's campaign in return for a reduction of a corporation's property tax bills. The documents were a muckraker's delight—elaborate calculations of what a corporation's taxes would have been, the company's reduced assessment, copies of canceled checks, and explanatory notes: "Enclosed is a check for your campaign for assessor that was volunteered last week after filing the American Can return."[8]

Newspapers and district attorneys concluded that many businesses were being assessed at unfairly low levels, resulting in revenue losses of hundreds of millions of dollars, made up for by small homeowners and ordinary citizens. At that time, the solution seemed obvious to two liberal State Assembly representatives from the San Francisco Bay Area, Nicholas Petris and John Knox. With their leadership, the Assembly passed the Assessment Reform Act of 1966, which required that all property, businesses and homes, be appraised at the same rate, 25 percent of market value. To see that its provisions were enforced, the law mandated periodic checks to insure that assessments were in line throughout the state.

But despite their good intentions, Petris and Knox had actually increased the homeowner's tax burden. The scandal in San Francisco focused attention on the corporations that had reduced their assessments through bribes, but these companies numbered only 7 percent of the total. In fact, the overall pattern in San Francisco was for businesses to be appraised at a *higher* rate than homeowners. Assessor Wolden may have been a little crooked but, on the average, business inventories and equipment had been assessed at around 50 percent of value, and business-owned land and buildings at 35 percent. Petris and Knox had unwittingly cut these business assessments to 25 percent. By contrast, single-family homes in San Francisco had been getting the real bargain— assessments on the average of only 9 percent of value, and 5 percent for older homes.

Assessment reform, in short, meant higher assessments for homeowners, bringing them up to the new 25 percent standard. A few months after the passage of the reform bill, the San Francisco County Board of Supervisors called on the state to delay implementing the reform. But it was too late. As the assessments on homeowners more than doubled, their reply was a sarcastic bumper sticker that read, "Bring Back the Crooked Assessor."[9]

In short, the politics of the California property tax in the 1960s seemed, at first, to be a model for the triumph of progressive reform. It was almost a textbook case of "good government" at work—using publicity to expose corruption, professionals to efficiently administer, expertise to resolve conflicts, and enlightened public opinion to make laws more just. In Los Angeles, Philip Watson was an expert civil servant, a UCLA-trained economist with a decade of staff experience in the assessor's office. In San Francisco, investigative journalists had written a series of exposes in the finest tradition of reformer and author Upton Sinclair. Through a free press, the public had discovered that the special interests—certain large businesses—had bribed the assessor. The resulting public outcry had sent the crooked assessor to jail.

And to complete the storybook ending, a law was passed mandating that all taxpayers would be assessed at the same percentage of market value. This reform law was supported by the League of Women Voters, the Assessors' Association, and a host of other groups representing labor, business, agriculture, and local government officials. There were no organized groups testifying in opposition. Everyone thought that assessments could now be based on hard evidence—the price of sales—rather than the assessor's estimate, whim, or favor. Assessments were becoming more rule-bound, more uniform, and more rational.

Real Estate Inflation and the Assessment Behemoth

But at the same time, the assessment process was becoming more rigid and less responsive to citizens' pressures. True, the old-fashioned assessor lowered appraisals when bribed. But in times past, he could also lower appraisals when homeowners complained that they could not pay their taxes, provided that they were party regulars. The old-time assessor generally kept valuations on homes low because it was the vote of the homeowners, after all, who kept him in office. The crooked assessor could heed special interests but could also respond to special needs. The former system relied on judgment, which was corruptible, but at least it was still the judgment of a human being.

Assessment reform supplanted this human consideration with rational, bureaucratic procedures. The law now required periodic checks and updates of appraisals. Computer-assisted valuation systems implemented the law with a vengeance, detecting every upward move in home prices, spewing out hundreds of thousands of yearly notices of higher assessments. It was the nightmare that sociologist Max Weber had fore-warned at the turn of the century—a procedurally rational system that nevertheless ground out substantially irrational results. While big government wandering among the banana trees in Vietnam pounded out its kill ratios and sorties, big government towering over the palms of Los Angeles tapped out year after year of double- and even triple-digit assessment increases. Elected leaders could only perfect the machinery of big government. It would take the groundswell of a mass movement to overthrow it.

Orange County, immediately to the southeast of Los Angeles, pioneered in using computers to appraise property. Assessed values in Orange County increased by three billion dollars between 1960 and 1969, as open land was rapidly transformed into the continuous suburbs of southern California. Home prices were soaring. To do his job the assessor needed a means of estimating every year the price of each of the county's 330,000 homes, so that all could be appraised at 25 percent of current market value—what someone would have to pay to buy the home now.

In 1965, statisticians analyzed a sample of Orange County real estate sales and developed regression equations that could do what every real estate agent likes to do in his or her sleep—predict selling prices from characteristics of houses such as location, age of structure, living area, and lot size. Then, the relevant characteristics on file for each residential property were entered into the computer. In 1969, the computer printed its first yearly estimates of the value of all the properties. No one had to see a home or talk to a homeowner.

It took somewhat longer to implement computerized appraisals in Los Angeles County, with its 1.8 million residential properties worth some $70 billion. By 1972, computers were routinely applying simple formulas to update the values of land and buildings. The same year, the Assessor's Office performed a pilot regression analysis that adequately predicted the sale prices of some one hundred thousand homes. Regression analyses were first utilized on a small scale two years later. Then, in fiscal year 1976, about 30 percent of county properties were reappraised, compared to about 20 percent in previous years. In 1976 assessed values in the county rose 7.4 percent. According to Watson, "The biggest increases are coming in the more expensive residential areas of the county, like San Marino," an upper-class town that had escaped reassessment since 1969 but was now hit with a 47 percent increase.[10]

By fiscal 1977, the price of an already-owned home in Los Angeles was increasing by about 20 percent a year. Assessor Watson's computer system was ready for a massive undertaking—using regression analysis to reappraise 800,000 single-family homes (60 percent of the county total) in order to raise assessments to match higher market prices. That year, total valuations in the county increased 13.8 percent, with the greatest increases in upper-middle-class neighborhoods (some areas in Northridge, up 111 percent; in Toluca Lake and Studio City, up 88 percent) and in neighborhoods in gentrifying beach communities (parts of Venice, up 90 percent; in Redondo Beach and Torrance, up 85 percent). In these communities, activists took leading roles in the tax revolt. Tax rates in the areas, at best, decreased only slightly; the higher assessments thus produced sharp increases in tax bills. The next fiscal year, assessments in L.A. County increased another 8.2 percent. Immediately before the June 1978 election, increases for fiscal 1979 were announced—a projected 17.5-percent rise countywide. That was enough. The voters endorsed Proposition 13 and rolled back their assessments to fiscal 1976 levels.[11]

Business or Homeowners: Who Pays?

Efficient and rational assessment techniques had been applied to California homeowners, with devastating results. But the assessor did not subject all types of property to the computerized mass appraisal. In the case of retail stores and industrial plants and equipment, assessed value could not be easily based on market price because business property is sold less frequently compared to homes. For business property, there usually was not a sale of a comparable property down the block that could be used to estimate market price. Business real estate was assessed by the good old-fashioned way—by an appraiser's estimates and hand calculations, which would take into account the cost of construction minus depreciation, benchmark land values, and the net income produced by the property (which capitalized would contribute to the business's valuation).

Since the assessment of commercial and industrial property relied heavily on human judgment, these appraisals could be marred by human error and corruption. Assessor Watson may have efficiently appraised homes without favoring any of them. But Watson stood trial in 1967 for allegedly conspiring to overlook a $350,000 tax deficiency of J. J. Newberry Company in return for a campaign contribution of $15,000. In 1977, as the valuations on homes shot up, the L.A. County Board of Supervisors was suspicious that commercial property was being underassessed. The supervisors voted to conduct an investigation, headed by Carmine S. Bellino from the staff of the Senate Watergate hearings.

Bellino concluded that, "Residential properties have borne the greatest burden of assessment increases over the past six-year period." Out of 50 commercial properties that had been selected by the supervisors, 14, including several owned by Watson's campaign contributors, were underassessed by a total of $15.3 million. A sports arena, Bellino further charged, was underassessed by $900,000. In Bellino's own sample of 120 properties, the appraisals of commercial establishments had decreased by 4.1 percent between 1971 and 1976, whereas adjacent homes had increased by 45.7 percent. Watson also allegedly helped two of his campaign contributors by cutting $350,000 off of an assessment and by canceling an audit. Although Watson heatedly disputed the charges of corruption, a year later the assessor's acting chief of commercial and industrial property admitted that the valuations of businesses had generally increased more slowly than residential property. This was precisely the trend that the Bellino report had outlined.[12]

Like the Watergate scandal, the Bellino investigation and the earlier trials of Watson and Assessor Wolden of San Francisco focused on the headline-grabbing issues of personal wrongdoing—who took the bribe, and who got the special tax reduction. Watson may have been the crooked assessor in disguise, lowering some assessments on businesses. Or he may have been entirely innocent of wrongdoing. In any case, individual instances of corruption did not affect the larger trend; the appraisals of homes were increasing faster than those of businesses. Business net incomes, which set the value of businesses, were just not increasing as much as the demand for single-family houses.

Throughout California, net assessed values between fiscal 1975 and 1978 increased 111 percent for owner-occupied homes, with only a 26 percent increase for commercial, industrial, and agricultural businesses. (Renter-occupied residences increased 34 percent.) The year before Proposition 13 passed, valuations on homes increased by 20 percent, whereas valuations on other types of property increased 10.5 percent.[13] This caused homeowners to pay an increased share of property taxes. Back in fiscal 1970, the property tax share paid by single-family residences had been kept in check because homeowners could deduct $3,000 from their market values ($7,000 beginning in fiscal 1974). But between fiscal 1974 and fiscal 1978, the share paid by single-family homes rose from 32.1 percent to 42.2 percent.[14]

In other states as well, market prices were driving the assessments on residential property higher than industrial and commercial assessments. In some states, politicians acted as they did in California and did nothing to provide tax relief earmarked for homeowners, thereby shifting the property tax burden onto them. For example, in Wisconsin between 1968 and 1978, property tax collections from residences increased by 126 percent while those from all businesses increased 62 percent. (Property tax payments from industries actually declined.) Reductions in assessments for business inventories, machinery, and equipment in Wisconsin accelerated the tax shift. Similarly, in Ohio, inflation in home prices outpaced the rise in business values. The property taxes paid by residences increased 53 percent between 1973 and 1978, while those on industries increased by only 25 percent and commercial establishments by 38 percent.[15]

In short, of all the types of property owners, homeowners throughout the United States were paying the largest increases in property tax bills. Meanwhile, the business share of the property tax burden in the United States fell from 45.1 percent in 1957, to 39.5 percent in 1967, to 34.0 percent in 1977.

The higher taxes on homes led majorities of the public to express their dislike of property taxes through opinion polls and through voting for ballot measures. The national trend of higher taxes increased resentments. In 1953 the average family paid 11.8 percent of its income for taxes to all levels of government. By 1977, this had risen to 22.5 percent. The percentage of the public who thought that taxes had reached the breaking point rose from 61 percent in 1969 to 69 percent in 1978, while the percentage who thought that taxes were unreasonable rose from 72 to 80 percent.

Of all the different types of taxes, the public singled out the property tax as particularly unjust. In 1978, only 10 percent thought that property taxes were the most fair, compared to 13 percent for the federal income tax, 17 percent for the state income tax, and 24 percent for the social security tax. The property tax was unpopular partly because it was so highly visible. In Los Angeles County many homeowners paid the property tax directly in two large installments, writing checks payable to the county. In contrast, the sales tax was paid more frequently (at each purchase) and was collected indirectly (by merchants rather than the government).

Obviously, the homeowners who thought that their property taxes were too high were the ones who were likely to vote for ballot propositions to reduce their property taxes. Massachusetts homeowners who felt their property taxes were very high voted 70 percent in favor of tax-cutting Proposition 2½, compared to 58 percent of the entire sample. California voters perceiving their tax burdens as high voted disproportionately in favor of Proposition 13 and other tax-cutting initiatives. Among homeowners, those who expected an imminent property tax increase of over six hundred dollars voted 83 percent in favor of Proposition 13, compared to 65 percent of the total electorate and 48 percent among those who did not expect an increase in their property tax bills.[16]

Tax Relief for Whom?

In short, the plight and the grievances of California homeowners were serious indeed in 1978. "Vote for yourself! Vote for Proposition 13!" This was the rallying cry for millions of Californians who voted to cut their property taxes. It is no surprise that given the chance to vote yes or no for Proposition 13, the voters chose "Yes!" by a two-to-one margin. Proposition 13 put almost two thousand dollars per year in the pocket of the average southern Californian who had owned a home for at least three years. As one tax protest activist described it: "It's a phenomenon that I've never seen in the past and I haven't seen since. People were at the polls almost salivating to go there and vote. . . . This is like standing in line to get a refund check. . . . These people would have waited three hours in line to vote. Normally, if the lines are five minutes long, people will leave. . . . Not on Prop. 13. They were just waiting."[17]

If that were not enough, voters were tantalized by the four billion dollar surplus sitting in the state treasury and were confident that huge amounts of "waste" could be cut from government budgets without affecting services. Voters were eager to take a swat at big government and were outraged when the latest round of assessment increases were announced. Some form of property tax relief was inevitable in California. But Proposition 13 was a particular program of tax reduction, which granted certain benefits that helped some groups more than others. What were the alternative tax reduction programs that could have been enacted? How did these alternatives compare to the specific program of tax relief as embodied in Proposition 13?

Given that property taxes in the 1970s were increasing the fastest on owner-occupied, single-family homes, one might expect that tax reduction programs would be designed to particularly benefit homeowners. Indeed, some states did adopt specific measures to channel property tax relief to homeowners. For example, single-family residences can be granted lower tax rates or lower assessments compared to other types of property. Fourteen states and the District of Columbia have enacted such property tax systems; Minnesota, for example, classified property into thirty-one types, each with its own tax rate. Massachusetts assesses industrial property at 55 percent of market value and homes at 40 percent. The plight of California homeowners could have led to a split property tax roll, with lower taxes for homeowners and higher taxes for businesses.

The homeowner's exemption is another mechanism that many states use to relieve escalating taxes on residences. Beginning in fiscal 1974,

California made the first $7,000 of a home's market value tax exempt. But within four years, the inflation of home prices in southern California had pushed the resale price of the average home to well over ten times this amount. California's property tax exemption, which reduced a tax bill by about $200, was scant consolation. One way of channeling tax relief to homeowners would have been to increase this exemption, say, to the level in Louisiana, which exempted the first $50,000 of a home's market value.

In Michigan, Oregon, Minnesota, Wisconsin, and several other states, another tax reform measure, the circuit breaker, provided relief to low-income homeowners. These homeowners only pay a limited percentage of their incomes for property taxes, with the state paying the remainder of the bill. California's circuit-breaker offered little help because of its extremely restricted benefits. Homeowners had to be over age sixty-two; those earning an income of less than $3,000 received the maximum rebate, around $1,000. Elderly homeowners with somewhat more income received much smaller rebates—$120 for those with an annual income of only $11,500.

The split roll, the homeowner's exemption, the circuit breaker, and other tax equity measures could have been enacted in California to provide relief to the homeowners, who were suffering from large property tax increases. Michigan provides an example of how the timely enactment of reforms can keep the homeowner's share of the property tax burden from rising significantly, despite sharp increases in home prices. In Michigan, local property taxes on residences increased by 293 percent between 1965 and 1978 while taxes on industries increased 136 percent. But because homeowners received a state tax rebate and businesses paid an additional value-added tax, the share of property taxes that homeowners ended up paying increased by less than 1 percent in the same thirteen-year interval.[18]

In short, the tax reduction movement in the late 1970s could have adopted a program of downward redistribution.[19] In many parts of the United States, political movements have pressured for such tax reform, calling for lower taxes for middle- and low-income earners and higher taxes for corporations and the wealthy. In Chicago, the Citizens' Action Committee (CAP) successfully campaigned to reduce property taxes for two residential neighborhoods and raise taxes on business properties, such as a new bank building, five race tracks, and U.S. Steel and other steel companies. CAP also succeeded in getting the Illinois legislature to give tax relief to elderly homeowners and renters. Similarly, the Ohio Public Interest Campaign, a citizens' group with a paid staff of twenty and one hundred thousand contributors, opposed the tax abatements that had been granted to developers in Cleveland. The Association of

Community Organizations for Reform Now (ACORN) also actively promoted downward redistribution. An organization called Tax Equity for America has established affiliate groups in New York, Ohio, Pennsylvania, and Texas to support reform of the property tax, as well as a proposed Tax Justice Act at the federal level.[20]

The California Legislature and the
Failure of Downward Redistribution

Similar political groups did exist in California, and these groups did work for equity in the property tax. The California Tax Reform Association (CTRA) and the Citizens' Action League (CAL) devoted themselves to influencing the state legislature, which, however, repeatedly failed to enact property tax reform. In 1977, for example, the CTRA and the CAL joined with a coalition of labor and leftist groups to sponsor Senate Bill 154. SB 154 was written by Senator Nicholas Petris (D., Oakland), the coauthor of the ill-fated 1966 law that ended up reducing business assessments to 25 percent and raising residential assessments to 25 percent. This time, Petris took care to formulate a program that would actually redistribute downward. SB 154 offered tax relief to homeowners and renters with low and moderate incomes. But for the affluent, the state income tax would be increased, and capital gains loopholes would be closed. Compared to the circuit breaker that had existed in California, SB 154 offered fairly large benefits. The average southern California homeowner would receive a state tax rebate of $900 to pay property tax bills.

Leftist groups campaigned for SB 154. In January 1977, the Service Employees International Union organized a rally in Sacramento. The Citizens' Action League and a coalition of senior citizens groups did likewise in the following months. But all was to no avail. The State Assembly heavily amended the bill, adding a provision that would benefit businesses by eliminating taxes on inventories. Then the State Senate blocked passage, voting down two conference committee reports reconciling the Senate and Assembly versions of the bill.

At the time Proposition 13 qualified for the ballot, the state legislature had failed to provide property tax relief for four years in a row. State legislators had repeatedly promised to reduce taxes, but now seemed incapable of agreeing on a program. A two-thirds vote of each chamber was needed to pass fiscal legislation in California. The Republican minority could easily gain a one-third vote, vetoing programs that channeled benefits to lower-income earners. Democratic governor Jerry Brown did not intervene forcefully enough to promote tax equity programs.[21]

With the stalemate in Sacramento, legislative politics would not decide the redistributive features of property tax reduction. As assessments continued to rise, taxpayers became more and more impatient with the wrangling at the state legislature. The ballot initiative, a legacy of the reforms of the Progressive Era, provided another means of achieving tax reduction. Citizens gathered one and a half million signatures on petitions to place Proposition 13 on the ballot.

The politicians made one last try. In 1978 the legislature passed Senate Bill 1, which reduced property taxes for homeowners and not for businesses and also slightly increased tax relief payments to renters and senior citizens. Senate Bill 1 would take effect only if voters rejected Prop. 13 and instead passed Proposition 8, a complex enabling amendment to the state constitution. But voters saw Prop. 8 as a move by the politicians which offered only a small tax reduction compared to Prop. 13. Proposition 8 went down to defeat, swamped by the two-to-one tide for Proposition 13. The citizens made Proposition 13 part of the state constitution, thus bypassing the legislature and making the law by themselves.

Homeowners' Movement, Business Programs

Which law, and what citizens? To explain the upward redistributive program that triumphed, one needs to explain why that program and not a downward redistribution was written into the text of Proposition 13. Programs that especially benefited homeowners could have easily been included in ballot measures that could win at the polls. For example, in the election of November 1978, voters in Texas approved a measure reducing property taxes for the elderly and increasing the tax exemption for homeowners. North Dakota voters passed an initiative that reduced the income tax rates for individuals and increased rates for corporations.

Proposition 13 in California did not extend the homeowner's exemption or the circuit breaker; nor did it enact a split roll or any measures that would have particularly benefited low- and moderate-income individuals. Proposition 13 reduced local property tax revenues by about $5.5 billion in the first year alone. A cut of this magnitude could also have been achieved by entirely abolishing the property tax on all owner-occupied residences in the state and then distributing an additional $1.5 billion to renters (who pay property taxes through their rents).

But instead, Proposition 13 in California provided no direct benefit to renters. Proposition 13 reduced property taxes for all types of property, not only for owner-occupied residences but also for apartments and business establishments, whose taxes had increased less sharply. Between 1978 and 1983 Proposition 13 reduced taxes by about $41 billion from what they otherwise would have been. Homeowners received about 36 percent of the reduction, including $2 billion in the first year (fiscal 1979) alone. Landlords, farmers, and the owners of commercial and industrial property received 64 percent of the savings, including $4 billion in the first year. Southern California Edison, for example, saved $54 million in 1979, while Chevron saved $47 million. As a result of this tax shift, four years after the passage of Prop. 13 the homeowners, in contrast to business, were paying a greater share of the property tax burden. Of every $100 of property taxes collected, single-family residence owners were paying $44, up about 5 percent from 1978 and 37 percent from 1974.[22]

In short, business property received most of the benefits from Proposition 13, despite the fact that assessments on business property were only rising by single-digit figures per year. Given that it was the homeowners who were facing double-digit increases year after year, how did the provisions of Proposition 13 emerge as the alternative for California's property tax system?

If one seeks to explain which program of tax reduction became concretized as Proposition 13, one must closely examine the process that succeeded in placing that proposition on the ballot. The million and a half Californians signing petitions to put it there were the last stage of a protest movement, a movement that began in the 1950s. Throughout its history, the movement stood for different programs and tried various tactics to achieve success. Dozens of leaders other than Howard Jarvis spoke for the tax protest movement.

For decades, higher property tax bills led Californians to attend mass meetings, denounce the assessor, appeal their property assessments, and sign protest petitions. The newspapers of Los Angeles featured stories about seventy-three major protest events, each attracting at least one hundred persons (see appendix). Back in 1957, thousands of southern California homeowners, incensed at their property tax bills, shouted at protest rallies; 153,000 signed to recall the county assessor. Protesters in 1964 stormed into a meeting of the County Board of Supervisors. In 1966 taxpayers organized a strike and refused to pay their property tax bills. A decade later, taxpayers burned their assessment notices during a rally. (See fig. 1 showing that attendance at protests and filing assessment appeals peaked in fiscal years 1958, 1965, 1967, and 1977.)

Angry taxpayers were in the mood to sign protest petitions; some 200,000 did so in 1964. Protest activists eventually discovered that enough signatures could place an initiative on the state ballot, which, if approved by a majority of the voters, would have the force of law. Howard Jarvis and Paul Gann were not the first to gather sufficient

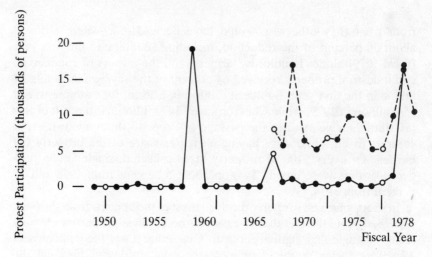

The top line represents the number of appeals filed with the Los Angeles County Assessor's Office.
The bottom line represents number of persons reportedly attending tax protest events during the year.
Figure 1.   Peaks of Tax Protest Activity in the Los Angeles Metropolitan Area

signatures to put a tax reduction initiative on the ballot. Oddly enough, it was Assessor Philip Watson who had the bold idea of soliciting the signatures of those who were irate at the assessment notices he had just mailed out. In 1968 and again in 1972, Watson collected the required signatures that placed his initiatives on the ballot. Both measures, however, were soundly defeated at the polls.

Nor was Proposition 13 Howard Jarvis's first attempt at an initiative. Jarvis launched his tax-cutting career in 1968 by proposing an initiative that would abolish the property tax entirely. In 1972, hundreds of volunteers associated with small tax protest groups and homeowners associations gathered 461,000 signatures (273,000 in Los Angeles County alone) to place one of Jarvis's tax initiatives on the ballot. Falling short of the number of signatures needed to qualify, the activists tried again. They collected close to half a million in 1976 and around the same number again in 1977, but still the number was insufficient.

Later that year, though, tax protesters amassed about one and a half million signatures, far in excess of the number needed. Almost all of these signatures were gathered by volunteers, in contrast to the paid solicitors used in most other initiative campaigns. In an era when special interest groups routinely spend $1 million to solicit signatures, the effort to place Proposition 13 on the ballot, which spent only $28,000, stands as a monument to the activism of ordinary citizens.

The Conservative Political and Economic Establishment and Tax Reduction Programs

In short, Proposition 13 was placed on the ballot by a grass-roots movement—by the protests and the petitions of homeowners. Yet that movement against high taxes on homes ended up by championing a proposition that gave away most of the tax relief to businesses. This is the central paradox of the tax revolt—a paradox that deserves careful explanation. What transformed a populist movement into one heralding a probusiness program, easily absorbed into the supply-side agenda of the Reagan administration?

One possible explanation is that the tax protest movement had to immediately come to terms with conservative politicians or the leaders of large businesses, who typically play a major role in tax legislation. These elites could have formulated the programs that initiatives copied and could have helped the right ballot initiative to succeed.

Perhaps Republican party politicians, who support low taxes and incentives for business, could have written a probusiness initiative. Republican leaders could have gathered signatures through their political organizations. Or they could have lent their support to groups that were proposing probusiness initiatives. There was one Republican, known for his espousal of controversial causes, who made an attempt along these lines. When Ronald Reagan was governor of California, he promoted a ballot initiative to gradually reduce state spending to 7 percent of total personal income in the state. Even this modest proposal was defeated at the polls. Republican leaders did not propose or even support ballot initiatives that would significantly reduce property taxes, despite strong grass-roots pressure. Between 1968 and 1977, when thousands of activists were collecting signatures on initiatives, almost no politicians offered their endorsements. One exception was Ronald Reagan, then ex-governor of California, who endorsed a Jarvis initiative (without involving himself in campaigning or other details). He was joined by James Hayes, a Los Angeles County supervisor who soon resigned.

Even after Proposition 13 had overwhelmingly qualified for the ballot, the California Republican party failed to endorse it. Republican leaders were still reluctant to embrace the issue that would later become their political bonanza—large tax cuts for the middle and upper classes, and especially for business, investors, and the supply side. Republican George Deukmejian (who would become California's governor in 1983) opposed Proposition 13 at the time. Republican Senator S. I. Hayakawa did endorse Prop. 13, as did an unsuccessful Republican candidate in the 1978 gubernatorial primary (Ed Davis), a candidate for lieutenant governor (Mike Curb), a dark-horse candidate for controller (Jimmy Ware), and a few candidates for the state legislature and local offices.[23] Yet most Republican officeholders and candidates did not even offer a token endorsement.

Another possible explanation for the probusiness program of the tax revolt is that its initiatives were influenced by business interest groups (such as the state Chamber of Commerce), large corporations, or organizations that represent large corporations (the California Business Roundtable). The most influential organization in tax matters is the California Taxpayers' Association (Cal-Tax), a lobbying group whose officers, executive committee, and sixty-person board of directors are entirely composed of high-level business executives, exclusively drawn from the large utilities, railroads, oil companies, banks, and other top corporations ranked by *Fortune* magazine.[24]

Business interest lobbies did not support the efforts of homeowners groups to reduce property taxes. In 1976, for example, the California Taxpayers' Association argued that homeowners who were angry about high property taxes should not campaign for limits on assessments or property tax rates. Instead, homeowners should work for economy in government expenditures. "Expenditure control is more essential than tax control—particularly control of only one tax." In an article in *Pacific Business,* the magazine of the California State Chamber of Commerce, the chamber's taxation director argued that initiatives, compared with legislative action, were a poor method of making tax policy.

Despite the fact that top corporations received large tax reductions from Proposition 13, major corporations and business lobbying groups did not support it. During the campaign for Proposition 13, the state chamber was neutral. The California Business Roundtable and Cal-Tax strongly opposed the proposition. Cal-Tax instead recommended a modest $1.5 billion reduction in property taxes, compared to Proposition 13's feared $7 billion cut.[25]

Cal-Tax's major concern was that the proposition would immediately trigger a backlash in the public and the state legislature, rapidly leading to higher taxes for business. Cal-Tax's position paper argued that if Proposition 13 passed, the legislature would probably put an initiative on the ballot allowing the tax reductions of Proposition 13 for homeowners only and not for business. Cal-Tax was uneasy about where the redistributive vengeance of the voters might strike next. "The 1.2 million who signed the petition [for Proposition 13] were mainly interested in property tax relief for homeowners, and would welcome the fact that their sales or income taxes would not be raised to fund relief for business. There would be inevitable publicity during the campaign of the huge tax savings of major industries. If placed on the ballot, the measure [to restrict Proposition 13 benefits to homeowners] would likely pass in the November [1978] election." Thus, business should not be tempted to support Proposition 13, because very quickly, tax 'relief' to business and agriculture would disappear."

In addition, Cal-Tax feared that if Proposition 13 passed, the state legislature and local governments would respond to lower property tax collections from homeowners with "massive new taxes" on business. An increase in the bank and corporation tax to at least 15 percent would be "inevitable"; counties could levy business license taxes based on gross receipts or on size of payroll, with the larger firms paying more. "There would be strong political pressure and ample opportunity" to enact a severance tax on the oil industry.[26]

Large oil companies, banks, aerospace and electronics corporations, securities-trading firms, steel producers, and utilities made thousand-dollar contributions or more to the No on 13 campaign. Large contributions from business totaled $652,000. Despite the fact that Proposition 13 would lower the Bank of America's property tax bill from $24 million to $13 million, the bank donated $25,000 to defeat Proposition 13. In a publicly distributed position paper, the bank stated that if Proposition 13 passed, "essential public services such as schools, police and fire protection, and public transportation, would have to be drastically reduced, or other taxes and fees increased significantly to maintain even reduced service levels."[27]

Southern California Edison contributed another $25,000; its president, Howard P. Allen, chaired the No on 13 campaign, organized fund raisers against 13 for top executives, and was instrumental in convincing the Los Angeles Area Chamber of Commerce to oppose Proposition 13. "I was led to believe . . . at the time . . . [that there] would be a sudden massive disruption of fiscal ability of governments to function in an orderly fashion."[28]

The No on 13 campaign relied on businesses who made donations of over $1,000. The money for the Yes on 13 campaign, on the contrary, was mostly donated by individuals who contributed less than $1,000. The striking fact about the tax revolt in California is that it won without receiving the support of large corporations.

Thus, the probusiness slant in the program of Proposition 13 did not come from big business pressures. The question remains: How did the tax revolt, a grass-roots movement of homeowners and other political outsiders, choose its program of reforms? If Proposition 13 would have arisen out of the legislative process, it would be relatively easy to trace how its provisions were adopted. One would study the first drafts, the amended versions, the testimony, the constituent mail, and the speeches. It would be easy if one could find the early drafts of Proposition 13 in a Bank of

America memorandum or in the platform of the California Republican party. But one cannot. A protest movement short-circuited the establishment, drafted Proposition 13, and made it the law.

Studying how a protest movement determines its program is a difficult undertaking. Within a new, volatile movement, debates are not transcribed and published as in the *Congressional Record*. Instead, the researcher must discover the social history of the tax revolt, community by community, complete with its forgotten leaders and its failures. These earlier efforts were part of a process that set the direction for a movement that eventually would triumph. In the next chapter, I develop a theory of social movement politics that helps to explain why tax protesters placed the provisions of Proposition 13 on the ballot rather than some other redistributive program.

2

Theories of Inequality and an Interactive Approach to Power

In trying to explain the very mundane problem of how tax protesters developed their program of economic redistribution, one immediately runs into issues that have perplexed theologians and philosophers as well as political scientists and sociologists. How free are people to make decisions and act, and how constrained are they by the first causes that operate in the world? Conveniently sidestepping the question of moral absolutes and divine intervention, political sociologists have asked, do the policies that a society pursues stem from the choice of free individuals? Or are policies determined by circumstances and conditions in society?

For some the answers are obvious. In democratic nations like the United States, some would argue, policies stem from the choice of voters. As comforting as this argument is, it still overlooks the fact that even in democracies, inequalities in society set trends and limit the options from which individuals must choose. In the case of the tax revolt, the vote of the citizens, of course, enacted Proposition 13. But the electorate only had the choice of voting yes or no for a particular package of tax reduction. To what extent was that package a product of the constraints of inequality in class, status, and political power?

There are some easy answers to this question, too. Some theorists argue that urban social movements are the product of class interest, the workers' interest in better social services. Other theorists argue for the primacy of status politics; still others argue that a structure of ethnic competition determines the programs of urban social movements. What I argue is that neither theories of class politics, status politics, nor ethnic politics are suitable for describing the structure of interests in American

27

suburbs that conditioned the development of tax revolt programs. The predominant interest of homeowners is consumerism. But this interest is by no means unitary. Homeowners are further divided by income levels and, in addition, often conflict with businesses in the community whose major desire is economic growth.

The program of the tax revolt was thus cast in the conflicting pattern of suburban economic interests, and it was forged by the crushing power of rationalized administration in government. As bureaucrats methodically matched higher home prices with ever higher tax bills, the result was devastating for homeowners. Neither politicians nor anyone else in the political system responded to the clear plight of the homeowners. Tax protesters faced the immediate problem of finding some way to overcome the unresponsiveness of the government apparatus.

The structures of political and economic inequality, together with the strategies that protesters devised to overcome those structures, shaped the programs of the tax revolt. Political action is best studied through an interactive approach. One must begin by charting basic political and economic inequalities. Then, one must examine how movement activists have a degree of freedom. Activists creatively interpret their confrontations with government and other opposing institutions and interests. In their fight against taxes, protesters developed strategies whereby suburban communities could oppose big city and big county government. As the tax activists invented strategies for gaining power, they shaped and reshaped their redistributive programs, altering the very interests that they pursued. Eventually, the redistributive programs of the tax limitation movement helped to form new patterns of inequality.

In short, social movements make their own redistributive programs, but not just as they please. They make them constrained by the structures of inequality in class, status, and political power inherited from the past. American citizens and political commentators have overlooked this truism because they are convinced that their country is a functioning democracy where the people rule. *Sic semper tyrannis.*[1]

The People's Choice?

Neither government officials nor business elites were celebrating on June 7, 1978, the day after Proposition 13 passed. As the airwaves buzzed with the news of Proposition 13—"mad as hell . . . ," "populism . . ."— the story went out: the people had won a great victory. Ordinary citizens, fed up with government, had written their own tax law and had overwhelmingly voted to make a huge tax cut for property owners and businesses part of the California constitution. *Eureka!*

The people of California had spoken; the voters had decided. Since the public had voted to reduce taxes on property owners and businesses, wasn't this exactly what the public had wanted all along? It had been a free election. Every citizen could have registered and voted; every ballot had been counted, and counted only once; each side had the opportunity to voice its arguments. The pro-13 and anti-13 campaigns had even spent roughly the same amount of money. This was not a rigged election in Mexico, nor a meaningless plebescite in China, but rather government for the people in the United States of America.

The folk wisdom about Proposition 13 matched the conventional wisdom of pluralist political analysis. Pluralists focus on voting and other observable actions that take place within conventional political institutions. Pluralist voting analysis attempts to discover the interests, feelings, and beliefs that lead individuals to vote one way or the other. Political institutions are seen as open to popular influence; in a democracy like the United States, voting is the supreme act of public choice.

Most of the research on the tax revolt has focused on explaining why citizens voted for Proposition 13 and similar measures in Michigan and Massachusetts.[2] This research has focused on the animus between the taxpayers and the government and has probed into voters' opinions about their tax burden, government spending, and the size and efficiency of government. In focusing on elections and on public opinions about government finance, however, researchers have missed some of the key developments of the past that made Proposition 13 what it is. The tax revolt was not only about how much the government got and how much the taxpayers kept. It was also about which groups in society gained and which lost. Tax policy is the supreme redistributive policy.

The vote for Proposition 13 was merely a plebescite, just the last step in a long journey of policy formation. One needs to look at the earlier quarrels over itinerary, when tax revolt leaders argued about the content of what was to become Proposition 13. At that time, basic redistributional questions of who gets what, and who pays what, were being settled. Proposition 13 and its tax cuts for business and homeowners were a ratification of an earlier rejection of downward redistribution.

Decisions to limit and set the agenda for the tax revolt, made in the decades before Proposition 13, were crucial because they established the general outlines of the program the tax revolt was to pursue. The process of agenda setting was greatly different from the election that ratified Proposition 13. Agendas are set more slowly and less publicly. The dropping of tax equity from the agenda revealed a fundamental inequality in the American political system: that different organized interests have widely differing powers in policy making.[3]

Establishing the agenda for the tax revolt involved non-decisions,

decisions not to act, not to target benefits to low- and moderate-income earners who could least afford their taxes. Explaining why something did not happen—or as historians term it, counterfactual history—is a task that can go awry. For every one event that did occur, there were many events that did not happen. Which one of these alternatives should the scholar pick to analyze? One should, of course, refrain from using personal preference or ideology to concoct remote possibilities to examine. Any nondecision selected for analysis needs to be an alternative that was in fact supported by some portion of the population. In this way, a nondecision can be treated as an empirical phenomenon in its own right, rather than just a fanciful dream of some outside observer.

It is, of course, more difficult to document possibilities that lost compared to causes that triumphed.[4] But as chapter 1 has demonstrated, there was a viable, alternative program for property taxes that stemmed from the interests and observable actions of homeowners in California. The owners of single-family homes, rather than businesses, were paying more and more of the property tax burden and could have decided to redistribute benefits downward, to themselves. Downward redistribution was an alternative that many states had adopted, that many activists knew of, and that was quite attractive to residents in working-class and lower-middle-class communities (see chapter 4). Some groups in those localities did in fact call for taxing big oil companies and providing property tax relief to homeowners only.

The possibility of downward redistribution was dropped from the agenda, opening the way for the very different program embodied in Proposition 13. A major reason for this nondecision was the political inequality brought about by economic inequality. Local government did not respond equally to pressures from different groups. The political system was biased against protesting groups from lower- and moderate-income communities, which lack resources—money, professional skills, information, media exposure, and access to government officials—and suffer from the generalized unresponsiveness of government and other institutions (see chaps. 4 and 5). In contrast to Robert Dahl's pluralist arguments that the American polity was a dispersed inequality where each group had some resources and power over some decisions, I argue that activists in middle-income communities were in a position of cumulative inequality and were powerless over a broad range of policies and arenas. When activists advocated downward redistribution, government simply ignored them once again.[5]

Thus, in order to better explain how the property tax revolt redistributed benefits from one group to another, one needs to examine not only the election of June 6, 1978, but also events in previous decades. In those years of fat government and lean taxpayers, the story of the tax revolt cannot be told by citing public opinion polls and voting returns. Back then, neither the weight of public opinion nor the votes of the electorate supported the tax revolt. Opinion polls rarely even asked about property taxes; newspapers may have discussed the problem once a year when tax bills were mailed out. Petitions to reduce property taxes failed to gain sufficient signatures to qualify for the ballot; initiatives that made it to the ballot were defeated by the voters.

In the 1950s and 1960s the 4.3 million Californians who would later vote for Proposition 13 were nowhere to be found. In these early decades, the tax revolt only attracted perhaps 15,000 supporters in the best of years. This was the white brigade that had the energy and the commitment to contact neighbors, gather signatures, and attend protest meetings. Although they may have been accustomed to standing on middle ground, they became caught in a redistributive battle and soon were to discover which side they were on.

Class Politics, Status Politics, and Communities of Consumers

Earlier in the tax revolt, many of the activists were homeowners in middle-income communities. Many had blue-collar jobs; many more were from working-class backgrounds. They did not own businesses or supervise others, and had little say over their own work. Their jobs provided only a modest income so that it took perseverance, luck, and overtime to be able to meet the monthly mortgage payments along with the other necessities of life. At their workplaces, trade unions pursued group interests by bargaining for more wages and less dividends and executive compensation. In tax policy, the first instinct of these homeowners was to pursue group interest through redistribution, paying less while business and the wealthy paid more.

In Western Europe and Latin America, unions and working-class political parties took the redistributive instinct and pressed it home. For example, in a deteriorating government housing project for workers in Spain, community organizations demanded well-constructed homes, clean water supplies, health-care facilities, and better schools—activity Manuel Castells calls "collective consumption trade unionism." In Italy, Communists elected to local government sought better government services coordinated with militant trade unionism, a strategy to redistribute to the working class.[6]

Throughout world history, workers have frequently pursued programs of downward redistribution and class interests, that is, the interests of all those with a similar position in the process of production.[7] The

United States, of course, has its own history of militant trade unionism and socialist, communist, and workingmen's political parties. Some of the legacy of this radical past can be found among the tax activists in working-class communities (see chap. 5). These activists scorned big business and expressed a faith in democracy and popular protest to win justice from errant elites. But all militancy aside, the tax protest movement became a multiclass coalition whose program was not downward redistribution and was not the class interest of the blue-collar homeowners who had begun the movement. The movement included not only the pizza delivery driver but the pizza-shop owner as well as the accountant who worked for him, thereby cutting across class lines at the workplace, mixing worker, owner, and professional.

The tax revolt may be atypical when compared to the urban social movements in the working-class suburbs of Paris, Turin, or Mexico City. But the tax revolt was similar to many movements in the United States such as the Progressive movement and the Temperance movement, which shunned the class-based politics of Europe and the rest of the world. What groups were involved in these movements in the United States, if not classes? What were their concerns, if not class interests derived from work? Some would argue that the tax revolt's mobilization of a multi-class base is part of a broader pattern of American exceptionalism, reflecting how American society was fundamentally different from those in the Old World.

Status Politics—And a Critique

In the 1950s, political leaders in the United States were confidently proclaiming that in America, unlike Europe, there was and would be no socialism, no proletariat. It was fashionable for the American scholar to claim that advocacy of economic redistribution was being eclipsed by status politics. Americans, for now satisfied with their material prosperity, could use politics to claim prestige and attack scapegoats and symbolic threats.[8]

American writers, seeing the past in light of their own era, went on to emphasize that throughout American history, many social movements were multiclass alliances that pursued status and not socialism. For example, Lipset and Raab's landmark study of right-wing movements analyzed nativistic organizations in the midnineteenth century.[9] Protestant craft workers joined groups such as the Know-Nothing American party because they feared losing their jobs from competition with lower-paid immigrants. The depression of 1893 led hundreds of thousands to join another nativist movement, the American Protective Association. At the same time, small businessmen and old-family Protestants in rural localities felt overtaken by the wealth of large corporations, the glamour of cities, and the power of the federal government. These local losers joined nativistic movements and the Temperance movement to establish their status and uphold their life style in a world that had left them behind. This same combination of the status-displaced with the intolerant working- and lower-middle classes led to the rise of the Ku Klux Klan in the 1920s. Local leaders threatened by political radicalism allied with a backlash movement against blacks and the looser morals associated with cities.

How do these multiclass movements hold together when, for example, one Klan member (a small farmer) was perpetually in debt to another Klan member (the town banker)? Or in the John Birch Society, when the business owner loudly advocated cutting local taxes while the policeman was a union member bargaining with the city for higher pay? The right wing was an uneasy coalition between the upper-middle class, interested in business and economic conservatism, and the lower-middle and working classes, concerned about race, family, and social issues. The tax revolt was also a combination of similar groups—small-business owners in communities, upper-middle-class homeowners, and middle-income homeowners. Discovering the collective aims, social processes, and bonds that joined different classes together in the past might provide insights as to how the tax revolt managed to cohere.

According to Lipset and Raab, status-oriented movements upheld a common program of restoring lost prestige, thereby providing a refuge from the disorganization of social change. First of all, Lipset and Raab argue that the status-deprived sought to gain prestige, self-image, or a sense of belonging by identifying with groups that had held high esteem in the distant past. Some may have used their ancestry to establish a connection to eminent groups such as the signers of the Mayflower Compact or the colonists who fought in the American Revolution. Through status politics, movement members placed their psychic investments in the past and adopted the "cultural baggage" and beliefs of bygone groups. Some joined the Klan to revel in the outlook of the Southern planters; others the Temperance movement to uphold the values of the old middle class of nineteenth-century towns.

The rise of movements that rhetorically revived group identifications, according to Lipset and Raab, indicates that the United States has become a mass society where individuals lack significant relationships and roots. In fact, claim Lipset and Raab, right-wing movements arose at precisely those moments when society was the most disorganized and when the populace felt particularly alienated.[10]

In short, Lipset and Raab argue that social disorganization and attachments to outworn eras have produced militant, cross-class movements.

Not so in the case of the tax revolt. First of all, tax protesters were not seeking attachments to the bygone past but rather were concerned with present-day problems. The tax protesters who filled the town meeting halls in California voiced an immediate grievance. The taxes on their homes, which had been among the highest in the nation, had sharply increased yet again.

Second, tax protests arose not from the disorganized and isolated individuals described in mass-society theory, but rather from communities that had developed their own organization and leadership.[11] Tax activists did feel disconnected from big government, which was unresponsive to their plight. But movement activists were not suffering from a general lack of social ties. In fact, the tax revolt spread precisely because it was able to tap into networks and associations at the neighborhood and community level.

Property tax increases affected entire communities at one stroke. Each year, as assessments were increased to match the increasing market value of homes, the assessor would revalue most of the homes in a particular town or community at the same time. The controversies over the property tax pitted communities against the government.[12]

The social life in communities contributed to the fight against property taxes. A tax protest could begin with a woman speaking to her neighbors and then arranging a meeting at her home. Supermarkets and community shopping malls were ideal locations to gather signatures on petitions. Much of the credit for mobilizing grass-roots support belongs to community-based associations of homeowners.

Tax protesters were attracted to movements that helped them to understand the concrete problems that touched the immediate world of their families and their communities. In this way, tax protest activists differed from the status-displaced individuals who sought comfort in the abstract ideologies of nationalism, fundamentalism, or anticommunism. The tax revolt cannot be adequately characterized by using theories of status politics, nor its competitor, class politics.

In theories of status politics, then, status is narrowly defined to mean prestige and social honor and, hence, loses its ability to explain the tax revolt. But the concept of status can be made more cogent if status is defined broadly, as Max Weber did, to include ethnic and racial status. The tax revolt was linked to the pursuit of ethnic advantage. Most of the activists were whites who thought that welfare programs for inner-city blacks consumed too much of their property tax dollars. In the United States, with its long history of intolerance, some would see the tax revolt as the latest example of ethnic conflict overshadowing class politics.

Ira Katznelson argues that class interests were indeed eclipsed in American cities of the nineteenth century, as local politics ignored the class-based issues of wages, conditions of work, and growth. The major institution in urban politics was the political machine, which provided patronage jobs in government and city services in ethnic neighborhoods. Local politics was restricted to deciding which ethnic groups would get the larger shares of jobs and services. By dividing any opponents into a system of competing, ethnic-neighborhood "trenches," urban political machines managed to defuse political challengers and make an anticapitalist redistributive program simply unthinkable. Meaningful solutions to urban problems, which would involve linking government services with broad programs of full employment and growth, were taken off the local political agenda.

Katznelson and other writers such as Paul Peterson conclude that local politics has become trivialized, consigned to the realm of small allocative decisions, disconnected from the major issues of class redistribution. The rise of the tax revolt, however, demonstrates that local politics can indeed decide an important redistributive policy.

Although Katznelson presents a compelling analysis of how the political machine overshadowed class politics, his findings cannot be applied to the case of the tax revolt because tax protests sprung up on a very different terrain, among suburban homeowners rather than urban ethnic voters. In California, weak political parties and a tradition of progressive reform have produced a political system that is the opposite of the political machine with its party boss, loyal aldermen, and patronage jobs. Many California cities, in fact, deliberately adopted measures such as strong city managers, civil-service rules, and nonpartisan elections in order to prevent the development of political machines. As a result, party organization at the precinct level was weak or nonexistent; the Democratic and Republican apparatuses did not have the power to name slates of candidates. Around the time the tax revolt began, although Los Angeles County had the most active Democratic party committee in the state, the committee was nevertheless weak compared to the campaign organizations of candidates for office. Furthermore, the mayor of Los Angeles, in contrast to the mayor of Chicago, had few patronage jobs to dispense and exercised little power over the city council.[13]

A Republic of Grasses and Suburban Consumers

If the political machine structured group interests in the city, how were group interests defined in the suburbs, in the absence of machines? In the 1950s, writers articulated one answer, that the suburbs fostered the outlook of the small property owner and, hence, political conservatism. As millions bought their look-alike homes in Nassau County, New

York; Cook County, Illinois; or Orange County, California, as the story goes, they found that despite their diverse backgrounds, their common interest was that of property owner. Some would argue that the suburban dwellers' ownership of property decisively shaped the interests that they pursued. Homeownership represented one's life savings; therefore it might have given the homeowner a stake in the capitalist social order and a common interest with other owners, large and small, business as well as consumer's property.[14] Property owners joined together to call on government to preserve the value of their possessions. Suburbs, so the argument went, turned their residents into Republicans.[15] Here were a thousand points of light forming one beaming presidential campaign.

The obligation of government to protect property, especially small property—this tradition of the property owners' consensus—has been a fundamental principle in the American republic. The political theorists of the American Revolution had agreed that the individual was entitled to enjoy the fruits of his or her labor. When latter-day big government increased property taxes to the point of confiscation, tax protest activists could recall the Boston Tea Party and the Declaration of Independence to justify their righteous anger.

But the planter's or the merchant's property was not the same as the homesteader's property. And in the twentieth-century American suburbs, there were great differences between different types of possessions, and between real estate of different values in different locations.[16]

First of all, it is important to recognize that the interests of homeowners center around property used in consumption, not production or investment. The interests of consumers can differ substantially from the interests of businesses. The property tax revolt was a protest against the rising cost of an important purchased good, housing. Tax protesters sought to preserve their standard of living, along with the styles and patterns of life in family and community which are the primary concerns of most people.

Tax protests expressed such fervor because high taxes threatened to curtail these patterns of consumption. For the moderate-income homeowner who could barely afford to pay a mortgage, higher taxes threatened the loss of a home and a move to a less desirable area, with all of the consequent disruptions to the family. For those who could afford to pay, spending two thousand dollars more each year in taxes meant cutting back the advantages of the good life that had motivated years of hard work—family vacations, home improvements, or savings for retirement or the children's education. Thus, taxes became a burning issue because economic losses threatened specific and immediate consumption practices.

The differences between the interests of homeowning consumers and the interests of businesses in the same community are evident in the political stands that homeowners associations take. Many tax protest leaders gained their political experience by working with these groups on previous issues; community associations provided essential support to tax protests. Some associations fought proposed freeways through their areas; many opposed new construction projects and other forms of urban growth that might crowd their community or overburden its services. In doing so, homeowning consumers found themselves opposing local businesses whose goals were metropolitan growth, more productive investments, and higher sales. As did other consumers, homeowners favored protective regulations, whereas business opposed them (see chap. 3).

In addition to conflicts of interest between homeowners and business owners in the same community, the pleasant suburban landscape concealed another major conflict, between suburbs with different life styles, ethnic and racial populations, and socioeconomic standings. Far from being homogeneous, suburbs are as different as the people who compose them. There were suburbs like Fremont, California, where half of the residents identify themselves as working class and four-fifths as Democrats versus one-tenth Republicans. There were suburban enclaves where black professionals and workers were able to find housing.[17] The residential segregation of ethnic groups and social classes has produced a hierarchy of communities that has hardened into a "stratification of places."[18] As I will argue in chapters 4 and 6, there were profound differences between middle-income suburbs and upper-middle-class suburbs, which led each to propose very different programs for tax reduction.

In short, political action in the cities was structured by political machines that rejected an encompassing, class-based interest and instead fostered a multitude of ethnic-based, fragmented interests. In the suburbs, the structure of interests was not a property owners' consensus; rather, business and different groups of homeowners had conflicting interests. Oftentimes, disagreements between the different groups of property holders simmered beneath the surface and were not articulated and resolved directly.

The ultimate outcome of these latent economic conflicts depended upon a political battle, between the different types of property owners on one side—and on the other side, their common enemy, state and local governments that had become unresponsive on the tax issue. Conflicts over economic redistribution, in short, hinged upon conflicts to gain political power. Class conflicts, such as they are in the United States or anywhere else for that matter, are inextricably connected to struggles for political power. Structures of political power can have a decisive effect on the lives of citizens—an effect that rivals the impact of structures of economic inequality.[19]

The suburban political landscape was dominated not by the partisan machine but rather by a bureaucratic structure of government, founded with the best intentions of honest and efficient administration. But unbeknownst to progressive reformers, plans for rational administration had turned into a behemoth of unresponsiveness. How groups attempted to restrain this behemoth shaped the redistributional programs that property owners adopted.[20]

Administrative Capacity and Unresponsive Power

Taxes that are administered inequitably and corruptly certainly provoke popular outrage. Unfortunately for tax collectors, the public can also revolt because of taxes that are rationally and legally administered. In California the property tax was a model of progressive administration. The law required all property to be assessed at the same rate throughout the state. Valuations were calculated by computers and checked by a State Board of Equalization. But all of this administrative efficiency and expertise in government made no sense at all, for when home prices inflated to ridiculous levels, property taxes did so as well (see chap. 1).[21]

The administrative power of big city and big county government had become unresponsive to the problems of ordinary citizens. This was the tragic flaw of the progressive reformers in California and elsewhere, who sought to do good, better than the political machine. At least the machine precinct captain was always arranging special benefits, trying to respond to the grievances of ordinary citizens. In fact, partisan machines arose not in Europe but in the United States, one of the few nations where many persons (most white men) had political rights early in the nineteenth century. Under the machine system, an alderman could fix a tax bill if a citizen could not afford to pay.

California, however, exemplified the states where progressives had triumphed and made the tax collection system a marvel of impartial administration. Here, inability to pay was simply not grounds for altering the assessment on one's home, which was invariably set at 25 percent of fair market value for all.

Attempting to reduce property taxes back down to affordable levels, homeowners groups and ad hoc protest committees contacted official after official for help—the assessor's office, the assessor himself, Los Angeles City Council members, the mayor of Los Angeles, county supervisors, and their assistants. Top elected officials and bureaucrats were not the least bit interested in a significant reduction in the property tax burden.

These political elites had great power, compared to the community-based organizations that protested property taxes. Government in the metropolitan areas of California was truly big government in its powers and its scale. The five supervisors of Los Angeles County represented seven million people; each supervisor had a constituency three times larger than a congressional representative from California.[22] The mayor of Los Angeles represented three million, compared to a typical community composed of perhaps fifty thousand residents. The mayor, assessor, and supervisors could safely ignore the complaints of the five or six communities who were hit the hardest by the yearly round of property tax increases.

The greater power of government leaders, compared to groups of suburban homeowners, does not necessarily mean that high officials are a "power elite"—a well-connected clique who coordinate their actions to pursue common aims. C. Wright Mills, who coined the term, sparked a huge controversy among social scientists. Much of the debate focused on the question of how centralized power actually was, with power elite theorists arguing that local governments were monolithic structures and the pluralists claiming that there was competition among the groups who governed.[23]

Whether or not top local officials are unified or fragmented among themselves, the fact remains that they are not very responsive to ordinary citizens who lack connections to government. Robert Dahl, a pluralist who vigorously argued that political power is dispersed, nevertheless admitted that the city is in no way ruled by the people. Dahl noted that the citizens he studied in New Haven, Connecticut, had no direct influence and only a moderate amount of indirect influence exercised through voting. Political leaders, regardless of whether they were cohesive or divided, had great powers over citizens, including the power to shape preferences and define the alternatives on the public agenda. Groups bold enough to challenge the system, according to Dahl, were likely to be isolated or defeated by insiders, who possessed superior resources and utilized them efficiently.[24]

The difficulties of gaining power[25] are a common problem for movements, which begin without sufficient money, reputations, donated labor, or other resources to work through conventional political channels and achieve victory. Local officials are not likely to bargain or to grant concessions to protest movements when they first appear.

During the civil rights movement in the United States, for example, local officeholders such as police chiefs and mayors, with the support of white merchants, exercised their power to jail and harass civil rights activists and otherwise defeat movement activity. Even movements that can claim a following throughout a nation are usually composed of groups based in a particular community or city, such as union locals, organization chapters, church congregations, party cells, or consciousness-raising groups. The setting for these local actors is the community and its authorities.[26]

If we are to explain how a social movement develops, we need to examine not only the interests and condition of individual participants when they first join together. We also need to study the process whereby the movement interacts with its local environment, particularly with local officials and other elites that are usually the movement's first opponents. Much about a social movement—the beliefs of the participants, the culture of the movement, its organization, tactics, and even its program for restructuring society—is shaped by interaction with the significant powers in society. A movement constantly attempts to test its environment and itself through action, and revise its beliefs and structures in light of successes and failures.

In short, we cannot understand a movement unless we examine how it has navigated and negotiated through a landscape of specific geographical places at a certain point in history. The social landscape of the California tax revolt was forbidding and sometimes even hostile. We have mapped that landscape, showing how it is contoured by the heights of power and the great plain of everyday life.

Tax protesters showed a determination to shape their urban social landscape. Learning about politics, they creatively responded when they found that normal political channels were ineffective. As they constantly devised original interpretations, reinterpretations, and novel actions, tax protesters managed to achieve a major social change against powerful adversaries. The tax revolt is best understood through an interactive approach to protest movements and social life.

Interaction, Power, and Redistributive Programs

An interactive approach focuses on portraying the activists' interpretations—the meanings that activists attach to situations they experience. As participants in tax revolts tried to comprehend the intricate political conflicts of tax reform, they showed a fundamental human urge to make sense out of the events that affect their lives.

The creation of meaning is an active and continual process. Humans can interpret their world in a range of various ways. People are constantly selecting among alternate interpretations. People check and alter the meanings conveyed to them by the institutions and rituals in a society. To be human is to formulate new meanings in response to changing situations. As the qualitative tradition in sociology has emphasized, people are constantly engaged in the process of negotiating their social world—reassessing their views as they reflect upon their own actions and the reactions of others.[27]

In social movements, activists become involved in patterns of interactions with local authorities, thereby devising new beliefs about power that make sense out of their situations.[28] Although new interpretations are obviously being formed in movements that overtly seek to change culture, new understandings can also be found in movements that deal with economic issues.[29] This includes even preservationist movements like the tax revolt, whose general tenor is not to herald the new but rather to defend existing styles of life. Even in the most traditional of tax reduction groups, whose meetings begin with the pledge of allegiance, whose leaders meet for golf, and whose wives form ladies auxiliaries— new ideas abounded about what local government does and what it ought to do.[30]

The changing interactions in social movements make for changing patterns of belief.[31] Different groups of property owners—homeowners in middle-income communities, homeowners in upper-middle-class communities, and small-business owners—developed different interpretations about their initial failures to get local government to reduce property taxes. Each protest group, because of its different economic standing and political history, formulated different views about big government.

In middle-income communities, protest groups were rebuffed by county government, by big city government (if they were part of the City of Los Angeles), and even by their town governments (if they were an incorporated small municipality), not only on the issue of property taxes, but on most other issues as well. Groups of middle-income tax protesters had limited resources and could find few community institutions to support them. Businesses in the community, for example, usually did not support tax protests. Movement activists interacted with unsympathetic elites and institutions, interpreted their experience of interaction, and concluded that they faced a situation of *generalized unresponsiveness*. This led to a strident sense of militancy among the activists (see chaps. 4 and 5).

Leading small businesses in a community had a different sense of their own power, since they had considerable influence over zoning and development decisions in their localities. But they too did not succeed when they tried to reduce their own property taxes. Community small business leaders interpreted their situation as one of *bounded power*. Their power was limited by the higher levels of government, county and state, which had the authority to assess property and collect taxes (chap. 6).

Chapter 7 shows how the same factors—power, interaction, and interpretation, operated in upper-middle-class residential suburbs. There, particularly on the issues of neighborhood zoning and development, homeowners associations had achieved some influence over government officials in towns, cities, and even at the county level.[32] But government officials did nothing about demands for major cuts in property taxes and increased participation in budget decisions. In this political setting, activists in upper-middle-class communities interpreted their experiences, producing beliefs that expressed their own frustrated advantage.

I use the term *frustrated advantage* to emphasize that the plight of the contemporary upper-middle class consists of advantages in class, status, and/or political power in some arenas, but relative powerlessness in other arenas. Tax protest activists felt proud to be influential professionals in their work; they were outraged at their comparative lack of power with big government. The activists in tax protests were leaders of homeowners associations. They were respected in their own communities but were powerless to affect decisions about taxing and spending at the metropolitan level of government.

Acting upon their sense of frustrated advantage, tax protest activists in upper-middle-class localities conducted highly professional campaigns in their communities to increase their power in metropolitan politics. In this endeavor, the homeowners allied with community small businesses, who were also trying to leverage and pyramid their standing in the community to influence big government. Both upper-middle-class homeowners and community businesses hit upon the idea of forming an alliance in their community directed against the larger political institutions outside their social horizons.

Alone, neither homeowners nor small businesses could succeed. But when they affiliated, they could pool their resources and use their communities as a base to attack the taxing and spending policies at the county and state level.[33] This coalition of small property upheld Proposition 13, with its common program of tax reduction for homeowners and businesses.

Thus, interpretations produced the strategies of a social movement. Opinions arose from the interaction between the movement and outside authorities; beliefs were tested and changed as the movement sought allies in its battle to make government more responsive. Just to form an interpretation is an affirmation of human subjectivity. Furthermore, meanings cannot be separated from the actions that they produce. Beliefs create motivations and generate activity that helps to shape the world.[34]

As I have argued, political action takes place in the confines of local settings structured by the inequalities of class and power. But those settings do not predetermine political outcomes. Each particular community formed a unique context, where people discovered for themselves the issues of the tax revolt. Countless small meetings and discussions among neighbors formed the ideas that shaped the political direction of the tax revolt. The negotiations at the community level had a cumulative effect. Patterns of local action, dramatized by the success of Proposition 13, and the slogans of that action then had a profound effect on national politics.

The alternative that came to pass, a tax revolt with a probusiness program, was in no way predetermined by the structure of local settings. The setting of suburbia gave the small property owner a host of conflicting interests—a common interest in protecting property, yes, but also divergent interests. Some small property owners were business proprietors, others consumers; some had wealth, others modest means; some were for, others against growth. Local activists needed to do something about their tax bills. The character of what they did was not a mechanical response dictated by the situation, however, but rather an action that affirmed the possibility for humans to transcend and alter their situation.[35] Even if history makes clear that the inequalities of power and class tend to persist, it also reveals the creativity of generations of activists who have reflected upon and then confronted those harsh realities.

Means and Ends in Movements

My interactive analysis of the formation of social-movement programs differs from the approaches that other writers have advanced in recent years. Others have also been concerned about political inequality—the power of governments and how protest movements can overcome it. But many important studies of social movements have focused not so much on the programs and goals of movements but rather on means—the tactics a movement adopts, the number of actions undertaken, or the mobilization of resources.[36]

For example, Doug McAdam's insightful analysis of the civil rights movement in the United States examines the power relations between national elites and black communities. Changes in the context of power contributed to the success of innovative protest tactics such as boycotts, sit-ins, and freedom rides. Authorities then succeeded in developing countermeasures that nullified the effectiveness of each new tactic. McAdam elaborates on the political processes of "tactical interaction," whereby insurgents make "tactical innovations" and authorities reply with "tactical adaptation."[37] McAdam, however, stops short of explaining the interesting succession of goals that the movement adopted from civil rights to black power to affirmative action.

Charles Tilly also analyzes social movements in the context of government power. His influential work, *From Mobilization to Revolution,* constructs strategic models[38] of movements which assume that participants start out with a certain interest in claiming goods for themselves at the expense of other groups. Tilly then uses a cost-benefit analysis that compares the advantages received for committing resources to win a conflict. He seeks to explain the level of resources a group actually committed and the forms of action that took place. Tilly's analysis begins with a group's interest in redistribution and then attempts to explain the success or failure of tactics ("repertoires") to achieve those given interests.[39]

This book will argue that political processes affect, and sometimes completely alter, the redistributive program of a movement. The interactions of a movement with the authorities can change much about a movement, not only its tactics, its organization, and its mobilization of resources, but even the program it advances.[40] Redistributive programs are not the simple product of preexisting group or class interest. Rather, through a process of political interaction, a group creates a sense of its interests that defines the programs the group promotes. What needs explaining is how movement participants continually construct and modify their programs through political interaction.[41]

Those scholars who have analyzed the changing goals of movements have emphasized a process—the bureaucratization of movements themselves—different from the one highlighted in this book. Roberto Michels described the growing bureaucracy in the European social-democratic parties. According to Michels's "iron law of oligarchy," movements inevitably became hierarchial institutions with leaders remote from ordinary members. Leftist parties began with a working-class base and Marxist doctrines but later developed centralized leadership that steered the parties in a conservative direction. By 1900 once-militant parties and trade unions had become tame members of the polity, the groups whose demands routinely influence government.[42]

To this day, political parties, labor unions, big business, professional groups, universities, agriculture, and other highly organized interest groups remain influential. In Sweden and France, many speak of the dominance of such a coalition of corporatist and technocratic interests. In this world of large bureaucracies, protest movements feel pressured to become large and bureaucratic themselves in order to exert any influence at all. According to McCarthy and Zald, even leftist social-welfare, civil-rights, and environmental movements of the 1960s have become centralized and professionally managed organizations with an agenda separate from the underprivileged beneficiaries who are supposedly served. Social reformers have become yet another bureaucratic interest group, whose advertising, marketing, and computer mail techniques rival those of any business.[43]

The tax revolt movement that succeeded in putting Proposition 13 on the ballot may have adopted more conservative goals, but it managed to escape the iron law of oligarchy. It was not professionally managed. From the early protests in the 1950s to the gathering of a million and a half signatures that placed Proposition 13 on the ballot, none of the leaders of the movement drew a salary. The movement was a shifting coalition of small groups of homeowners and taxpayers. The groups maintained only a tenuous connection to an umbrella group, the United Organizations of Taxpayers, and directed their own community activities to reduce property taxes.[44]

The decentralized tax protests contrasted sharply to the organized interests that already had a voice in tax policy. In fact, the tax revolt became a battle between community groups versus the corporatist and technocratic interests monopolizing local government, all of which opposed Proposition 13. Large utilities, banks, and other businesses donated large sums of money to fight Prop. 13. Leaders of both political parties denounced the measure; most media outlets editorialized against it. Labor unions, teachers' associations, and school and university administrators joined in the No on 13 campaign. The victory of Proposition 13 was an angry rejection of the entire establishment. It also unravelled the very structure of interest-group politics. Individual firefighters voted for Proposition 13 despite the recommendation of their union; managers in the Bank of America voted for it despite the bank's public stand against. Small businesses worked for it in their communities despite the fact that the State Chamber of Commerce did not favor it.

The tax revolt, then, was a revolt of communities against big government and the bureaucratic interest groups associated with it. This revolt left its mark upon the large patterns of economic inequality between rich and poor, between those who owned businesses and those who did not. With Proposition 13, billions of dollars year after year would not be channeled into local government services; most of the benefits would accrue to business owners rather than homeowners. The formula of Proposition 13 would be repeated in other states and at the national level during the Reagan administration.[45]

Communities Against the State: The Formation of Class Programs

What the tax revolt demonstrates is that movements advocating major redistributive programs are not only formed at the workplace through conflicts between employers and unions but are also formed through political activity in communities. It is the community and the group with its own social order which provide resistance to adverse conditions and the vision of the justice to be won.[46]

The relations of work and production, now structured by far-flung international interdependency, no longer take place within the confines of communities. Communities have become centers of consumption. The issues of consumption sparked protests and organizations which contributed to the mobilization of a powerful tax protest movement.

Throughout history, classes with the power to remake the economy of a nation were first formed in small communities. In the early industrial revolution, the working class took shape in the villages of England and France, where new small-scale industries had to find their place amid local ties and traditions. As social movements arose to protest the conditions of work, the strength of movements and their inspiration stemmed not so much from the new relations of class but from the established relationships of the residential community and the status group. Ongoing communal relations set the goal for the movements: to mitigate the disruptions of social life brought on by the industrial revolution.

Edward P. Thompson traces how English workers began to articulate programs advancing their common interests, in opposition to the interests of their employers. These class-based redistributive programs, grounded in class consciousness, were formed through political activity within communities. As they organized the London Corresponding Society, challenged the state in demonstrations and uprisings, and campaigned to reform Parliament, English workers developed a sense of their own identity and interests.[47]

In the villages of Yorkshire, a struggle for political rights and power was the making of the English working class and its challenge to industrial capitalism. In the suburbs of California, the small property owner's campaign for lower taxation with representation has been the making of the American middle class and its fascination with business conservatism.

3

Probusiness Leaders and Consumers' Movements in Communities

I'm always for the consumer. If the consumer gets the best deal that's what I'm for. And so the consumer is king in my mind. And whoever benefits the consumer—he's got my vote.[1]

I thought of it in terms of my own personal, my selfish reasons. I wanted my house to be saved and that was utmost in my mind. My husband was an engineer and he made a fair salary, but if I followed it with my property tax, that's taking money I could spend on something else, mainly my son's college education. And your home and your children's education are the two biggest things that people consider in their lives. Your husband's job first because without that you don't have anything.[2]

[I]t's only a question of reaching people so that they are able to see beyond the tunnel vision of the problems that face them . . .—job, insurance, mortgages, and whatnot. If they see a little daylight they'll move, and if they see a little common sense, they'll move. But it takes collective thinking, and it's not hard to get collective thinking, not hard at all. I think that Proposition 13 was . . . a community manifestation. . . . At a given point people get together and they have a Boston Tea Party.[3]

The property tax protesters in California ended up enacting a proposition that gave most of the tax relief to business. The victory of Proposition 13 inspired probusiness conservatives to organize a national tax limitation movement, which succeeded in cutting taxes on businesses and upper-income individuals. But as tax cuts became the talk of corporate boardrooms and the Cabinet Room, forgotten were the owners of the modest suburban homes who had started the tax revolt.

Homeowners had the simple desire to reduce their property tax bills. But in order to understand their fate—how their movement adopted a redistributive program that undercut this goal—one needs to comprehend the homeowners' broader concerns. The homeowners' interest was consumerism, which they pursued not just as individuals in a market but also as social folk in a suburban community. The outlook of the homeowner, which was crucial in shaping tax protests, is best understood by examining some other movements that arose in California suburbs during the 1960s and 1970s. As homeowners took part in antibusing movements, antigrowth movements, and movements to increase government services, their message was clear: let the consumer be king. This message, however, has been blacked out by the probusiness conservatism that was humming through the air.

The Probusiness Creed

In the 1970s, the media was full of the words of probusiness publicists and organizations. While writers such as Milton Friedman and George Gilder were extolling the virtues of free enterprise, groups like the American Enterprise Institute and the Heritage Foundation planned a conservative policy coup. These probusiness conservatives were the champions of lower taxes and government spending and were the inspiration for President Ronald Reagan's economic policies.

Here, then, was one influential force for lower taxes. But what was its relation to grass-roots movements—especially the homeowners who protested against their property tax bills? Probusiness writers and groups had national visibility, expertise, and resources which might have helped the tax revolt in California.

But probusiness leaders and conservative groups gave only sporadic assistance to the tax protesters in California, and then only late in the game. In fact, the probusiness conservatives and the tax protest movement were worlds apart, as can be seen by comparing the themes and the issues that each has raised.[4] Probusiness conservatives emphasized the supply side, growth without regulation, and stringent monetarism. This creed directly contrasted to the theme of preservation of consumption that was dear to the community groups forming the tax revolt.

The central premise of probusiness conservatism was that the free enterprise system in general, and business corporations in particular, were a force for accomplishing good in society. Probusiness proponents agreed that taxes and government spending must be significantly cut.

Although lower taxes and lower spending had always been a sacred incantation for conservatives, in the 1970s these homilies inspired a crusade. Taxes had to be cut. But the reason was not that people could barely afford to pay. Representatives David Stockman (R., Mich.) and Jack Kemp (R., N.Y.) spoke incessantly about how tax and budget cuts could spur a great economic revival. If tax rates on individuals were eased, then people would supposedly work harder, be more productive, earn more, and save more, thus producing capital for business. If the tax burden on business were reduced, then corporations would have even more capital to invest. Thus, cutting taxes and the budget would supposedly stimulate investment on the supply side.[5]

The supply side! What transpires in this ethereal realm? George Gilder portrayed the supply side as entrepreneurs, with the intelligence and vision to make the investments that create productive wealth. Thus, the prophets of the supply side spoke of investment; they relentlessly criticized the liberal Keynesians, who emphasized the demand side and consumption. The liberal Keynesians, the story goes, had given money for the poor and for government agencies to spend, hoping that increased consumption would bring prosperity. The conservatives argued that all Keynesianism had achieved was public bankruptcy and inflation. To the Keynesian injunction to fight recessions by increasing demand, the conservatives countered with Say's old law that supply created its own demand. Conservatives argued that priorities needed to be changed from stimulating consumption to fostering investment.[6]

Stimulating investments, according to another variant in the conservative economic creed, was merely a matter of getting the government out of the way so that the free enterprise system could work its miracles. Free marketeers such as Milton and Rose Friedman condemned the Interstate Commerce Commission, the Federal Drug Agency, the Consumer Products Safety Commission, the Environmental Protection Agency, and other regulatory agencies for ruining the economy. For economic conservatives, deregulation became another sacred incantation. Mismanagement of the money supply was another obstacle that the government had created, which, according to the Friedmans, had produced the ruinous inflation of the 1970s. The Federal Reserve Board needed to take stringent control of the money supply, allowing only modest growth.[7]

Without government meddling the American economy could become the shining New Jerusalem. But this miracle could only come to pass if the United States forsook the false prophet of protectionism, and if the United States opened itself to the adjustments inevitable in a dynamic world economy. Capitalism was change, and capitalism was growth: individuals moving up to better jobs, the nation enjoying a better standard of living, new technologies being applied and marketed. Conservatives saw change, and it was good, whenever it occurred on earth, even on the morning and evening of the seventh day.[8]

The probusiness conservatives made a sharp contrast to the tax protesters in the suburbs, who also opposed high taxes but came to that concern through a very different set of beliefs and social circumstances. For tax protesters, the large issues of economic policy, redistribution of wealth, and business growth were seen and understood as local phenomena that impacted on their neighborhoods. For many residents, probusiness policies, the supply side, monetarism, and growth and deregulation sounded fine as pieties but were irrelevant to making political choices in their communities. To the grass-roots tax protester, stringent monetarism meant higher interest rates on mortgages and home-improvement and automobile loans. Tax protesters, particularly those in middle-income communities, were often skeptical or hostile to large corporations. In many communities regardless of income level, tax protesters worried that growth and deregulation meant that they would have to live next to a towering apartment complex, or worse still, next to a polluting industry. Economic growth, despite its benefits, had shown itself to be a great destroyer of communities and people's place in those communities. The community activists who created the tax revolt wanted not growth and change but rather preservation. And finally, in contrast to the probusiness conservative's emphasis on the supply side and investment, the tax protest activist was primarily concerned with enhancing consumption and consumerism.

Lords of the Mall, Stewards of the Middle Class

The immediate goal of the tax protesters in California was to reduce their own property tax bills, thereby lowering the price they paid for an important consumer good. The tax revolt was akin to a number of other movements that also sought to enhance consumerism at the community level.

Consumerist movements seek to advance the interests of the purchaser of consumer goods, that is, the final products and services that are used for such purposes as housing, food, child rearing, leisure, and personal development.[9] Consumer goods can be distinguished from raw materials, intermediate products, and plant and equipment, which are directly utilized by businesses to produce other commodities. Consumerist movements accept the premise that commodities, things that can be bought and sold, are the major way in which human needs are satisfied. Within this constraint, consumerist movements attempt to increase the quality and volume of goods for purchase, while at the same time trying to reduce the price of those products.

Since consumer purchases require a source of income and usually employment, consumerism is closely related to issues of work such as rates of pay. In the 1970s, as tax protests were mobilizing, consumerism became a charged issue because many thought that the standard of living in the United States was falling, especially for the middle class. Spendable weekly earnings, after rising steadily from 1949 to 1969, actually decreased by 1.7 percent between 1969 and 1979. Between 1979 and 1984, all income brackets suffered declines in income after taxes and inflation. Declining real incomes were particularly pronounced in wholesale and retail trade and in the finance, insurance, and real estate sector. The jobs in these sectors are mainly low-paying and dead-end positions as clerks, secretaries, and cashiers. Some predict that as these low-paying service jobs become more prevalent, and as the number of well-paying jobs in manufacturing declines, the middle class in the United States will continue to shrink. Families earning incomes between $15,000 and $35,000 in constant 1982 dollars comprised 53 percent of all families in 1970 but only 44 percent in 1982.[10]

Most trade unions aid the consumerist interests of their members by organizing credit unions and discounted automobile insurance. But in the twentieth-century United States, the general pattern has been for consumerist movements, such as the cooperative purchasing movements popular in the 1930s and 1960s, to be relatively independent from unions and other work-related organizations.

Thus, consumerist movements have been specialized, focusing on the issues concerning buyers, even when these movements have attacked the same large corporations that trade unions fight. Among militant consumerists, Ralph Nader is no doubt the best known. Nader campaigned to obtain compensation for children who had been deformed by the drug thalidomide; he wrote *Unsafe at Any Speed,* alleging that there were gross defects in the Chevrolet Corvair. Nader's publications, investigations, and citizens' lobbies have charged that hot dogs were unhealthy, clothing was dangerously flammable, tire advertisements were deceptive, and that nuclear reactors and waste disposal procedures were unsafe. Widely believed by the public, Nader's charges have compelled government and business to take remedial action. To both his friends and foes, Nader is a leftist reformer who stands for citizen pressure to initiate government regulation and limit corporate power.[11]

Throughout the history of the United States, consumerism has sometimes been a doctrine of the left, sometimes the right. Consumerism was promoted in the 1920s by farsighted capitalists such as Lincoln Filene and Henry Ford, who hoped to sell more commodities mass produced by large corporations. In the name of consumerism, Filene and Ford introduced the assembly line, mass marketing, and higher wage scales. Ralph Nader's attacks on the next generation of merchants and auto makers redefined the consumer's interests in leftist directions. In local communities, consumerist movements have also raised issues that led sometimes to the right, and sometimes to the left. A prime example is the tax revolt, whose leader was Howard Jarvis—but could have been Ralph Nader.

Communities as Sites for Consumption

For many Americans, the most costly consumer transaction they will ever make in their lifetime is the purchase or rental of a home. In recent years, the portion of family income spent on shelter has increased as rents and homeownership costs have increased faster than inflation. The monthly expense of owning a new home increased by 120 percent between 1970 and 1976, whereas the consumer price index rose by 46 percent. A home involves a major financial investment—the security deposit if one rents, and the down payment and equity if one owns.[12]

Economists encourage us to think of the consumption of housing as an isolated choice by free individuals. At the center of the neoclassical model of consumption is a sovereign household that decides how to maximize personal preferences, subject to the constraints of its financial resources. Popular sentiment also claims that housing is a realm of individual freedom. Particularly when houses are owner-occupied, the home is mythologized as a haven where individuals can find refuge from the demands of one's boss and all the rest of the outside world. One's home is one's castle: secure but isolated, where one locks out but is also locked in.[13]

Despite these views, the fact remains that a household's consumption of shelter is a public, social phenomenon—rather than just an individualized, economic choice. Purchasing a home involves a major commitment not only to a particular piece of property but also to the neighborhood and local institutions around it. Housing is a collective consumption good, because many qualities of housing are shared by other residences in a particular area. One's property value is determined by the character of the surrounding neighborhood. The style of life of one's neighbors affects the quality of one's own. The term "public safety" emphasizes the fact that urban crime is a highly patterned phenomenon which exposes people in a specific locale to a similar level of risk.[14]

In addition, housing is collective consumption because many residential amenities are the product of the public interactions among inhabitants. Most householders, in addition to having a financial stake in their neighborhood, develop a social stake as well. Residents usually make some effort to gain knowledge about their community and develop acquaintances in the vicinity. Although these attachments are less intense than the bonds in the idealized small town of the nineteenth century, community affiliations, albeit in a limited form, have persisted into contemporary times.[15]

A variety of social interactions help residents to improve the quality of their housing and related consumption in communities. Through conversations with one another, residents collectively devise a shared mental map that indicates, for example, the areas where it is safe for children to play. Parents and senior citizens who spend much time around home monitor the comings and goings of residents and take notice of strangers on the streets.

In addition to defending their neighborhood through informal contacts and understandings, residents join groups such as neighborhood watches, parent–teacher associations, improvement organizations, and homeowners associations in order to see that the people, institutions, and environment nearby are compatible with their own consumption style.[16] Inhabitants are mainly interested in issues that directly affect their localities—whether the streets are safe, the schools are good, and polluting industries are far away. Thus, residents collectively seek to maintain and improve the desired patterns of consumption in their neighborhoods.

Frequently, community organizations exert pressure on local government, which has the formal responsibility to provide many of the goods and services desired by community consumers. James O'Connor used the term *social consumption* to describe government spending for such services as schools, roads, parks, sewers, and police and fire protection. The government provides consumption items not only through its direct expenditures, but also by granting subsidies such as the tax deductions allowed for home mortgages. Local governments, furthermore, make decisions on zoning that determine which types of businesses and people will locate in a community, which in turn produces patterns of social life. These issues of spatially grounded consumption are a major concern of community groups.[17]

Community organizations, located in California suburbs, generated the grass-roots activity that placed Proposition 13 on the ballot. Despite the reputation of Los Angeles for alienated transience, scores of homeowners and residents associations flourished there. As high property taxes enraged the one million inhabitants of the San Fernando Valley in 1976, a newsletter listed seven valley groups working mainly for lower property taxes and government spending and another eighteen home-

Table 1   The Varieties of Community Consumerism

---

1. Lowering consumer costs:
   Tax protests, tax reduction movement
   Proposition 13

. . . .

2. Obtaining ethnic advantages in consumption:
   Antibusing movements
   Movements against open housing   Right affiliation

. . . .

3. Improving quality of consumer goods:
   Environmental preservationism   Left affiliation

4. Improving government services

---

owners associations concerned about taxes and other issues. One, the Hillside and Canyon Associations, was itself a coalition of twenty-eight homeowners groups. Through a homeowners association, a constituency of some fifty thousand persons (several orders of magnitude more than a block club) mobilized to fight taxes. In 1977, while a million and a half signatures were being collected for Proposition 13, a "Taxpayers Congress" convened, with representatives from sixty taxpayers and homeowners groups in four counties. After Proposition 13 passed, one statewide mailing list of tax activists included 334 addresses and, in Los Angeles and Orange Counties alone, forty-eight organizations including twelve specializing in tax issues and twenty-eight homeowners associations.[18]

These homeowners associations in suburban communities provided much of the support for the tax protest movement and gathered most of the signatures on tax-cutting initiatives. Homeowners groups pursued a variety of goals, which advanced community consumerism in different ways (see table 1).

A close examination of these consumerist issues can provide much evidence about the political views of tax protest activists, who usually were, after all, officers in the community groups.[19]

The Moral Revolt to Preserve Consumption

To begin with, the tax revolt can be considered a type of community consumerist movement. The grievance was high property taxes, which further increased the price of housing, a costly purchased item. In the years before the passage of Proposition 13, large increases in property tax bills had a drastic effect on the consumption and living patterns of middle-income and even upper-middle-class households.

Take the case of Marilyn Noorda, the head of the Taxation Committee of the Sherman Oaks Homeowners in 1976, who tirelessly worked out of her house with thirty other volunteers, gathering signatures on petitions. That year, the tax bill on the Noordas' modest three-bedroom house increased from about $1,200 a year to over $2,400. With an annual income of about $24,000, the Noorda household was well-off, compared to the median family income of about $14,000 in Los Angeles. But even the Noordas' could not stretch their income to pay the tax increase. Glen Noorda's paycheck as a stagehand at a movie studio, after federal taxes and union dues, was $1,341 a month. The $200 a month in property taxes, a $218 mortgage, $240 for food, $134 in church donations, and $110 for entertainment and baby sitters boosted their total monthly expenses to $1,375. Marilyn just managed to pay her tax bill that year by shaving a few dollars here and there from her household budget. That same year, the dilemmas were even more sharply posed for Helmut and Carmen Foster, whose property taxes increased from $750 to over $1,700. With a household income of $15,000, still above the Los Angeles median, the Fosters were forced to cut their auto and disability insurance and, beyond that, would have to sell a small plot of recreational land and take their two children out of Catholic school.[20]

People fought high property taxes when they were forced to abandon consumption patterns that they had valued and perhaps cherished. Citizens became outraged when high taxes raised the specter that the government would confiscate homes if owners could not pay their tax bills. Unpaid taxes produced a lien on the delinquent property. In time, the chilling words, "Sold to the State" would be stamped on deeds in the county recorder's office. And this would happen not in the Soviet Union but in the United States of America.

Few persons actually lost their homes directly to big government. But some did have to sell in the market because they could not pay tax bills; many more had good reasons to fear this grim eventuality. Selling one's home, even though it might fetch a high price, was no solution. To quote one overtaxed homeowner: "If I sell my home, even at inflated prices, I have to replace it at equally inflated prices or find a rental at exorbitant rates or move out to the hinterland." The home was not simply another financial asset but also the center of a household's social relations of consumption. As another put it:

We did not buy our property for investment purposes—we bought it for our home. . . . Of course we could sell our home and buy some other property at an inflated price, but what would we gain? After the real estate agent gets his cut, we would have a larger mortgage at a higher interest rate and still have the tax burden, so we would be worse off than we are now. If we do not reinvest [in a new home], then the capital gains tax will dissipate our "profit."[21]

Thus, high property taxes threatened to make owning a home even more expensive and unaffordable for many, forcing existing owners to sell and potential owners to despair. High property taxes were a menace to something immediate and concrete, as well as inviolate and private—a person's home. One bumper sticker for Proposition 13 proclaimed, "Save the American Dream: Yes on 13."

The possibility of losing one's home created further anger because the cause, big government, was supposed to protect and encourage property owners. American politics has been dominated by the assumption that property owners, particularly small landowners, should have the opportunity to improve their property and use it in productive activity. They should have the right to be protected as they enjoy the resulting wealth and advantages—secure in the pursuit of happiness. The American Revolution established a republic, which guaranteed the property owner the right of due process under law and the right to participate in politics as a "freeman" and a "freeholder." Property owners had a stake in society and, hence, would be the ideal citizens.[22]

When Thomas Jefferson dreamed of the United States as an agrarian republic and spoke of small property, he meant small farmers. But today, farmers have become a tiny fraction of the citizenry. The owners of tract houses and small plots of suburban land preside over homes but no longer homesteads. Still, these suburban yeomen believe that the small property owner who improves his or her property is an ideal citizen who has earned the state's protection and not confiscation. As Helmut Foster argued, "I put all my efforts in my spare time to build up the house." After remodeling the kitchen and dining room, adding a bedroom and a brick driveway, and tending the plants that had grown into a shady garden, Foster's improvements made his tax bill even higher. "It ends up as a penalty if you do anything to your property. Our taxes would probably be lower if we had done nothing, just not made any improvements." The Fosters became angry tax fighters and gathered signatures for tax reduction initiatives.[23] They would defend small property that the owner improved and then enjoyed; they could sympathize with a small business owner who had built up his own enterprise. But it was quite another matter to defend big property, a large corporation where the hard work and virtue of an owner was not apparent. Big business conservatism did not necessarily flow out of the concept that property was the fruit of one's labor which the government was duty bound to protect.

High property taxes raised the price of an important consumer good, housing, and led the Noordas and the Fosters to make the tax revolt a consumerist movement. But this movement was very different from the triumphant consumerism of the 1920s and 1950s, which offered Americans even higher standards of living, based on the economic growth promised by probusiness conservatism.

Glen Noorda captured the mood of preservation-minded consumers of the 1970s and 1980s: "Now I just want to hold onto what I've got." Defending the home that one had remodeled with one's own hands, and preserving one's accustomed standard of living from the tax collector who threatened to take it all away, was an obvious thing to do. Commonsense reactions gave way to indignant self-righteousness and then to a populist moralism that decorated the bare self-interest of consumers. An economic issue had produced a moral movement.[24]

The end result was a protest whose rhetoric and character brings to mind the artisans and peasants of two centuries ago. These common folk sought to uphold their own moral economy and defend their way of life against markets and the state—against a rampant inflation in the price of necessities and against the tax collectors of the absolutist governments.

Since Marx's exhortations in *The Communist Manifesto,* those with economic discontents have been motivated by "the world to win," the promise of a better life. But even in Marx's day, workers had more often sought to preserve their economic and social positions in a chaotic world that threatened to erode both. The urge to preserve living patterns and communities and protect crafts and livelihoods induced workers to join protest movements throughout the nineteenth century.[25]

Antibusing Movements and Ethnic
Advantage in Consumption

The tax revolt, then, was a consumerist movement based in community organizations. Many tax protest activists had participated in other types of community consumerist movements that helped to shape their beliefs. One such movement was an antibusing movement that arose as white suburbanites fought plans to bus their children to schools closer to the largely black and Hispanic areas of central Los Angeles. The antibusing movement originated in community organizations such as the PTA and sponsored constitutional amendments to limit busing, challenged busing in court, and sought to elect sympathetic candidates to the school board.

The antibusing movement and the tax protest movement were closely related. In Los Angeles, both were strong in outlying white suburbs, such as the San Fernando Valley and the Harbor area. Activists from

BUSTOP, a coalition of community antibusing groups, helped in campaigns to lower property taxes, as did two major leaders of the antibusing movement, Bobbi Fiedler and Roberta Weintraub. Conversely, antitax crusader Howard Jarvis was a founder of the Taxpayers School Reform Committee, formed in 1977 to campaign for an antibusing ballot initiative. In 1978, a leader of a campaign organization for Proposition 13 in the San Fernando Valley teamed up with Roberta Weintraub and formed a committee to recall L.A. School Board president Howard Miller. Miller had angered antibusing activists and had clashed with Jarvis in a series of debates on Proposition 13.[26]

Both the antibusing movement and the tax revolt enjoyed very high levels of popular support, and many of the people who supported one movement also favored the other. In one opinion poll, respondents who favored an antibusing proposition in 1979 and who objected to government efforts to help blacks were particularly likely to vote for tax reduction initiatives. Studies of antibusing movements in other regions of the country also revealed a blending of sentiments against busing and taxes. When asked if the costs of school busing resulted in increased property taxes, 81 percent of a sample of Boston residents said yes. Among those agreeing, 81 percent were "outraged" or "very dissatisfied" that this was the case; those who agreed were particularly likely to support and participate in the antibusing movement.[27]

Whites joined antibusing movements because they sought to maintain advantages for their racial or ethnic group in the consumption of government services. For some participants in the antibusing movement, the advantage was apart from the quality of the school and was merely the opportunity for their children to associate only with whites. This was an important advantage for the white supremacists in the movement. These activists, who were likely to be older, less-educated persons raised in the South, were prejudiced against blacks, making prejudgments and holding negative stereotypes. For prejudiced individuals, school busing evoked images of mandatory, close contact between white and black children. Busing was a potent symbol for the racially prejudiced.[28]

Many who joined the antibusing movement, however, did not necessarily harbor old-time white supremacism but rather were more subtle about seeking consumption advantages in public policy for whites. Here, the issue was not so much the personal characteristics of blacks but rather conflicts between black groups and white groups over resources. Many whites resisted black demands because blacks allegedly had already made too many gains that had not been deserved. By the 1970s, many Americans believed that blacks had made enough progress, that blacks no longer suffered discrimination in public education, and that the problems of blacks were not important. In Boston, the residents who thought that blacks were gaining faster than whites and had unduly benefited from favored treatment tended to oppose school busing and participate in antibusing activities.[29]

In short, antibusing and other movements that sought community-based ethnic advantages are a type of community consumerist movement. Consumption, as Thorstein Veblen revealed, is a competitive process. Veblen argued, for example, that the conspicuous consumption of the wealthy incited others to strive to emulate it. Consumption in communities sometimes entails excluding other groups from sharing advantages. Max Weber pointed to the aristocracy in Europe at the turn of the century as just such a status group, one which claims high prestige based on an exclusive style of life.

In metropolitan areas in the United States, it is race and ethnicity that sets apart life style from life style. Racial and ethnic communities strive to exclude the seemingly less desirable from dwelling in their midst and compete for quality environments, better government services, and other consumption advantages. A racial minority exemplifies what Weber called a negatively privileged status group. For Weber, " 'Status groups' are stratified according to the principles of their *consumption* of goods as represented by special 'styles of life.' " Consumption, then, was the key concept that included ethnic advantage and yet was more universal.[30]

The antibusing movement could be termed right-wing, in the general sense that it sought to defend privileges and at times was tinged with prejudice against minorities. But the antibusing movement differed greatly from the probusiness conservatism portrayed at the beginning of this chapter. Like other community consumerist movements, the antibusing movement sought to enhance consumption rather than investments and the supply side. Rather than favoring growth, expansion, and change, the antibusing movement was preservationist. It attempted to maintain customary patterns of residential segregation and school policies that sent white, middle-class children to the white school in the white neighborhood.

The antibusing movement also differed from probusiness conservatism because antibusing was about ethnic allocation—specifically, what children attended which particular school. Much local politics in the United States deals with such allocative questions—deciding whether an Irishman or a black is hired as police sergeant, or whether the Polish or the Italian construction company gets the contract. The antibusing movement did not address redistributive questions such as whether business or some other social class or economic group would lose or gain. Neither did the antibusing movement deal with the broad issues of production and work; most antibusing movements did not even make an attempt to enter national-level politics, where these issues are debated. The anti-busing movement remained apart from the probusiness redistribution that conservatives were pushing at the national level.[31]

Welcome to the Peninsula, and Now
Go Back Home

The antibusing movement, which arose in the leading centers of the tax revolt in the San Fernando Valley, reveals some of the interests and orientations among community activists in southern California suburbs. Another community that took a leading role in the tax revolt was the Palos Verdes peninsula, a very affluent residential area along the coast, twenty miles south of downtown Los Angeles. For a decade prior to the passage of Proposition 13, residents in the peninsula fought not only high taxes but also property developers. Community organizations on the peninsula sought to limit economic growth and preserve the environment, typical goals for the homeowners associations that supported the tax revolt.

> First we were little pockets of homes. People came up here and they built tracts and people came in and built homes up here. This was the end of the world, and it still is in a way. . . . Have you looked out on the coast here? Look it, out there, right there, there's hundreds of acres open on those bluffs. This is the only [open] place on this whole coastline from Malibu practically to down past . . . Camp Pendleton [a distance of one hundred miles].[32]

If L.A.'s the place, then the Palos Verdes peninsula was the escape. From work, the way to the peninsula was a grueling one-hour crawl on the Harbor Freeway from downtown. Or, from the aerospace companies around the Los Angeles International Airport, it was an even more miserable half-hour stop-and-go past the twenty-three traffic lights on the ten lanes of Hawthorne Boulevard. But then, safely across the Pacific Coast Highway with only five curses and two near accidents, one gradually ascends into the peninsula on gently curving highways. From rolling hills one can gaze out over the deep, clear blue of the Pacific Ocean and can sneeze at the sea breeze and not cough in the smog.

Year by year, though, the traffic on the once-serene hills began to resemble the noisy gridlock below. More homes built and more homes quickly sold brought more new residents with two- and even four-car households, one for each teenager. Land developers formulated a new master plan that would increase the population on the peninsula from 30,000 to 144,000, creating a population density of about 20,000 persons per square mile (four times as dense as the City of Los Angeles) in a largely uninhabited coastal strip. Developers wanted to construct high-rise condominiums along the scenic Palos Verdes Drive, which provides spectacular views of cliffs and ocean. One developer planned to build a complex containing 400 residences, a hotel, and a shopping center.

"We were going to have nothing but condominiums all along the coast . . . !" The existing homeowners on the peninsula were shocked at these plans and fought to preserve the open spaces and restrict construction to the single-family houses characteristic of the peninsula:

> The owners [developers] of large parcels of land . . . want every possible dollar of return on their investment at the expense of the residents; to obtain this, they propose to develop this undeveloped space in high-density, multiple-dwelling units ranging from eight to forty or more units per acre. If this were to occur, the effect of these wall-to-wall apartments would be to smother our traffic system, our public safety system, and our school system—in short, all of our community services—in a thick blanket of additional people adding up to more than twice the present population.
>
> This development would result in increasing major elements of your tax bill, since these additional people would bring more incremental demand for services than incremental tax base. It would permanently change the character of our semi-rural, open-space community to that of a conventional urban environment such as Glendale, Anaheim, or Burbank [middle-income communities].
>
> Finally, our magnificent coastline, a natural resource to the entire community, would be obliterated in a cascade of glass, aluminum, concrete, and macadam, while bulldozers would destroy the natural contour of the land and cliffs, replacing it with high-density development.[33]

On forty-three occasions, a coalition of peninsula homeowners associations tried to block the planning permits and the zoning changes that the large developers requested. The homeowners failed forty-three consecutive times. In 1969 the homeowners and civic organizations formed a new group, Save Our Coastline (SOC), which sought to create a new town on the peninsula that would have the power to veto new construction.

More than a thousand SOC volunteers gathered signatures supporting the new town from three-quarters of the registered voters in the area. However, the owners of large plots of land who favored development struck back. Persons owning 55 percent of the property value on the peninsula (including the owners of Marineland of the Pacific theme park and its dolphin "Flipper") filed a protest, which was sufficient under California law to stop the new town. SOC eventually mounted a constitutional challenge to this law that gave dollars of property value a vote along with persons. In one last feeding frenzy in 1971, developers began construction on one thousand multiple-dwelling units and had received approval for another thousand units with two thousand more awaiting approval. If the builders succeeded in pouring their foundations they could not be stopped. "If you go down [to] the ocean like you're going to Marineland and turn right . . . there's a great big chunk of open land, and they were trying to get that done before the city was formed. And they got a lot of bulldozing done down there. I think they were working three shifts."[34]

At one stormy hearing on land use, Robert Ryan of the Abalone Cove Homeowners Association called the developers "carpetbaggers" and exclaimed, "We want no more high density. Get the message . . . no more high density. . . . It's zoned for greed." The SOC filed more lawsuits against developers for violating the state's Environmental Quality Act and existing deed restrictions.[35]

In 1972, the California Supreme Court overturned the law that the large property owners had used to block the new town—a law that openly violated the one-person, one-vote Supreme Court ruling. A year later, 82 percent of the voters supported the formation of the new town, Rancho Palos Verdes, and chose the leadership of the Save Our Coastline movement as the first town council. The council imposed a moratorium on development until a general plan was drafted, which eventually allowed only one dwelling per acre on the coastal strip. Of the five members on the first town council, three became leaders of Citizens for Property Tax Relief, the peninsula's tax-fighting organization that arose three years later.

During their long and heated conflict with real estate developers, peninsula homeowners found themselves at odds with probusiness conservatism and its emphasis on entrepreneurial opportunity, economic growth, profits, deregulation, and business activism in politics. Responding to the developers who promised that new construction was an opportunity to create a great new city on the peninsula, Fred Hesse, the mayor of one peninsula town, retorted, "This is one 'opportunity' we definitely want to miss." Pledging his support to the Save Our Coastline Campaign, Hesse wryly added, "It's going to be necessary for us to work very hard to continue to miss this opportunity." According to Hesse, the residents were trying to preserve their environment while the developers just wanted profits. "The four principal landowners have a different profit between the plan which the community proposes . . . and the plan which they propose in the neighborhood of $30 million."[36]

Robert Ryan rejected arguments that the economy is a free enterprise system and that the government should stay out. "Free enterprise—baloney. . . . [D]evelopers are really one of the worst people who want subsidies. They come in and build something in the city and they want everybody else to build the infrastructures. They build their project and then walk away and leave you with the traffic jams and everything else that the city has to improve." For the SOC activists, the solution was not deregulation but rather regulation, which would finally hold businesses accountable to the citizens. If such a regulatory apparatus did not exist, it was necessary to create it, and an entire town government as well. Activists such as Robert S. Gruhn, chairman of the Rancho Palos Verdes incorporation committee, continually pointed out how large landowners were thwarting the political will of the people. Even after the favorable California Supreme Court ruling,

> [p]owerful economic interests organized and presented a campaign to political figures at the County level, hoping to delay incorporation by this means. . . . [O]pposition forces have arisen, backed by the large landowner/developer who has opposed our movement since the founding of Save Our Coastline. . . . These people have a vested, monied interest in overdevelopment.[37]

Another activist railed against the personal influence of large developers in politics:

> The developers, they're an insidious group of people, I feel. I think that there's more to fear from them than . . . anything. . . . Having been in sales myself, to sell something big you've got to get close to people, and you do that socially. And these guys do it. They have the yachts and expense accounts and theater tickets. I've worked that myself but at a very low level, but these guys work it at a high level. It's so intertwined, I think, their business and social and personal lives are wrapped into one big bucket, and they're scary. . . . [W]hen you see the power they've got it's really frightening.[38]

Although the conflict on the peninsula over growth was perhaps a little more heated than usual, most other upper-middle-class communities in southern California raised similar issues. In the San Fernando Valley, the Encino Homeowners Association and the Tarzana Property Owners Association campaigned for and won a city ordinance limiting the height of new construction along Ventura Boulevard, a major thoroughfare for the community. Elsewhere in the Valley, a coalition of homeowners groups opposed the expansion of the Hollywood–Burbank airport.[39]

Homeowners in middle-income communities also sought to limit and regulate growth; they fought urban redevelopment projects and the construction of high-rise office buildings and condominium complexes (see chap. 4). In other parts of the United States as well, efforts to regulate developers and control the use of land resulted in such legislation as the

Florida Environmental Land and Water Management Act (1972) and the Vermont Environmental Control Act (1970).[40]

The homeowners groups that fought growth in their communities soon were to provide the organization, expertise, and resources enabling tax protests and signature-gathering campaigns to begin. In their first political battles, the homeowners groups had fought for preservation of the environment rather than economic growth, government regulation rather than free markets, political power for citizens rather than for business, and the quality of consumption around homes rather than the volume of production of housing. Theirs was still a consumers' and not a probusiness movement.

The Two-Martini Free Lunch

Everywhere, homeowners seek better public services for their communities. Perhaps what distinguishes southern California is how quality public services have been part of a California dream that drew millions of residents from back east in the 1950s and 1960s. Those who migrated to the Los Angeles metropolitan area during those years did so partly because of the weather—winter high temperatures normally above sixty degrees, summer highs around eighty. But there were also the promises of quiet residential neighborhoods, safe streets, and educational opportunities. The president of one residents group in the San Fernando Valley reminisced about the golden age of Los Angeles, around 1960:

> At the end of the day you were in your castle—a back yard filled with fruit trees and a monthly payment of $183, a price most people could afford. . . . Los Angeles was safe. Its police department was among the best in the country. If you needed assistance, it was provided immediately, with courtesy. . . . Schools were good. A young man or woman attending public schools in Los Angeles had as good a chance to attend the best universities as a graduate of any exclusive private school, assuming equal performance. . . .
>
> Then suddenly in the 1970s the city that worked stopped working. . . . Thus we have a city with mediocre schools, poor police protection, planning and transportation in chaos . . .
>
> The question is, how can the average citizen force his local government to give him safe streets, good schools, good transportation, roads free from traffic congestion and pollution, and residential neighborhoods free from the fallout of unrestrained industrial and commercial growth nearby?[41]

Homeowners kept up their appetite for improved services, even as they railed against big government and called for slashing the property tax. Just as tax protests were mobilizing rapidly in the San Fernando

Valley around 1976, the Tarzana Property Owners Association was pushing for better government services, including improvements on two busy streets, a new electrical substation, horse trails in a park, and favorable routing of a proposed rapid transit system.

Throughout California, the pet projects may have been different, but the result was the same: more demand for government services. Citizens continued to favor service spending even as Proposition 13 was being passed by a huge margin. At that time, public opinion polls indicated that pluralities actually favored increases in spending for mental health, police, fire protection, prisons, schools, and transportation. Even among those who felt that their own taxes were "much too high," a majority wanted an increase in service spending. Questions about specific programs, except for welfare, elicited favorable responses, even though questions about government in general evoked negative reactions.[42]

Similarly, nationwide polls around the time of Proposition 13 reveal support for specific government programs combined with sentiments for overall reductions in government. Over 90 percent of the public wanted the same or increased government spending for crime control, health, drug addiction, and the environment. Over 80 percent supported spending at the current or even higher levels for education and cities. (At the same time, majorities of around 85 percent believed that the federal government spent too much; clear majorities of around 60 percent favored a "smaller government providing fewer services.")[43]

Howard Jarvis once gloated: "I debated a school superintendent in Southern California. He said, 'Why, if you pass 13, we'll have to shut the schools down.' And everybody stood up and clapped. They wanted the damn schools shut down. . . . [An opponent of Proposition 13 admitted,] 'Whenever I tell an audience that Jarvis will bring local government to a halt, all I see is smiling faces.' "[44] To some degree, Howard Jarvis was correct in portraying a diffuse antigovernment mood among his supporters. But the activists of homeowners associations were poles apart from the libertarians who had principled objections to government providing social services. Tax protesters could not fondly imagine, let alone live in, a community where the public schools are shut down and where government grinds to a halt. Even in the heat of the tax revolt the public desired more, not less, specific services.

In their stands on local issues, residents associations throughout southern California were similar to the civic associations in suburbs elsewhere in the United States. One study of the town of Forest Park, Ohio, is noteworthy because it documents the forty-year history of residents associations in the town. These organizations pressed for improved city services and took steps to reverse the growing presence of lower-income blacks. Homeowners in Forest Park fought plans for high-density devel-

opment by organizing an initiative petition and by electing new representatives to the town council.[45]

The End of (Conservative) Ideology
and the Beginning

The homeowners and residents organizations that campaigned against
high property taxes had also been involved in other community issues, all
of which tended to predispose them against the probusiness conservatism
articulated by leaders such as Howard Jarvis, William Simon, and Milton
Friedman. Instead of taking a probusiness stance, homeowners involved
in controversies over new construction learned to combat the political
power of business with their own organization. Rather than emphasizing
production and the supply side, antibusing protesters focused on how the
consumption of public services would be allocated among ethnic groups.
Not laissez-faire and market expansion but rather regulation and no-
growth were the homeowners' slogans. And finally, the relish that
probusiness conservatives felt about cutting government programs was
distasteful to the residents groups, who wanted improved services to their
communities.

Thousands of community activists—the presidents of homeowners
associations, the founders of residents groups—created the property
tax revolt that culminated in the passage of Proposition 13. Rather
than probusiness conservatism, these activists sought to advance community consumerism. Consumerism, like Janus, turned to the left and
the right at the same time. Community consumerists took up leftist
issues such as the quality of the environment and democratic participation. To be sure, community consumerists also sought to preserve their
existing privileges—their suburban home and their children's assign-
ment to a nearby school with white students bound for UCLA and
maybe even Stanford. The preservationism of consumerists makes
them "conservative" in a very general sense.[46] But if by "conservative"
one means the articulated, probusiness doctrines and programs of the
American Enterprise Institute, then community consumerism was drastically dissimilar to ideological conservatism. When compared to black
renters, the head of a homeowners association may have a world of
advantages to defend. But compared to the Heritage Foundation, a
homeowners association stands for equality.

After 1978, as the tax limitation movement made its probusiness
program clear and changed from community-based protests to election
campaigns managed by consultants, it may have attracted some support
from political conservatives.[47] But the conservative political action com-

mittees that took over the tax limitation movement in 1979 were worlds apart from the homeowners who had begun the tax revolt in California. The homeowner and the ordinary citizen had not jumped on the bandwagon of probusiness conservatism.[48]

Many a pundit did not recognize this and instead saw the two-to-one vote for Proposition 13 as a sign that there had been a fundamental shift among the American people toward the right. Many thought that a groundswell of public opinion was endorsing the probusiness conservatism of Howard Jarvis and some of the other leaders of the tax revolt. *Newsweek* pointed out that Proposition 13 expressed "a reaffirmation of free-enterprise priorities. . . . Just as the New Deal of the 1930s launched Big Government, the Great Tax Revolt of 1978 may herald a conservative reaction." Lewis Uhler, the president of the National Tax Limitation Committee, asserted that the tax revolt demonstrated that a majority of the public had become favorable to private-sector and market-oriented solutions.

Public opinion polls cast doubt on this view that the tax revolt was a mass upsurge of conservatism. Despite the publicity given to conservative causes, only a minority of the public has identified themselves as conservative when asked whether their views were conservative, liberal, or moderate. This conservative minority had not increased since 1968, despite the decisive reelections of Presidents Richard Nixon and Ronald Reagan. According to the Harris Poll, the percentage of self-identified conservatives has fluctuated between 30 and 37 percent between 1968 and 1985. Thirty-four percent called themselves conservatives in 1978, the year Proposition 13 passed, and 36 percent did so after the 1984 election.[49]

But what did the one-third of the public mean when they called themselves "conservatives"? It was certainly different than what a new right leader or a business lobbyist advocated. Even among self-proclaimed conservatives, strong majorities favored government programs and criticized business. Sixty-eight percent of conservatives, and even 65 percent of extreme conservatives, agreed that big business has too much influence. Among conservative respondents only, a strong majority of 67 percent nevertheless agreed that the government should guarantee fair jobs and housing for blacks. Around the time of Proposition 13, only tiny percentages of conservatives thought that the government was spending too much for big cities, education, the environment, and health. From 44 to 56 percent of conservatives actually thought that the government was spending too *little* for these programs.[50] Further evidence comes from a series of in-depth interviews of residents of Orange County, California, who expressed vague and abstract conservative views. At the same time, however, the residents approved of many specific liberal policies and sentiments—quite unexpectedly, given the reputation of the county for right-wing extremism.[51]

What, then, did people signify when they called themselves conservatives if not a stand in favor of business and against government social programs? Philip Converse suggested that it is something more vague, incoherent, and idiosyncratic than the programs and ideologies of a right-wing political group. Converse argued that only a fraction of the mass public uses abstract ideologies to organize their political beliefs consistently. Less than one-fifth of the public thinks of conservatism as broad philosophical differences over issues such as the welfare state, free enterprise, social change, and individualism. About one-third of the public thinks that the difference between conservatives and liberals has something to do with government spending and saving. The majority of the public has even more vague or incorrect notions, or no idea at all, about what constitutes conservatism.[52]

Citizens who define themselves as conservatives do so for a variety of reasons. Homeowner activists, as I have argued, may have considered themselves "conservative" in that they seek to preserve their consumer possessions[53] and their ethnic-group advantages. Many ordinary citizens consider themselves "conservatives" only because of their general attitudes toward change and action. When one poll asked, "What do you have in mind when you say that someone's political views are conservative?" a 43 percent plurality mentioned such characteristics as resistance to new ideas as opposed to acceptance, slow rather than rash responses, and cautious rather than irresponsible actions. When Gallup asked respondents, "What is the first thing that comes to your mind when you think of someone who is a conservative," 35 percent had no opinion; 16 percent made comments like "saves, doesn't throw things away"; 12 percent stated, "does not want to change, does not want to take a chance"; 10 percent, "cautious, careful"; and 9 percent, "close-minded, intolerant, self-centered."[54]

A political belief—conservative or liberal—can arise from the rubbish heap of incertitude and become charged with meaning when it is removed from the realm of abstraction and is connected to specific concerns and actions. Activists in homeowners associations began their political pursuits with clear grievances—higher property taxes, which were set in the context of larger concerns about the consumption of housing and public goods.

The common action of an association is the crucible for the formation of interpretations.[55] A group learns by interacting with its political environment, thereby defining who its allies and who its enemies are. As the group tries to find solutions to its problems, sometimes failing, sometimes succeeding, political interpretations emerge that summarize the group's experience and serve as a guide to further action. Although political scientists have studied how attitude change affects actions such as voting in elections, this book focuses on noninstitutionalized actions such as protests and social movements.[56] The tax revolt is of particular interest because it spread certain political interpretations far beyond southern California into American politics.

The major political lesson that tax protesters learned was that they could expect little support from metropolitan and state political and economic leaders. Without access to big government, tax protesters worked at the community level to build a power base. The homeowners in middle-income communities, compared to the upper-middle class, experienced government power and sought to empower themselves in different ways.

Interpretations about the unresponsiveness of government and affiliations made in search of power had a decisive impact on the programs that tax protesters pursued. The process of contending for power determined the most important issue in tax policy—which groups benefit and which groups pay—in short, the very interests that the tax reduction movement pursued.

4

Middle Americans and Generalized Unresponsiveness

We don't consider ourselves of the rich class. We don't consider ourselves of the lower class. . . . We're middle class, but poor.[1]

Our tax protest movement has been characterized as a grass roots revolution set in motion by a beer truck driver in Alhambra. It's true and thank God for people like Mike. We hope that it is never forgotten that the American Revolution was started by farmers in work clothes.[2]

The average working guy gave us a much fairer shake than the fat-cats did. Fortunately for us, the little guys had a thousand times as many votes as the fat-cats did.[3]

Alhambra, Chinatown

Alhambra is middle America, in spite of its place. Located eight miles east of downtown Los Angeles, it stands at the foot of the sprawling, suburban San Gabriel Valley. In 1960, Alhambra was an incorporated town of fifty-five thousand inhabitants with fewer than one hundred blacks; it was 94 percent Anglo despite its close proximity to the Mexican-American barrios of East Los Angeles. The families of Alhambra were of modest means, earning a median income just about that of Los Angeles County. Alhambra was a city of small, two-bedroom stucco houses and plain apartments in need of paint. The name Alhambra, like so many names for real estate in California, is a creative misnomer, for this town has nothing in common with the palace of Alhambra in Spain.

Michael Rubino was a regular guy. A forty-year-old beer truck driver, he was outgoing and unpretentious. Through his deliveries and by once owning a gasoline station, Rubino had won many acquaintances. He was engaged to be married and was caring for his elderly mother who lived nearby. Energetic and sometimes brash, Rubino described himself as a "sucker for the little guy."

In November 1964, Rubino received a notice that his property taxes had increased by six hundred dollars, at a time when apartments in Alhambra were renting for eighty dollars a month. With a group of friends, Rubino organized a protest meeting, attended by over one thousand homeowners whose taxes had also drastically increased. Outside, one thousand more protesters were caught in a three-mile-long traffic jam around the meeting site. Inside, public officials faced a storm of catcalls, boos, and roars of disapproval that led Rubino to wonder aloud to the audience, "Are we a mob?"[4]

Rubino claimed that he was offered a government job if he would call off protest activities. Indignant, he refused. A week and a half later, passions still ran high. Rubino led one thousand demonstrators in a caravan of buses to confront the Los Angeles County Board of Supervisors. "Citizens surged forward from their seats to press against the wood rail in front of the supervisors' desks. . . . [Protesters] shook fists, shouted, [and] tried to get control of microphones . . ."Rubino shouted to the officials, "When an Italian gets his temper up, look out!" After an impassioned speech, Rubino strode out of the room, only to collapse in a faint. As his fiancee rushed to his side, the crowd called out, "What have you done to him?"[5] The demonstrators then booed the county assessor and the supervisors and even a protest organizer who meekly announced that the buses were about to leave.

Those buses, however, were the start of Michael Rubino's problems. He had chartered one hundred of them and had personally guaranteed to pay the bill. Fewer than expected had bought tickets, however. The bill for the buses and other expenses left Rubino with a personal debt of over seven thousand dollars. The leader of the movement to save people's homes was forced to sell his own house.

Although Rubino organized one more large protest meeting, public pressure did not result in lower property tax bills. Activists then formed an ongoing group, Property and Homeowners of the San Gabriel Valley. Periodically becoming involved in local issues, the group later gathered signatures and campaigned for Proposition 13. Looking back over his efforts to reduce property taxes, Rubino reminisced: "I wouldn't say I was a failure, no. I've said this a couple of times to certain people I know and they said, 'No, Mike, you were never a failure because from what you did Proposition 13 came about.' "[6]

A year after the tax protest, Rubino was elected to the Alhambra town council; a decade later he was again elected and was chosen as mayor. Then, he was accused of punching a political rival and was convicted of accepting a bribe from an ambulance operator, who was actually a police undercover agent in a sting operation. Rubino was forced to resign. Shortly before his sentencing, his mother died. A sixty-year-old bachelor, Rubino wept as the judge spared him a prison term. Now his solace is not so much his religion as a scrapbook of newspaper clippings about his dogged political career.

Today in Alhambra, middle Americans speak little about their former mayor. They watch uneasily as thousands of Chinese immigrants bring their savings from Taiwan to Alhambra, buying new condominiums and opening seafood restaurants with large red signs in Chinese characters. Michael Rubino and the white residents of Alhambra share the same fate. Their worlds have become as inauspicious and as incomprehensible as Chinatown. They feel relentlessly pursued in strange, foreign surroundings that they did not create and cannot control. On occasion, however, middle Americans take their stand.

Interpretations: Unresponsive Big Government

For Michael Rubino and other tax protesters throughout California, the tax revolt was something more than the simple reluctance to pay more money. It was also a protest against big government, which had the power to tax but had failed to respond to the citizens. The government seemed to have the power to arbitrarily wreak havoc and, worse, the authority to increase tax bills in the future to the point where all would lose their homes. Some of the daring went to the County Administration Building to appeal the assessments on their homes. They won only token changes and, moreover, witnessed proceedings that dramatized the power of the state over the individual:

> One time I went down and I appealed . . . when they raised the assessment. It must have been in the early 70s. . . . [T]here's something called an Assessment Appeals Board, and you go down there and you state your reasons. . . . And they had a very arrogant head of the board. . . . I started to testify and he interrupted me and overruled me and said I couldn't quote the *Wall Street Journal* because it wasn't proper legal authority. . . . So I went a little further and I quoted the Constitution, and he said, "Well, that doesn't apply." And I said, "Do you mean to overrule the Constitution?" And the man said, "Constitution overruled!" And they

were so impressed by my testimony, they gave me some small benefit that amounted to not more than ten dollars a year but that's the best they would do.[7]

When citizens visited the halls of government to express their grievances, they were, to their surprise, rebuffed. Tax protesters found it difficult to get the opportunity of presenting their views to the County Board of Supervisors, which could have reduced tax rates. When Richard Carman took the protests of San Gabriel Valley citizens to the supervisors, he discovered that they actively hindered him.

> Local government did everything in the world to discourage us. We'd be on the agenda to speak, and I'd be the last one to be heard because they figured the press had plenty of stories and they'd have to get out and file their stories and they'd be gone. . . . Then they'd do everything possible to belittle you or even entrap you. You'd be halfway through your thing and they'd say, 'That's enough time,' and they'd give their sheriff a wink and he'd come over and take the microphone away. . . . No cooperation— it's a wonder we lasted as long as we did.[8]

During one of Carman's presentations, "Two of the five supervisors were talking behind their desks, two others were reading, and a fifth was making an effort to appear he was listening." Government was unconcerned about the taxpayer's plight. Carman received similar treatment from officials in state government. "When we showed up at Sacramento, and we couldn't afford to go there very often, they treated you very badly because they just didn't want to be bothered. We got to talk to the officials very little because they cloak everything so that the ordinary person wouldn't even know what they were passing—everything was cloaked in secrecy."[9]

Even when government officials took the time to meet, they did not take the taxpayers' grievances seriously. At the height of 1964 protests, Michael Rubino met with the county assessor and his staff, who all flaunted a condescending attitude.

> The . . . Assessor did explain a tax graph, the type often seen in school books. . . . Then Rubino was ushered out of Watson's office and into the arms of waiting newsmen. . . . The TV lights flashed on. . . . Smiles slowly spread over the faces of Watson's [the assessor's] employees as they coughed and turned away. Rubino said the first thing that came to mind. "We certainly learned a lot about taxes."
>
> Later, driving away from the County building with its marble floors and inlaid wood paneling, Rubino commented, "He [the assessor] never really did say very much, did he?"[10]

Another government official gave a junior high school lesson in civics to a tax protest activist, in a manner almost calculated to induce feelings of inferiority: "[I had] a hard time getting to see him but I saw him. I'm very persistent and I saw him personally. And you know, he took . . . a great big book . . . in very small print to show all of the different departments and what they call them. He practically laughed at me. . . . I got nowhere, absolutely nowhere."[11]

Before Proposition 13, the tax protesters had an unbroken losing streak. No concessions were granted, and property tax assessments and rates continued their inexorable climb. But more than that, the protesters felt that they were not even a part of the political game. In the supervisors' meeting room, a oak railing was the barrier. Solid oak divided the citizens who tried to express their plight in the allotted two minutes from the insiders who did not care. The top floors of the county administration building were a social world unto themselves, where citizens like Mike Rubino realized they were but strangers.

Strangers at City Hall

Although citizens thought they could obtain help from smaller governmental units such as towns, no favorable response was forthcoming.[12] Mike Rubino brought the problem of property tax increases to the Alhambra town council. Their reaction, in his words, was "It's tough." The mayor of the town, Norma Yocum, "did a good job of cutting our throats." After establishing an office in Alhambra where taxpayers could file an individual appeal, the mayor then argued that Rubino's planned protest was no longer necessary. Mayor Yocum, emphasizing that Rubino was only a beer truck driver, helped to establish a rival taxpayers group. The president of that group claimed to be more respectable than Rubino and attempted to become president of Rubino's own organization.

School boards at the community level, which activists hoped would be more responsive than big state and county government, nonetheless imposed taxes without heeding the wishes of citizens. In 1967, the California legislature passed a bill that enabled school boards to increase taxes without approval of the voters. The San Gabriel Taxpayers Association reacted angrily: "If you are unhappy about the constant increase in your property taxes and the fact that your inherent right to vote on school taxes has been stolen from you, then you have the privilege of letting your opinions and wants known." Activists sought to arrange a debate with school board members and administrators, but no officials were willing to attend. The taxpayers association sent a delegation to Sacramento to press for repeal of the bill, without success.[13]

Tax protesters in the middle-income towns of San Gabriel Valley found to their dismay that all levels of government were unresponsive or actively hostile. An activist concluded that elected officials "were against any controlling of taxes by the people. . . . They felt that as long as they were elected . . . they had the right to do just as they saw it. Another summarized: "It's unfortunate that the citizens, the consumers, the people, the so-called we the people—are only recognized on election day. The day after election, 'Fine, thank you very much,' but business is as usual. . . . [T]hat's the Federal right down to the little township."[14]

The unresponsiveness of local government, not only on taxes but also on a host of other issues, contributed to the activists' sense that they had little voice. Immediately before a major tax protest in Monterey Park, homeowners had failed in another battle, against a costly urban renewal project promoted by a prominent state senator. In another community in the San Gabriel Valley, a tax protest group had also unsuccessfully fought a redevelopment project that consumed many tax dollars. One activist had learned, "There's always a gimmick behind everything that city hall does. Remember that. There's nothing for the people."[15] Another activist in a middle-income community, who led a campaign to pressure Los Angeles to limit noisy air traffic at a nearby airport, summarized his group's dealings with local government:

> First of all, they don't want to see you. You have trouble getting in to see them. You'll see an aide. . . . When you do see the supervisors, your position is denigrated, or at best, listened to but only given lip service. . . . At other times you cross a politician. They write you off, and they have to deal with you, but they'll do the least they possibly can. . . . [The mayor of Los Angeles] has never been cooperative. . . . Only in a confrontational situation would he send a polite word process[ed] answer, but not really deal with the gutsy sort of issues that we want.[16]

Studies of localities throughout the United States reveal a similar pattern. In one medium-sized city, the mayor ignored the middle-class homeowners and instead cultivated support from city agencies, political parties, and community institutions. One official ridiculed middle-class homeowners as "cheese and cracker millionaires" who lacked political clout but nevertheless made demands on public officials. In Levittown, the community that Herbert Gans studied as a typical lower-middle-class suburb, power was concentrated in an "actual government" composed of the developer and a caucus of Democratic party leaders. The residents believed that a corrupt political clique ruled their community and that local politics was a series of schemes by the powerful to sell out the residents.[17]

Interpretations and Actions

Two centuries ago Americans were incensed that England could impose taxes while the colonies could not make government decisions. As Howard Jarvis put it, " 'No taxation without representation.' In a very real sense, the American Revolution was the first American tax revolt. Proposition 13 simply followed in that hallowed tradition."[18] Once again, although citizens found it self-evident that their government should be a democracy, citizens instead encountered a multitude of offices and repeated injury in answer to repeated petitions. The resulting anger animated the tax revolt.

Michael Rubino was one to directly vent his anger at big government. During a protest demonstration, Rubino pointed his finger directly at the county supervisors and exclaimed, "Your seats are getting a little bit too comfortable. . . . We have come to this conclusion—you might not know where Alhambra is now, but hereafter when you walk in, you're going to take your hat off." In order to get just a little respect, a little break for the homeowner, Rubino had to protest again and again, preaching his message—politicians "don't give a damn." The people had "lost faith in the politicians."[19]

The story of Michael Rubino is also the tale of many other tax protests in middle-income communities throughout southern California, where local politicians failed to support the tax revolt. Table 2 lists the communities in Los Angeles County that reportedly held a tax protest event attracting at least one hundred persons.[20] All of the middle-income communities, with a relative affluence index of at least 0.60 and less than 1.30, are indicated by an "a" in column E.[21]

The protests that were supported by community political leaders are marked with a "p" in column F.[22] Among the twenty-four middle-income communities (which erupted in a total of forty-nine events), community political leaders failed to support the protests in twenty-three of the twenty-four cases.

For example, in the community of Baldwin Park (with a relative affluence index of 0.64) an activist in the Taxpayers Committee for Lower Property Taxes complained, "I didn't know the government would do this. Not to the working man. The government is breaking him into little pieces." Tom Klein, the leader of the group, alleged that the government responded to their petition by deliberately cutting needed services rather than waste and administrative costs, thereby discrediting the protesters. "I think they did a number on us. . . . The experience taught property owners a big lesson. They learned that there is a need to organize," like the unions, to gain power.[23]

And organize they did. Angry taxpayers shouted abuse, refused to

Table 2 Tax Protest Events and Community Leaders' Response, 1950–1978

(A) Fiscal Year	(B) Name of Community	(C) Attendance at Tax Protests	(D) Number of Events that Year	(E) Relative Affluence Index	(F) b = Facilitation by Business in Community p = Facilitation by Political leaders
1. 1952–1953	Glendale	250	2	1.19[a]	
2. 1957–1958	Pomona	250	2	0.97[a]	
3. 1957–1958	Temple City	725	4	1.04[a]	b
4. 1957–1958	Glendora	500	1	1.08[a]	b
5. 1957–1958	Covina	2,750	4	1.12[a]	
6. 1957–1958	Downey	900	1	1.13[a]	
7. 1957–1958	West Covina	7,325	4	1.30	b, p
8. 1957–1958	Woodland Hills	300	1	1.51	
9. 1957–1958	Highland Ave., Hancock Park, L.A.	400	1	1.92	b
10. 1964–1965	Lomita	250	3	0.78[a]	
11. 1964–1965	Alhambra	3,190	5	1.00[a]	
12. 1964–1965	Glendale	480	3	1.10[a]	
13. 1965–1966	Glendale	450	2	1.10[a]	
14. 1966–1967	Alhambra	200	1	1.01[a]	
15. 1966–1967	Glendale	400	1	1.09[a]	
16. 1968–1969	Temple City	180	1	1.04[a]	
17. 1970–1971	La Canada–Flintridge	300	2	1.80	b
18. 1971–1972	La Canada–Flintridge	900	1	1.80	b
19. 1974–1975	Manhattan Beach	550	2	1.47	b

Table 2   *(continued)*

(A)	*(B)*	*(C)*	*(D)*	*(E)*	*(F)*
Fiscal Year	Name of Community	Attendance at Tax Protests	Number of Events that Year	Relative Affluence Index	b = Facilitation by Business in Community p = Facilitation by Political Leaders
20. 1975–1976	El Monte	200	1	0.690[a]	
21. 1975–1976	Westchester	1,100	1	1.28[a]	
22. 1975–1976	San Marino	150	3	2.89	p
23. 1976–1977	Baldwin Park	100	2	0.639[a]	
24. 1976–1977	Lakewood	630	4	0.935[a]	p
25. 1976–1977	Alhambra	110	1	0.965[a]	
26. 1976–1977	Van Nuys	5,800	3	1.03[a]	b
27. 1976–1977	Covina	1,000	1	1.07[a]	
28. 1976–1977	Glendale	160	1	1.07[a]	
29. 1976–1977	Torrance	550	1	1.27[a]	
30. 1976–1977	Hacienda Heights	190	3	1.29[a]	
31. 1976–1977	Woodland Hills	3,740	1	1.30	b
32. 1976–1977	Northridge	1,250	1	1.40	b
33. 1976–1977	Sherman Oaks	1,110	4	1.48	b
34. 1976–1977	Palos Verdes Pen.	1,950	3	2.16	p
35. 1977–1978	Alhambra	150	1	0.964[a]	
36. 1977–1978	Manhattan Beach	500	1	1.50	b

[a]Indicates middle-income community.

pay taxes, demonstrated at the county administration building, tried to recall public officials, burned their tax bills, and reenacted the Boston Tea Party, complete with colonial garb. In the seaside community of Venice, a low- to moderate-income area in 1975, tax protesters went to the office of their representative on the Los Angeles City Council. "She had a meeting there one night so we had a candlelight march there. . . . [T]he Venice group was quite militant."[24]

Tax protest associations set upon the goal of increasing their political influence. One group in the San Gabriel Valley summarized its aims: "To promote a constructive and equitable property tax program and a reduction and/or limitation of governmental expenditure . . ." and, "To encourage participation in management of government affairs. . . . We the people insist on remaining informed so that we may retain control over the instruments that we have created." Throughout southern California, groups with similar aims emerged.

Some protesters tried to use their voting rights to reduce taxes. But as they gathered signatures to place initiatives on the ballot, the activists felt that big government again was hindering them. The government required that for each of the hundreds of thousands of signatures, the signatory's voting precinct needed to be determined and listed. Activists worked long hours, looking up names in voluminous precinct books during the limited time allowed. Tax protesters alleged that county government was deliberately interfering in their basic democratic rights:

> The demands made upon the public by the Los Angeles County Registrar of voters pertaining to the precincting of petitions . . . reeks of obstructionist self-imposed controls. We also feel that some of our county Supervisors have lacked in cooperating in addition to our county Counsel.
>
> These controls have [been] deliberately designed to obstruct and discourage the average non-professional group from ever attempting to qualify any petition of any kind for placement on a statewide ballot.
>
> In addition to illegal demands, the . . . registrar's lack of cooperation, delays in fulfilling orders for the proper precincting books and maps vitally necessary to fulfill their arbitrary demands are intolerable. The REGISTRAR'S lame excuses are pathetic and must be eliminated. The County Counsel's arbitrary decisions have been discriminatory. . . .
>
> The shameful politics, pressure tactics, and deliberate withholding of full and proper information and instructions upon receipt of a Title and Summary from the State Attorney General is [sic] tantamount to suppression of the voters right to have placed an initiative that they themselves can vote on.[25]

A Land of Strangers

The activists in homeowners groups who were so angered with local government were neither chronic malcontents nor atypical agitators; rather, they were expressing sentiments common among the American public at the time. A public opinion poll in 1978, for example, indicated that 81 percent of the citizens had "only some" or "hardly any" confidence in local government; only 19 percent had a great deal of confidence. These sentiments were not some volatile flash in the pan; on the contrary, they persisted through the 1980s (18 percent in 1983 and 23 percent in 1984 had a great deal of confidence in local government). Similarly, only a small portion of the public (19 percent in 1978) expressed a great deal of confidence in state government.

The views of tax activists also resembled those of the public in that both groups were dissatisfied not only because big government spent too much but also because it was unresponsive to the citizens. When pollsters asked, "How much attention do you feel the government pays to what the people think when it decides what to do," the percentage answering "a good deal" fell from 32 percent in 1964 to 14 percent in 1978, the year Proposition 13 passed.[26] The percentage who thought that political parties pay attention a good deal of the time also fell (from 41 percent to 21 percent between 1964 and 1978). The public in 1978 doubted that the government was run for the people; rather, 67 percent believed that it was run for the benefit of "a few big interests" (up from 29 percent in 1964; the percentage remained above 60 through 1982).[27]

The sentiment that government was unresponsive was widespread among citizens earning moderate incomes. One survey identified "middle American radicals," who believed that the government unfairly favored the rich and the poor at the expense of the middle class. Most middle-American radicals earned moderate incomes and lacked a college education. They expressed much alienation from institutions and felt that local government did not serve their needs. Middle-American radicals were more likely to support the tax revolt.[28]

In short, the public in the 1970s concluded that the government had become unresponsive. Some concluded this because government did not respond to their calls for withdrawal from Vietnam. Others were disaffected because they wanted the government to respond to whites instead of blacks; still others during the Watergate hearings witnessed a presidency that combatted public criticism with dirty tricks.

Tax protesters operating in the very different arena of state and local politics had also learned about the unresponsiveness of government. Tax activists spoke about big government with a passion that could only come from firsthand experience. The activists in middle-income communities, in contrast to the ordinary alienated voter, were informed about government, were confident about their own abilities, and at least cared enough to be involved. When these activists denounced the unresponsiveness of big government, they could easily find an audience of alienated voters who were willing to cheer loudly. Tax protesters found many a stranger who needed little convincing to join a campaign for representation and no taxation. The truly estranged who felt that they were "not well represented" in government were more likely to vote for Proposition 13.[29]

Feelings that the government was unresponsive mobilized ordinary voters in other states as well. A study of voters in Michigan revealed that, "Far and away the strongest support for the [Headlee] Amendment [a limit on state revenues and local property taxes] came from those who felt that it would increase either government efficiency . . . or voter control of government." The feeling that one is cut off from political decision making is the best predictor of public support for the tax revolt nationwide. Pollsters Yankelovich and Kaagan characterized the mood of Americans with the phrase, "take-back psychology"—the desire to retrieve from government the authority that belongs to the people.[30]

The Antibusiness Moment

To take back political power and to win back tax money—these were the twin objectives of the tax revolt. Accomplishing these goals would be difficult, given the lack of support at all levels of government. What strategy would overcome the political roadblocks to tax reduction? What groups or forces could help? These were the questions that would confound tax protest activists for decades.

One possibly ally for the tax revolt was business. The support of small business in the final stages of the movement would prove decisive. But in the 1960s and early 1970s, activists from middle-income areas found that large corporations and even the leaders of small businesses in the community were unwilling to assist homeowners in their battle. Homeowners responded with dislike, distrust, and sometimes anger at business. These negative feelings affected the programs that the middle-income tax activists adopted.

Tax protesters counted among their enemies the industrial giants, utilities, and banks large enough to be listed in the *Fortune* magazine directories of top corporations. Large companies sought to reduce their own taxes and showed no interest in helping the homeowners' movement throughout its long history, to the very end. Many large firms took a public stand against Proposition 13 and donated large sums of money to fight it; the California Taxpayers Association, whose directors are senior managers in large businesses, actively campaigned against Prop. 13. One community activist exclaimed, "The large corporations opposed it. The Bank of America opposed it. . . . They pretend to be for lower taxes, but in practice they were getting great benefits out of high property taxes." Not only did large companies allegedly have a different economic interest; they were also unwilling to help the homeowners gain political influence because they already had great powers in government: "Government listens to financial interests. . . . Government is dictated by financial considerations mainly. The rest of it is a show, I think. It's what will make money for someone, and the people who run our government are large corporations and banks, financial institutions. . . . Politicians make a pretense of working for the common man but in practice they don't, unfortunately."[31]

Another activist agreed:

Most of our legislation favors big business. . . . It's going to be difficult to change this. We just don't have the lobbying power even though we are the biggest special interest that should be recognized. . . . Big business is out for itself. Because of its inefficiency, it needs to get out of us as much money as it can. . . . Since big business's interests are different from those of the consumer, its stance on public issues will reflect this.[32]

Large institutions, both business and government, work together and concentrate power at the expense of the citizenry:

The big people work together. They may not always work directly together but they're working indirectly together. . . . This is a normal function of business. . . . Whenever a ruler, say, has gained power, he's sought more power, and learning the road to power he's learned the tricks. Like Caesar—once he learned to conquer one county he learned how to conquer another one, and then five and then ten and then twenty more. Same things happened here among the big corporations. They got a corporation. They see how to merge and take over another one and they get bigger and bigger and concentrate power. . . . The problem is that they're taking this power at the expense of the common man, the average citizen.[33]

The activists' views about large corporations were quite in keeping with what the general public was saying in opinion polls during the late 1970s. For example the percentage agreeing that, "There's too much power concentrated in the hands of a few large companies for the good of the nation," rose steadily to 78 percent in 1975, remaining around there through 1981. Another question tapped opinions about the economic power of corporations: "In many of our largest industries, one or two companies have too much control of the industry." The percentage agreeing also steadily rose from 58 percent in 1965 to 82 percent in 1975, fluctuating to 79 percent in the first year of the Reagan administration.[34] When respondents were asked to state their opinions of industries on a five-point scale, the average percentage of "very favorable" and "mostly favorable" responses steadily declined, from 68 percent in 1965 to 35.5 percent in 1977. When tax activists criticized the power of large corporations, the activists found many others in the community who were inclined to agree.[35]

Small Businesses in the Community: Backslapping or Back Stabbing?

Through their experiences in tax protests, activists developed negative views of big business. Activists had more direct and frequent contact with smaller businesses in their communities and, as the movement developed, it was this contact that decisively shaped the views of the activists. Most of them believed that small business had different interests and powers than large corporations:

> I think that when you say business, we have to make a difference between business and monopolism, and what we've got today are two types of business going on—monopolism, which is the operation of large corporations and large banks that are using government to further their own ends at the expense of the average man. In contrast with that is small business and entrepreneurs and individuals and little businesses of five employees or less who are working in a really competitive situation and they aren't monopolists. They can't be.[36]

In middle-income communities, a few owners of small retail outlets supported tax protests; after all, many of them paid high property taxes on their personal residences. "Some of our members were small businesses, so yes, we sought their help when we started our tax reduction activities. . . . Many small businesses did not want to join because they didn't want to get involved."[37]

Michael Rubino was irritated at the businesses in Alhambra for opposing his tax protest in 1964. Rubino thought that businesses did not support him because they had the money to pay their taxes and could work through established political channels rather than protests. Real estate businesses did not help, despite that fact that land and buildings, their stock in trade, were the targets for higher property taxes. Rubino charged that after homeowners could not make their tax payments, real estate agents were "buying up homes cheap." Rubino alleged that the attitude of the agents was, "Why should we help you? We stand to make more money." The lack of business support made it difficult for the tax protest to succeed, for "it takes money, and we didn't have a lot. And it takes a lot of influential people, and we had very little of that."[38]

In the middle-income communities of the San Gabriel Valley, Richard Carman also found it difficult to gain the support of community businesses:

> The majority of the people I was working with were people who were medium class back in 1969. . . . We worked with down-to-earth people, grass-roots people. . . . I approached business owners for support . . . with very little success. The business community was not responsive in general. . . . I was wasting my time going to business people. . . . When you walk into a business place, number one, they've got customers and they're interested in serving their customers. The boss isn't in. If the boss is in and you state your case, by the time the clerk goes back to the boss, "Oh well, another one looking for a handout." They haven't got time to listen to it.[39]

Although a few small retail outlets offered support to tax protests in middle-income communities, leading small businesses and business organizations in the community usually did not help. These community business leaders typically included the heads of organizations such as the community's chamber of commerce and real estate board, the managers of supermarkets and other business chains, and the owners of retail outlets and wholesale and manufacturing firms employing between five and fifty persons. In middle-income communities, according to a tax protester:

> The chambers of commerce are a joke because where do they get their handout? They get it from the city. Where does the city get its money to give them a handout? From property taxes. . . . They're not going to bite the first hand. They're not going to give you anything, and they're not famous for the number of individual household tax participants. . . . Local real estate boards were practically no help. They didn't want to buck the politicians.[40]

Another tax reduction activist who lived in the middle-income community of West Hollywood criticized the chamber of commerce:

> I resigned from their board of directors because of the fact that they were all for business—of course that's the name of it—chamber of commerce. They were all for business, and the heck with the homeowner. And they don't live here. There isn't hardly a business in West Hollywood that the owner lives in West Hollywood. They live in Bel Air and Beverly Hills [two very affluent communities] and the [San Fernando] Valley and all over. They make their money and put it in their pocket and run home with it.[41]

The newspaper accounts of tax protests indicate that in other middle-income areas, community business leaders usually failed to support tax protests. In table 2, those protests that community business leaders supported are marked by a "b" in column F. Of the twenty-four middle-income communities, community business leaders supported the protests in only three localities.

In one of the three instances (Temple City), the evidence for support is scanty. Newspaper articles reported that citizens could contact the town's chamber of commerce to obtain petition forms or learn when the next meeting would be held. Community business leaders clearly supported protests in two other cases, Van Nuys–Sherman Oaks, discussed in chapter 7, and Covina, discussed in chapter 6. The strength of these protests, as indicated by the attendance totals above two thousand, could account for the support of community leaders. Furthermore, in these two cases protests also arose in adjacent, more affluent areas where community business leaders supported the protests. Perhaps the business leaders in Van Nuys–Sherman Oaks and in Covina were following their more upscale compatriots.

These three middle-income localities where community business leaders supported tax protests are the exception, amounting to only 12 percent of the cases (compared to 75-percent support in upper-middle-class communities; see table 3). As the activists in middle-income communities pressed their grievances, they discovered that the institutions around them, from the largest corporations to the local chamber of commerce, from the governor to the town councilor, were either indifferent or hostile, creating a situation that can be termed generalized unresponsiveness. Activists reacted to this situation with angry antielitism, targeting the well-to-do and political leaders: "[W]e're wasting our time to pay taxes. For who? Some politician. What's he do with it? He goes [sic] buys a Lincoln limousine two blocks long and puts eighty gallons of gas in it and runs it down to Las Vegas."[42]

Table 3 Community Business Leaders' Facilitation of Protests by Income of Protesting Community

	Upper-Middle Income		Middle Income	
Not Facilitated	3	(25%)	21	(88%)
Facilitated	9	(75%)	3	(12%)
Total	12	(100%)	24	(100%)

Lambda = 0.50.

The Social Origins of Antibusiness
Redistribution Programs

Where antibusiness views were particularly intense, tax protesters supported proposals to increase the taxes on business and to lower the taxes on homeowners, consumers, and workers. Mike Rubino's protest in Alhambra was one of the 88 percent in middle-income communities that did not gain the support of business leaders. Rubino spoke out angrily against business and advocated tax benefits for moderate-income earners at the expense of business and the wealthy. Rubino argued that his movement championed the "little people" who owned only one house or, at the most, one in front and a cottage in the back. The Alhambra protesters of 1964 insisted that special tax relief should be targeted to senior citizens, many of whom could not afford to pay their tax bills. Rubino contrasted himself to Howard Jarvis, who allegedly was more concerned with big corporations and the people who own "fifty thousand acres" and "five apartment buildings." Rubino opposed Jarvis's plans to reduce property taxes for businesses as well as residences.[43]

In the moderate-income areas of the San Gabriel Valley, the San Fernando Valley, and the coastal area, past conflicts, particularly those over urban growth and redevelopment, left a lingering negative view of business. This led activists to articulate and campaign for tax reforms that would redistribute downward, away from business.

Both in Alhambra and throughout the San Gabriel Valley controversies about the redevelopment of "blighted" areas pitted homeowners against small business leaders in the community. Through urban renewal projects, local governments acquired and cleared land and encouraged the construction of office buildings, industrial parks, and shopping centers. When improvements in the redevelopment area resulted in increased property tax collections, the revenues were not spent by the city operating budget but rather were used by the redevelopment agency to meet its costs and pay off bonds. Tax protesters saw redevelopment simply as one big subsidy to business, which siphoned off revenues from the city budget and imposed higher taxes on homeowners to pay for needed services.

Tax protesters in the San Gabriel Valley began to oppose urban renewal projects around 1970, leading to direct conflicts with community business leaders: "In nearly every city, the chamber of commerce supports redevelopment. In Alhambra, for instance, the chamber of commerce is supporting the redevelopment agency, and the BGA [the tax protest group] sued, the case called *Fossilman* v. *Alhambra*. We're certainly on the opposite side there. We're on the opposite side in Downey." Activists in the town of San Gabriel distributed one leaflet arguing, "The 'big money' in this city is working to form a redevelopment agency. . . . A lot of little people 'working together' can fight the big machine."[44]

Richard Carman was a major activist in the movement that fought urban renewal and high property taxes in the west San Gabriel Valley. His program was that property taxes should be cut in half. State government could subsidize the localities, replacing lost revenues. "They can tax the freeloaders. The insurance companies, the banks, and others who benefit through tax loopholes should be forced by legislation to take up the slack." Another one of Carman's redistributive programs, which he attempted to place on the California ballot in 1975, would have given tax reductions to residential property only, and not to "hotels, motels, business, industrial, or commercial properties."[45]

In Monterey Park, a community in the San Gabriel Valley where the median family income was 1.09 times that of Los Angeles County, the issue of urban growth also sparked hostility against small business leaders. In 1976, the Monterey Park Taxpayers Association opposed the town's $13 million redevelopment program and later contested new construction by private developers. Another homeowners group in the town sponsored an initiative, which won the support of 85 percent of the voters, to limit the construction of new condominiums. But at a later election, "the developers knocked us all [the homeowners] off the city council. . . . They sent out a hit piece [negative ad] and, the last weekend of the election, they killed us." The lengthy conflict between homeowners and developers led many activists to conclude that there were fundamental differences between the interests of homeowners and businesses. As Irving Gilman, a past president of the homeowners, stated: "Our local chamber of commerce is our enemy. . . . They're promoting business and . . . [that] requires customers. The more the merrier. . . . They wanted developing; we wanted control." The board of realtors, which aggressively promoted development schemes, was "just murder."

In conflicts over development, activists formulated antibusiness stances that they applied in their programs for tax reduction. Before Proposition 13 was enacted, the Monterey Park Taxpayers Association supported the Tax Justice Act of 1977, which proposed to channel tax relief to moderate- and low-income homeowners and renters.[46]

Growth became a major issue dividing homeowners and community business leaders in the middle-income parts of the San Fernando Valley as well. Here, increasing traffic and jet noise led homeowners to oppose the expansion of the Hollywood–Burbank airport, despite the many business opportunities there. Homeowners grew antagonistic to business leaders who supported airport growth. "You have to understand that the chamber of commerce and homeowners associations on many issues clash. And even when we agree on things there's not really a close working relationship."[47] One activist from the middle-income community of North Hollywood summarized how his opposition to airport expansion, billboards, developers, and high taxes shaped his views about business in the community:

> When I was with North Hollywood Homeowners, we had folks that were in a much lower SES, socio-economic status, than let's say, the Encino crowd. . . . In North Hollywood . . . you had more of a blue collar mentality. . . .
> Small business . . . they tend to keep to themselves . . . mom and pop kind of operations. They're usually marginal operators, just breaking even. They don't have the time and money and resources to devote to community efforts. All they can do is stay in business at a profit. Bigger corporations of course are a little different. They've got the money to help. . . . By and large businesses have not been cooperative. Their principal measure of what they want is based on dollars in the short run. . . . As a result, I've gone head to head with the chamber of commerce for as long as I can remember. We've always been opposed to the chamber because the chamber has not been generally interested in homeowner concerns. . . . [W]e've not had cordial relations and right through the years that's been pretty much true.
> [Banks and savings and loans?] . . . We've had contacts with them. Those have not been fruitful. I think they tend to be exploitative. . . . We approached a while ago a bank on a project. . . . I think they felt that our tactics and strategy were . . . not a suit and tie kind of thing, and as a result were not really supportive of what we did. Those have not gone anywhere, those kinds of things. . . . We've battled pretty much the real estate agents, developers. Real estate houses have not been overly cooperative with us. . . . We want to see tougher zoning and controls that are not consonant with the goal of an agent who is interested in getting and selling a piece of property and turning it over for cash.

This activist opposed Proposition 13, partly because it provided tax advantages to business rather than the homeowner. Since property under Prop. 13 would be reassessed upward with each sale, and since homes were sold more often than businesses, assessments on homes would follow more closely the upward trend of property values.

> There is the matter of the turnover, . . . [that is,] when a business turns over its property for reassessment versus how often a [home turns over], and it's my understanding that homeowners are turning over faster than businesses, and as a result . . . homes were winding up by paying and were moving up on the [assessment] scale, whereas businesses have tended to be a little more static than the transient homeowner. . . . I see a definite conflict of interest between an apartment owner and a single-

family dwelling owner. . . . Much of . . . the Jarvis mentality was R-4
property owners [apartment owners] who . . . were paying a pretty hefty
tax, who wanted to get out from under that and were one of the prime
movers behind this [Proposition 13]. The homeowners bought into
that. . . . What is good for the owner of a sixteen-unit apartment is
probably not what's in the best interest of a single-family homeowner.
And I feel very strongly about that.[48]

From the Valleys to the Oceans,
Views for Sale

In the coastal plain of Los Angeles County lies the middle-income
community of El Segundo. Over one hundred thousand commuters
stream into the town to work in the refineries, aerospace industries, and
office-building complexes. Beginning in 1964, the El Segundo Taxpayers
Association worked to lower tax rates, expose corrupt officials, reduce
airport noise, and improve zoning regulations. When the association
tried to influence local government, activists soon discovered that government had established close relations with the nearby large corporations. One leader of the association concluded that "the entire city was
run by Standard Oil." The leader of the taxpayers group organized
campaigns that succeeded in replacing all the probusiness members of
the city planning commission and defeating three city council members.

This activist thought that the town's government should take an active
role in solving traffic, pollution, and other problems caused by the many
businesses operating nearby. She favored what she termed "planned progress," including stricter regulations over proposed office buildings. "The
developer has certain rights, but his rights end where his property line
stops. And if he's creating a problem for the community, then there
should be some limitation put on it." When it came time to pay for solving
the problems created by business, many members of the association favored increasing business license taxes and instituting a split roll for property taxes, which would tax business property at a higher rate than homes.

Oh, we'll have to tax industry. . . . Example. The city business license tax
here has not been increased since 1947. It's $24 a year for the entire 20
stories of the Prudential Towers. (Now Palos Verdes [the affluent coastal
community discussed in chap. 3] is $30 per employee.) And again they're
paying absolutely nothing in the way of property taxes. But they desper-
ately need some street improvements. I have no objection to creating a
special assessment district enabling them to pay for the street improvements that they require. But I object vehemently when the public works
director takes the money that he gets on gas tax which comes to the
community on the basis of the number of residents and uses it to service
the industry, who's getting off Scot free.[49]

In short, the operations of the large businesses in El Segundo, usually invisible to residents of suburban bedroom communities, had led activists to support antibusiness tax programs.

Another coastal community, Venice, is an area where the median family income in 1976 was 90 percent that of Los Angeles County. But this one statistic does not capture the great contrasts in the town. Venice includes a largely black neighborhood where incomes hover around the poverty line. Nearby, blue-collar Portuguese and Greeks could still afford in 1970 to buy their tiny houses lost amid a maze of alleyways and, yes, canals. But one person's alley is another's charm. Flocking to Venice are the young professionals, whose favorite haunts include Beyond Baroque, an old city jail now resplendent with art exhibits and resounding with poetry, and the Rose Cafe, the fine purveyors of fresh croissants, quesadillas made with brie cheese, and fish with blueberry sauce. Among these Venetians of fashion, "industry" refers to film-making and not to the oil refinery a scant five miles away. In Venice one can also find a network of political organizations favoring women's rights, rent control, environmentalism, and nonintervention in Central America.

Although the liberal climate made tax protest hardly the proper cause, real estate inflation made it a necessity. One activist recounts how his neighbor paid $2,700 for his house; by 1975, the market value had topped $100,000, and $300,000 the year Proposition 13 passed. This activist volunteered with the American Association of Retired Persons to improve social security benefits and services for the aged. He campaigned to reduce noise levels at a nearby airport and pressured developers—"the big interests"—to build more housing for seniors while preserving the natural habitat in the wetlands by the beach. But his major political work was to organize the Coalition of Homeowners and Renters of Los Angeles County, which campaigned against the privileges of large property owners. As he wrote in an open letter in early 1977:

[L]arge and affluent property owners . . . pay only a small, if any, share of their fair taxes, especially those who made substantial campaign contributions to the Assessor. . . . A sampling of properties owned by some of [Assessor] Philip Watson's contributors along Wilshire Blvd. show an underassessment of $500 million and may reach $2 billion. . . . Among properties enjoying assessment advantages are reported to be the 53-story UCB [United California Bank] building; . . . American Savings and Loan–Sherman Oaks—unchanged since 1970 although residential property 2 blocks away was reassessed higher up to 300%. . . . Because of the Assessor's conferring of assessment advantages to his favorite special interests, the historical 1966 collection ratio of 55% of the taxes from the income producing [business] properties has been reduced now to 45%, thus shifting 10% of the taxes to the residential taxpayers.

This activist's program for tax reform included making homeowner-occupied property tax exempt, which would help accomplish the larger objective of "reduction of the combined total property and income tax now burdening the low and middle incomes."[50]

Generalized Unresponsiveness

During their protests to reduce property taxes, activists in middle-income communities discovered that the governments of their towns, cities, counties, and states were unresponsive to their petitions. Through their own experience, activists learned that small businesses would offer little assistance and that community business leaders and large corporations would not help at all. Activists gave tirades about the unresponsiveness of big business and big government and, in doing so, were able to tap the feelings of many citizens who felt powerless against all dominant institutions.

Such feelings, widespread in the 1960s and 1970s, are a recurrent feature in the American polity. According to Samuel Huntington, suspicion of the power of government and other institutions such as big business is a long-standing American creed. Periodically, in times of "credal passion," democratic ideals were used to challenge existing institutions. In these periods, "[A]uthority . . . [was] widely questioned or rejected. . . . Traditional American values of liberty, individualism, equality, popular control of government, and the openness of government were stressed in public discussion. . . . Hostility toward power (the antipower ethic) was intense, with the central issue of politics being defined as 'liberty versus power.' . . . Movements flourished devoted to specific reforms or 'causes.' "[51]

The tax revolt was one cause that dramatized activists' and citizens' feelings that government and business had become unresponsive. Many leaders and institutions stood in the way of lower property taxes—the office of the county assessor, whose computers inexorably printed out the higher tax bills; the chiefs of government agencies, who built their bureaucratic empires at public expense; the politicians in Sacramento, who endlessly haggled over tax relief and never delivered; and finally, the executives of corporations, who along with politicians, labor union leaders, school administrators, the media, and the experts warned that Proposition 13 was folly.

In their confrontation with unresponsive institutions, tax protesters sputtered sparks of angry rhetoric that inflamed middle-income communities. But although it was like a fire that refined them, it was also an anger that isolated them from the allies that might have brought success.

5

Middle-Income Communities in Search of Power

At the race track it's the two-dollar window that makes money for the race track. It's the same thing when Jarvis under Prop. 13 had probably the premier mailing list in the world. . . . Even though you only get ten dollars or five dollars a person from your property owners, there are so many of them that if you collect from five percent of them ten dollars apiece you've got $15–16 million.[1]

In the early years of the tax revolt, activists gathered together in small groups that usually encompassed only one community. These groups suffered a precarious existence. They continually had to worry about soliciting donations; volunteers worked for a few weeks and then quit; sparsely attended meetings were an embarrassment. Protesters turned to organizations in the community, seeking donations of money, supplies, staff, and office space, and also nonmaterial help such as reassurance that their cause was worthwhile, explanations of their plight, suggestions about how to proceed, and justifications for their actions.

Such help was hard to find, particularly in middle-income communities. Even obtaining the facts about taxation and spending was difficult, as government tried to give the best possible interpretation of its performance and budget requirements. From newspapers, protesters were lucky to get a fleeting mention, let alone a favorable story. The limited formal education of most residents of middle-income communities was a further hindrance. The traditional high school civics course, praising America as a land of freedom and democracy, was strangely irrelevant to the challengers' experience of unresponsive government.

Middle American activists eagerly sought to understand their own circumstances but received no help from established sources. The activists had to turn to whatever was at hand. Sometimes, they created their own pet notions. In the San Gabriel Valley, for example, several turned to fundamentalist religion. They formed their own Bible study class to discuss what they called Biblical Economics for Full Employment Parity, which argued that tax laws should follow God's laws. Their biblical economics attempted to use divine standards to determine how all taxpayers should pay their fair share. After all, "Saint Paul was a tax man. He was a crook, but he turned Christian." Another activist pointed out that "the problem comes when wealth . . . turns one away from the Heavenly Father."[2]

In Search of the Democratic Right

Another possibility was obtaining assistance by affiliating with a political group. Although most in the tax revolt were not sympathetic to probusiness varieties of conservatism, a few of them eventually gravitated toward right-wing political groups that capitalized on feelings that government was unresponsive to citizens.

Those who did affiliate with the right picked certain right-wing groups that catered to the anti–big-government and anti–big-business sentiments in middle-income communities. For example, after Mike Rubino's tax protest in Alhambra had organized itself into the Property and Homeowners of the San Gabriel Valley, the group chose as its president Houston Myers, a partisan in the American Independent Party (AIP) who ran for lieutenant governor of California on the AIP ticket. Myers was not attracted to right-wing groups that were the champions of big business, but rather ones that talked about the little guy. He was shaped by the hardships of the Great Depression:

My father, he was a farmer . . . back in Arkansas. My dad had a place; we gave it away when '29 hit. We just walked out and left it and came to California in 1929. My dad, he was a carpenter out here . . . but he didn't have any job for a long time during the Depression. He worked some on PWA [the federal Public Works Administration].

I worked in a bakery during high school . . . at night . . . all through high school. I went to . . . trade school. . . . I studied to be a sheet metal worker, I studied auto mechanics . . . body and fender work.

Myers opened an automobile repair shop on Main Street in Alhambra. When segregationist governor George Wallace took his presidential

campaign to California in 1968, Myers became an enthusiastic supporter. He ran for state assembly in 1970 with his slogan, "A friend of
the working people, for lower taxes, with a more equitable tax system . . . for God, Country, and freedom." Later he argued: "[President]
Reagan is going to have the biggest budget ever. . . . So where does that
leave the poor working people? We're the ones paying—the middle
class. The high-ups don't pay a dime. That's proven. . . . We believe
really that everybody should pay taxes. We don't believe in the loopholes that they have for the big boys to get off the hook."[3]

Around the time that Proposition 13 qualified for the ballot, right-
wing groups were not the well-financed operations they later became in
the 1980s. The membership of right-wing groups in 1977, such as it was,
cannot be attributed to glossy advertisements or computer-aided marketing. The American Independent Party was a struggling political group
whose resources were not much larger than those of the tax protest
movement. In the November 1976 elections, the AIP fielded thirteen
candidates for the California State Assembly. The expenditures of most
of the AIP candidates were less than $200. The highest was $5,900,
compared to the average of $72,000 for all assembly candidates includ-
ing major party nominees. AIP spending was comparable to that of the
leftist Peace and Freedom party, which ran fourteen candidates, most of
whom also spent less than $200. The Peace and Freedom Party and the
AIP each won only 0.7 percent of the California votes for president in
1976.

The handful of tax reduction activists with affiliations to the American Independent Party were attracted not to the AIP's money but to its
stand in favor of the middle-income earner. The AIP also gained followers by emphasizing that the government was undemocratic and that it
wielded excessive power over citizens. The AIP platform condemned
illegal government surveillance and harassment of citizens and called for
full public disclosure of governmental affairs. Myers opposed regional
government because it was a "dictatorship" of appointed officials. "You
and I can't vote for the people that's running it. . . . No place should we
have anything that we don't have an opportunity to vote on." Myers also
believed that judges should be directly elected, rather than appointed,
and should serve for shorter terms.[4]

Some tax protesters were so alarmed about the unresponsive power
of government that they became eager believers of conspiracy theories
popularized by right-wing groups. Since tax protesters in middle-income
communities had received so little support for their cause, they concluded that ruling elites and institutions must have formed elaborate
conspiracies against the people. Some activists spoke of their suspicions
that major banks and the Federal Reserve Board controlled America.

John Noehl Schmitz organized the Tax Rebellion Committee of Los Angeles County, which was against

the whole monetary system of the United States, . . . and the big, like an iceberg . . . part sticking out is the IRS. That's the collection agency for the bankers to collect money. . . . We picketed the banks. Every Friday night we picketed the Federal Reserve Bank downtown on Olive and Olympic Streets. . . . We moved from bank to bank all the way from Orange County clear up to . . . Burbank. . . . We had picket signs, "Banks cause poverty." They cause poverty 'cause they cause unemployment. And banks also cause inflation. So they cause all of these problems we've got today.[5]

Others dramatized their distrust of big government and big business by describing the secret networks of influence among the elites. Howard Farmer, for example, pointed to the "Rockefeller brain trust" and the Trilateral Commission as the ruling forces in the world. According to Farmer, a conspiracy was centered at the Center for Public Administration in Chicago, which promoted regional planning and the concentration of power in the hands of city managers, who formed an "invisible government." Locally, the conspiracy involved the powerful *Los Angeles Times* publishing and media corporation, which editorialized against Proposition 13 and was allegedly well-connected to the Trilateral Commission.[6]

Some like Pablo Campos, who did not believe in conspiracy theories, used libertarian beliefs to passionately argue that more citizen participation was needed to control the power of big government to tax and spend: "And so what we're saying, there should be no taxation without the direct participation of the taxpayer. In other words, we no longer can afford the luxury of delegating the power of taxation to our elected officials. If you want my money, for God's sakes, ask me. . . . The feeling was there's two groups. Them and us. The them are in government, and the us are out."

Campos organized a citizens' group to fight to repeal the sales tax because it unfairly burdened moderate income earners. Although he favored a libertarian philosophy, his version of it was far removed from the fountainheads of free enterprise. Campos's arguments recruited people into the movement from middle-income areas.

The lower the income, the higher the representation in the movement [and] the more they contributed. . . . Little people, little nobodies . . . they are the ones . . . who are more easily persuaded that, hey, if you['re going] . . . to be taxed, you should at least be asked. . . . The little man—even though you say, well he's the recipient of all this [govern-

ment] largess, right? He is the easist one to convince: have them ask you
before they take your buck. . . . Because he has less power. He perceives
himself as having less power. And here's someone saying, wait a moment. You should at least have power over what you've created, as mea-
ger as it may be.[7]

In Search of the Participatory Left

Since activists in middle-income communities were hostile against
business elites, one might expect that protesters would affiliate with the
political left. Irving Gilman, for one, was attracted to a leftist tax reform
group and participated in one of their demonstrations:

> I once participated in a march on Wilshire Boulevard which pointed out
> some of the bigger buildings that were undertaxed. . . . Again it was early
> on in the beginning and it was an educational process. So I guess we were
> reaching for any contact that we could make. . . . I participated in their
> march because in a broad sense it was the same thing. They were pointing
> out that here's this big, humongous building and because somebody knows
> somebody, it didn't get reassessed, and it's way undervalued. So we did
> that and at the time we attracted some media attention. . . . [W]e
> marched up and down for about three hours . . . down Rodeo Drive [the
> luxury shopping district in Beverly Hills]. I think one of them was the
> Wells Fargo Building and another one was on Wilshire [Boulevard], was
> another bank building. . . . It created a little stir.

This leftist group also went to the county assessor's office and staged a
guerrilla theater performance, telling of an insurance company that was
presenting its case that day for a reduced tax assessment. The troupe
marched into the hearing, as television news crews followed.

Gilman began to get involved with the group: "They wanted me to
attend their meetings to supposedly 'keep them straight.' So I did go to
some of their meetings. . . . [Interviewer: How big were those meetings?] Not a hell of a lot bigger than ours." Besides the small size of the
group, its stance toward big government led Gilman to question his
affiliation to the left:

> Their membership was composed mostly of . . . government employees
> and/or union people. So their philosophy was not necessarily to give the
> [Prop.] 13 benefits back to the people but rather to spread it around to the
> government employees and the union people. . . . [They were] more wel-
> fare oriented, more philosophically aligned, I guess, with big govern-
> ment. . . . [Our Monterey Park group] was not, was anti. . . . Their phi-
> losophy was that whatever savings they could get, it should be poured

back into the welfare area of government and not given back to the people. So I didn't stay with them very long.[8]

Although the left's antibusiness stance evoked sympathy among activists in middle-income communities, Middle America was also angry at the institutional power of big government. Activists hesitated to affiliate with left groups because they equated the left with the most visible portion of it—the institutionalized left. Since this institutionalized left was in charge of administering programs in education, housing, health, and welfare, the left had become identified with powerful bureaucracies and entrenched constituencies of clients and professionals. The activists were not aware that there was another section of the left, the "new left," which like the homeowners opposed urban redevelopment, argued that poverty programs benefited bureaucrats and not people, and sought to revitalize politics through meaningful participation. Although a few activists spoke of their sympathies toward the antiwar movement, they did not know that it had spawned community organizations whose leaders had first articulated the phrase, "participatory democracy."

Another activist worked with leftist groups to organize both renters and homeowners into a movement for property tax reduction. He understood that renters, too, pay property taxes by way of their rent payments to landlords. Renters were "a group that [Howard] Jarvis certainly had no use for because it didn't go along with some of his earlier plans. . . . After all, Jarvis was the secretary or something for the landlords' association so he wouldn't do something that would harm them." Shunned by Jarvis, this activist affiliated with a coalition of leftist groups that included the Democratic Socialist Organizing Committee, two activist Democratic party clubs, and a local of the Service Employees International Union. At the founding meeting of the coalition, the groups agreed that low-income homeowners and renters should receive property tax relief in the form of tax credits from the state, that businesses should pay a higher property tax rate than homeowners, and that the coalition should even press for "the public ownership of key enterprises such as utilities, [a] state bank, and [a] state insurance company, etc." The coalition also made a commitment to fight against cutbacks of social services throughout Los Angeles County.[9]

Only two groups of homeowners, both based in the liberal town of Venice, joined the coalition. Furthermore, its drastic program guaranteed that local government leaders would continue to be unresponsive:

Obviously we never got anywhere, because our plans, you might say, were so radical from their conservative, or already established things. . . . [T]hey probably . . . [wanted to] have pleased their campaign contributors, their so-called special interests in many areas—the real estate lobby, for instance, which is one of the most powerful, together with the bankers and the insurance lobbies. They're so powerful so it's pretty hard to get through them, and there are not enough of our elected representatives that are not connected in some way with those, and therefore obligated to them, unfortunately.

The leftist tax coalition tried supporting a petition that called for progressive tax reforms combined with maintaining levels of social services. The petition failed to get the required number of signatures, however, and therefore was never put before the electorate. As an activist from Venice put it, "The results were always negative, so you just give up on that score."[10]

In Search of Rank-and-File Trade Unionism

In middle-income communities, trade unions could have provided assistance for incipient tax protests. But for the most part, tax protesters did not seek such help. Only two activists from blue-collar backgrounds did attempt to raise tax issues with union locals. The worst response came when an electrician wanted to distribute leaflets about property taxes at a meeting of his own union in 1966:

At that time things were pretty rough. I'll give you an illustration. . . . I went to a union hall, IBEW, the International Brotherhood of Electrical Workers. . . . And I tried to pass out some explanations of what was needed in the fight for our right to limit taxation. . . . I brought this material to the union hall and they said, Bill, you know you can't bring that in here; that's too political. We are not going to allow you to get up here and talk to these people, you can't do that. That's too political. And I said, well, what will I do? I'm going to do something, you know I am. . . . Before you guys were all born, I'm already born and working. . . . And they said, all right then, if you want to do something, get your chair and go out in the hall and sit out in the hall out there and talk to the people . . . which I did. And what did they do? . . . They sent somebody out there to take the light bulb out. Now it's dark in the hall. . . . And so I said, now that's a dandy, ain't it?

But taking the light away from this electrician with fifty years of seniority is like trying to sue a lawyer: "So I went in the toilet and stole a lamp out of the toilet and climbed up there, and I really had to go get a step ladder from another room to reach it. So I kept that up."[11]

Howard Farmer, another activist with long experience in trade unions, wrote some angry letters to the editor about high property taxes and the excessive salaries of politicians, thereby attracting the attention of some members of the United Auto Workers Union. The president of the union local invited Farmer to dinner in 1976 and backed Farmer's fledgling tax protest group, the United Voters League. Although the local president attended some meetings of the league, he offered only limited assistance, according to Farmer:

> I asked him to let me bring my proposition before the membership, but he would never give me the right to speak before the members. . . . I wanted three thousand leaflets published, and he said, OK, I'll tell you what I'll do, I'll run them off on my machine. So these [shows interviewer] are the leaflets that was [sic] run off at the United Auto Workers Union. He never gave me one cent of cash. The only thing that he ever gave me was just this and his personal appearance at our meetings. . . . I tried to get . . . [the local president] to run against Ed Edelman [the incumbent city council representative] . . . and he said no, he was not interested in politics.[12]

For many tax protesters living in middle-income communities, trade unionism had been a vibrant part of their life's story.

> I had a socialist father. . . . On May Day you would go to the May Day demonstrations. . . . Talk about your early police brutality—that was it. . . . Here you had policemen on horseback and policemen with billy clubs controlling a crowd by hitting them on the back with billy clubs and break up [sic] the demonstration, and all they're doing is listening to somebody speak. . . . I carried leaflets at one time. I was a great supporter of Harry Bridges's International Longshoremen's union. I was in favor of Caesar Chavez and . . . the creation of the farmworkers' union.[13]

Some activists were union members; one, as we shall see, had become a union organizer in the 1930s. Yet by the time of Proposition 13, they felt that trade unions were irrelevant to their immediate plight. How could they continue to own their homes when property taxes were increasing past two thousand dollars a year? Those, like Howard Farmer, who did try to work with unions, were disappointed. Many others did not even try because they knew it would be fruitless.

Scarcely any of the activists in middle-income communities had been conservatives since their youth; nor had they undergone a personal reversal from union activist to conservative ideologue, as did Ronald Reagan. All were proud that they had been and still were fighters for working men and women. They had not sullied their union cards with slick affluence. "I can't afford that kind of stuff. I'm not in that class. I'm a working man, not a capitalist." "I ain't got nothing. I'm just a poor working bastard just, just running out of life and running out of money."[14]

The unions that they had known, now had changed. Did John L.

Lewis ever say, "No, it's too political"? Activists had apocryphal stories to express their disillusionment with contemporary unions:

> You're talking to the right person about unions. I will have to go way back, though. Both my parents were very much involved in union organizing. And those were bad days for the unions. Those were the days when you had sweatshops, 14-hour-a-day work, low wages, and very bad working conditions and so on. And those were militant things. There was a lot of violence in those periods. But the leadership there was representative of the working classes. But now they eventually got the unions, got them recognized, and so on, and that's when a lot of—what would you call them—underworld figures got into control of many of them, unfortunately. I recall a friend of mine was . . . a member of [a] . . . union in New York; they called a meeting, the purpose of which was to oust their leadership because of their underworld associations and so on. Well, about half hour or hour or so before the meeting, the bomb was set off, which broke up that meeting, and I guess broke up the attempt to oust their leadership. That was kind of representative. . . . You read about the huge salaries and expense that their leaders build up.[15]

Trade unions, rather than guiding the tax protests in middle-income communities, instead had become yet another remote, bureaucratic institution that needed to be shaken by a taxpayers' revolt.

In short, left political groups and trade unions did not build on spontaneous antibusiness sentiment; they failed to help tax protesters develop and fight for a downward redistributional program. In order for the left to succeed in middle-income communities, there needed to be something more than just a bigger campaign for Hubert Humphrey. Regis Debray wrote of "the revolution in the revolution," arguing that in order for revolutions to succeed in third-world nations, activists had to shake off older, Western Marxist theories. In middle-income communities, there had to be a left within the left, which would have shaken off trade union bureaucrats and would have addressed the problems of middle-income Americans in ways that made sense of their life experiences. But it was not the left that would build the tax revolt, give it leadership, and shape its program. Welfare-state bureaucrats and union business agents had dropped the banner of democratic participation in communities. Who would pick it up?

Half the Way with Jarvis Today

Enter Howard Jarvis. In 1977, when Jarvis unveiled his petition that would be approved as Proposition 13, it embodied a program much different from the antibusiness proposals common in middle-income communities. In contrast to proposals for downward redistribution, Proposition 13 targeted one-third of its relief for homeowners and two-thirds for business, with none for tenants. Activists like Bill Hutton of North Hollywood grumbled at Jarvis's program: "Having been a businessman in the past and now a man of wealth . . . Mr. Jarvis is [not] much concerned with those who really carry the burden of a corrupt tax system in the state or the United States." Hutton supported Jarvis and Proposition 13, nevertheless, as did others with antibusiness resentments.[16] Another activist, who campaigned against the Vietnam War and characterized himself as "almost extreme liberal in most areas," coordinated civic associations in areas of the San Fernando Valley where homes were "average or a little above average" in value.

> We were also focusing on the unfairness at that point, where the homeowners were being charged an unfair portion . . . to what the business community and the commercial community was paying. And we were attempting to get them to bring that into balance. . . . This is what preceded the whole concept of the Proposition 13 discussions and battles. . . . At that time the homeowners were carrying most of the burden. And the businesses were paying less proportionately. Gann and Jarvis came along and presented their proposition to the people and most of us didn't really want that but had no choice. It was the only thing . . . that offered any kind of alternative to what was actually happening in the local communities. All of us . . . particularly we of (if you will) the liberal bent, we realized we were selling some people down the tubes. It really got down to bothering a lot of us conscience-wise. Because it boiled down to them or us, almost a kill or be killed kind of thing, a military mentality which was quite sick.[17]

Activists who had promoted their own antibusiness programs, then joined Howard Jarvis and the campaign to put Proposition 13 on the ballot and pass it. A veritable army of volunteers, many from middle-income neighborhoods, gathered one and a half million petition signatures. Mike Rubino, for one, threw his support to Jarvis. Despite his misgivings about Jarvis's probusiness positions, Rubino advised the protest groups that he once had instigated that they should affiliate with Jarvis's coalition. Rubino delivered twenty-five speeches in support of Proposition 13.[18]

Why did these tax protest leaders in middle-income communities campaign for Jarvis and Proposition 13? Richard Carman's group issued a news release supporting Prop. 13, emphasizing that it was an expression of the citizens' fight against unresponsive government power:

> What is property taxation all about? Let's not forget that it is a privilege . . . that the voters give [to] their elected officials to set property tax rates.

During the past 20 years, lawmakers and bureaucrats have managed by their tricky manipulations to pass many laws, that actually take away the people's right to vote on most local tax issues. Their goal is to be able to tax at will, and they have almost achieved it.

"Abuse a privilege—lose a privilege." That is what we are now telling these government manipulators. That is what the Jarvis–Gann amendment is saying.[19]

Grievance and Militancy in Middle America

Activists in middle-income communities, unmoved by Jarvis's program, affiliated with him partly because he promised to use citizen activism to fight government power. Jarvis's fight generated enthusiasm because of his militant style and rhetoric.

Jarvis became known for his irate mannerisms, which middle Americans adored. Jarvis's militant talk about drastic solutions captured the angry mood of activists who saw that elected officials and business leaders would not respond to their grievances. The activists, like others of moderate means in their community, also were angry because higher property taxes brought on personal crises of somehow trying to pay for shelter and other basic needs.

The higher income of upper-middle-class homeowners gave them discretionary funds that they could use, albeit reluctantly, to pay higher taxes. Not so for most residents in middle-income communities, whose earnings were totally spent just paying for the mortgage and other necessities. The security of sheltering one's family in a home whose payments did not increase gave way to panic as tax bills rose higher and higher. The president of the homeowners association in North Hollywood originally paid $250 per month for the mortgage to his house. In the mid-1970s he had to pay an additional $150 per month in property taxes. This "devastating" burden led him to become active in the homeowners group. As another protester described it, "People were really threatened because, you know, their taxes were astronomical. A simple little two-bedroom Burbank home, the taxes had been, what, $400, $500—all of a sudden $1,300, $1,600, $1,800. People were going crazy!"[20] One thousand of these Burbank homeowners flocked to a rally to cheer Howard Jarvis on.

Since higher property taxes in middle-income communities meant less money for necessities, the resulting sense of desperation led protesters to be quite willing to demonstrate and otherwise resort to protest actions. Two activists, squeezed to pay their bills, asked the interviewer's help in obtaining pension benefits that were due and then proclaimed that their platform was "fight school bonds, fight the city, fight anything that was gonna hurt our property taxes. . . . It's a fight, fight, fight, and even when you fight it doesn't matter."[21]

At times activists in middle-income communities had been involved in militant leftist movements that provided a legacy easily transformed into militant tax protests. Howard Farmer for example, had joined the Communist party in the 1930s, organized unemployment councils in New York's Lower East Side, and led a march of unemployed seamen on the U.S. Capitol. Years later, he turned his anger against the Los Angeles City Council. Once again he set up a picket line, this time to protest the council's attempt to vote itself a pay increase.

> [T]he city council down here had just voted themselves a huge increase in pay. . . . I told my group . . . I'm getting tired of sitting here in a debating society, and see nothing happen. And I'm going to move, and so if you want to join me fine, if you don't, well, goodby. And so I wrote a letter into the *Valley News* . . . and told them on Monday morning I was going to set up a one-man picket line up around city hall as a protest against this increase in salaries. . . . By one o' clock I had about twenty people on the picket line. . . . And so this was my first action, direct action, in the tax fight right there.

Farmer decided to confront his city council representative:

> So I went into his office with a chip on my shoulder and demanded action. . . . And I said, I'm getting damned tired of all this horse shit going on around this city hall down here. And I said, you claim that you're a man of the people and I said I want to see if you are. I said here, here's two hundred and fifty signatures that I collected out here in the three hours that we've been picketing. . . . I want to see what you will do. Will you get up tomorrow and object to this pay increase. . . . And he said, yes, I will . . . I went out and I thought I had won a victory there.

But Farmer found out otherwise at the city council meeting the next day.

> I was the last one to speak there at the city council meeting. So help me God, when you go in there, here's the barricade around the city council and they put the microphone right there where the fence is. . . . From the time I walked from this microphone . . . and before I could sit down, they had already voted on and passed 13 to 2 in favor of the increase. . . . And I blew my top when it happened, because I was so angry.

From this encounter with unresponsive government, Farmer carried on with a militant spirit. "If you want anything you got to go out in the streets and get it. They ain't gonna give it to you on a free sample. . . . You got to go out and fight for everything you get."[22]

Activists in middle-income communities adopted militant tactics not only because of their pasts but also because militancy seemed to prod unresponsive officials with unfavorable publicity. In Monterey Park, for example, Irving Gilman organized seventy-five people to picket city hall to protest a tax increase. This "taught us . . . that if you want to get the media involved you have to have . . . action. . . . They won't come out and cover a meeting. But if you say, 'Hey, we're gonna picket,' then that's a different story." This advocacy of militant tactics contrasts with the ethos of upper-middle-class communities (see chap. 7). "Wealthier . . . [communities] handle things more in a professional way. . . . They fight city hall with their own tactics. . . . If necessary, we'll put up a demonstration."[23]

In some middle-income communities, homeowners resorted to another militant tactic, the tax strike—an organized, mass refusal to pay property tax bills. In Culver City, seven hundred taxpayers met in 1966 and booed a deputy to the county assessor. Amid shouts of "Taxation without representation!" and "Remember the Boston Tea Party!" the noisy assembly supported the twenty thousand citizens throughout the county who had reportedly pledged to stop paying their property taxes. Bruce Kay told the angry crowd, "We must have immediate relief. . . . We're not talking about five, ten, fifteen years from now. We've got to have relief now. . . . The voice of the people will be heard." That same year, the tax strike was a popular cause in the middle-income community of Glendale, where the median family income was $10,016 (1.06 times the figure for L.A. County). One resident pledged, "We'll support any organized tax strike. . . . The taxes are outrageous. . . . And many people in our neighborhood are retired or widowed. Most have a fixed income and can't afford to have taxes raised." The secretary of the Los Angeles County Tax Protest Association told of the spread of the tax strike: "There have been about 25 meetings throughout the county. . . . At each one there were 300 to 500 people and almost 100 percent indicated they would withhold their taxes."[24]

Symbolic Militancy and Anti-Elitism

Howard Jarvis's wrathful mannerisms and his verbal broadsides against the establishment expressed the spirited militancy that taxes and unresponsive government had generated in middle America. Jarvis peppered his speeches with comments such as, "[W]hat we were trying to accomplish was to put a fence between the hogs and the swill bucket. . . . Proposition 13 was intended to forge a chain around the necks of all elected officials and their coteries of bureaucrats so that they could be dragged away from the feed bag." At the peak of tax protests in 1976, he announced that he was refusing to pay his own property tax bill, arguing that the right to strike extended to the overburdened taxpayer: "[J]oin with us and thousands of others in refusing to pay your property tax on December 10, 1976. We the taxpayers are constantly burdened with strikes by public employees, and as all the people are presumed to enjoy equal rights in this nation, we taxpayers who pay the salaries, fringe benefits, and pensions of all public employees have the same right to strike as do the public employees." Jarvis summed up the spirit of militancy in his movement when he remarked, "Our small group of taxpayers in California . . . slew the giant. They had the will, the persistence, and the guts to fight and win."[25]

For many middle Americans, Jarvis evoked the reaction, "I admire him. He's a fighter." Another activist remarked, "Jarvis . . . did a great job just by being such an angry old curmudgeon. No one has ever talked back to these fellows before. . . . There was a brush fire waiting for a match and Jarvis was the match. . . . Sometimes he was a little extra abrasive. . . . But I happened to think that it was a necessary element."

Like other charismatic leaders throughout history, Jarvis evoked a personal, emotional response from his followers. Some called him "the savior." Another explained, "[Jarvis] was the kind of personality that was appropriate for the time because people were very angry. They could relate to him because they all had the same feelings . . . of frustration and anger—that we were being robbed by the city. The robber barons were out to confiscate our properties. . . . [T]he threat was so great to so many people that they just all reacted spontaneously. . . . [P]eople were so turned on by it at the time because they all felt the same way and didn't know how to express it. So when he expressed it, . . . we were all one. We were all Howard Jarvises waiting to be discovered."[26]

Attracted to Jarvis's militant style, middle Americans were willing to overlook the often-repeated accusation that, "All you really need to know about the property tax initiative on the June ballot is that Howard Jarvis . . . is also the paid director of an association of apartment house owners in Los Angeles."[27] Many middle Americans did not notice that Jarvis and the United Organizations of Taxpayers stood for a program of tax reductions for both residential and business property. Activists in middle-income communities set aside their suspicions of business and ended up supporting a leader whose program gave most tax relief to business. Style had prevailed over the conscious choice of a redistributive program.

As the June 1978 election approached, even leftist activists whose first choice was tax reform for low- and moderate-income earners, decided to support Proposition 13. In Venice, the founder of the Coalition of Homeowners and Renters supported Proposition 13 because the choice had boiled down to Prop. 13 versus its rival, Proposition 8. Proposition 8, placed on the ballot by a vote of the state legislature, authorized the split roll—a lower property tax rate for homeowners compared to business. If Proposition 8 had passed, then Senate Bill 1 would have taken effect, which would have lowered the homeowner's property tax by 30 percent. A poll before the election showed that the public, by a two-to-one majority, did favor the general idea of taxing homes at a lower rate compared to businesses. Here, at last, was a redistributive program to benefit the homeowner, but it was too late. Most were suspicious of Proposition 8, because they saw it as a bogus, last-minute concession by unresponsive politicians. The text of the proposition did not even specifically mention the planned tax reductions (which were listed in the State Senate bill). The Venice activist opposed Prop. 8:

> Now they constitute a 27-page fine-print Bill together with cross-references to at least 28 major sections of the Property Tax Laws, and worded in legal gibberish apparently designed deliberately to be incomprehensible to the average taxpayer, and make him dependent on its spokesmen's interpretations and claims about its benefits. . . . [The] 30% reduction of the property tax of homeowners . . . could disappear by next year's assessment. . . . The total lack of concern or response of the Legislature to the peoples' needs is further unerringly demonstrated when it heard, but refused to listen to, the message of the Peoples' Prop[osition 13] clearly indicating that a change is urgently needed in the present archaic and regressive tax system that ignores the basis of ability to pay, and burdens the low and middle income taxpayers.

Although this activist was clear in his rejection of Proposition 8, he was not an enthusiastic supporter of Prop. 13 and expressed his judgment this way: "[O]n a scale of ten, we generously gave it a four, even though we gave it our wholehearted cooperation in getting it passed because it was the only game in town."[28]

Middle-Income Communities and the Growth of the Tax Revolt

But how had Howard Jarvis and Proposition 13 become the only game in town? Part of the explanation one needs, is why Howard Jarvis and his coalition, the United Organizations of Taxpayers, actually gained strength until it could claim to speak for all the taxpayers of California (see chap. 6). The other part of the explanation is how tax reduction groups in middle-income communities failed to provide leadership to groups elsewhere. For example, the Monterey Park Taxpayers

Association, the El Segundo Taxpayers Association, and the North Hollywood Homeowners Association were based in a single community, had limited memberships and resources, and had to contend with many issues other than taxation. Groups such as these could join confederations formed by others but did not have the capability of starting their own coalitions with a distinctive program. Similarly, when tax protests in the San Fernando Valley began in earnest in 1976, Howard Farmer's group had only eight members and did not lead the other groups in the valley.

Although a few activists in middle-income communities did attempt to become countywide leaders of tax protests, these efforts quickly failed. Michael Rubino was the undisputed head of the tax revolt that flared up in Alhambra and surrounding communities in 1964 and again in 1965. Then, he was asked to lead a coalition of homeowners groups. "When all this first started they wanted me for their president. . . . But I was in the hospital at the time and I turned it down. . . . And I says [sic] give it to someone down there who knows what the devil he's doing. . . . That's how Howard Jarvis first came into the picture." After that, Rubino's little people, the moderate-income taxpayers of the San Gabriel Valley, never achieved the same levels of anger and mobilization, thereby denying Rubino another chance at tax revolt leader.[29] But if Michael Rubino did not have the pleasure of seeing his program for tax reduction triumph, at least he could take his stand on June 6, 1978, and gloat as Howard Jarvis struck back at the politicians.

In 1972, Richard Carman raised the two hundred dollars required to file his statewide initiative, which would have granted tax relief to homeowners only. He failed, however, to get anywhere near the number of signatures required to place the measure on the ballot. The Venice activist formulated his proposals for progressive tax reform and sent detailed and passionate letters to the governor and local elected officials. These letters were soon filed and forgotten. Again, government was unresponsive.

Activists in middle-income communities had begun tax revolts and had continued to support tax reduction through the years, but what made the tax revolt win were the homeowners from more affluent areas who increased their participation as victory neared. In the 1960s, all tax protests took place in middle-income communities, where the relative affluence index ranged from 0.78 to 1.10, and the weighted index (weighted by the attendance in each community[30]) was 1.02. These protests did not accomplish their objectives. Similarly, in fiscal year 1977, tax protests in the San Gabriel Valley mainly attracted activists from middle-income communities, which had a weighted affluence index of 1.02. The protesters assisted in activities that had been organized by other groups such as the Taxpayers United for Freedom and the Sherman Oaks Homeowners, which were headquartered in affluent areas outside the San Gabriel Valley.

Homeowners in middle-income communities participated in tax revolt activities through the decades—thirteen thousand in the 1950s, six thousand in the 1960s, and eleven thousand in the 1970s. But by themselves, the protesters in middle-income communities were not sufficient to reduce property taxes. In order to succeed, the tax revolt had to spread beyond middle Americans to the managers and professionals that compose the upper-middle class.

But frequently, taxation generated rivalries between communities of different income levels. As Mike Rubino argued: "Some cities even got clobbered [with tax increases] worse than we did. Beverly Hills didn't get hit at all. . . . Beverly Hills, Bel Air, Brentwood [wealthy neighborhoods]—at that time, those cities out there weren't touched. [Question: Why do you think that is? Rubino: chuckles] You can play politics and you can play dirty politics with people's lives. . . . Beverly Hills was paying a tax rate of $1.05 while Alhambra was paying $3.98."

The disparate economic strata in the tax revolt coalition held together because of political issues rather than economic ones. The redistributive questions of taxation tended to set middle Americans against businesses against professionals. It was the issue of government power that united small property owners into the tax revolt. Each middle-class group experienced in its own way the unresponsiveness of government on the tax issue. Each group responded to Howard Jarvis's rhetorical blasts against big government.

Conclusion

The history of tax protests suggests that there is a recurrent conflict between small property and big government. The homeowners' worst suspicions about politicians were confirmed when government officials did not even seriously respond to the taxpayers' plight. Unresponsive government incited angry protests but, still, no tax relief was granted. Homeowners also protested against urban renewal projects, which epitomized government's worst traits: wasting money and driving people out of their homes. But on this issue, too, government was unresponsive.

Tax protests are also indicative of a conflict between small and big property. Today the most common form of small property ownership in America is home ownership. Homeowners began their political actions with a distrust of big business. They were suspicious of the developers and financiers of high-rise office buildings that encroached on their residential communities. And as homeowners fought to lower their own property taxes, they discovered that big property was not fighting the same battle, but rather a competing one to reduce taxes on special interest groups. Some homeowners protested when they determined that office buildings and other large parcels of property had been granted lower assessments. Many homeowners learned that the best stance was to demand a program of tax relief for owner-occupied residences and let the owners of business property be damned with the rest of them.

The emphasis here on the conflicts between small and big property owners is a departure from the approach of Louis Hartz. Hartz's influential book, *The Liberal Tradition in America,* argued that American politics has been based on a consensus of property owners, large and small, who agreed on the principles of representative and limited government. Hartz believed America was a unique civilization because it had avoided the conflicts over property that had racked the old world. In the United States there had been no feudal aristocracy to monopolize the land and no peasantry lacking property rights. For two centuries the United States was populated with independent farmers who owned the land that they worked. As America industrialized, its workers were enthralled by the hopes that they could own a workshop, a home, or a farm. Here, argued Hartz, where there were no sharp class distinctions or class struggles, socialism and communism could only be alien ideologies.

In Hartz's America, naturally, the assumption was that the owner should have the right to enjoy the fruits that stemmed from his property and labor. Thus, the first obligation of the American republic was to protect private property, both large and small. Hartz admitted that differences sometimes arose between large and small property owners. Occasionally the small yeomen attacked the large merchant's riches; sometimes, the large industrialist castigated the American commoner for considering the expropriation of wealth. But for Hartz, these were misunderstandings, the result of temporary passion and exaggeration. Throughout most of American history, the property owners' consensus reigned, a "Lockean settlement," enshrined in the American Constitution. Twentieth-century reformers, despite their cries for change, worked within the property owners' consensus. The Progressive movement sought to revive a democratic capitalism, where individuals could find the moral equivalent of entrepreneurship. The New Deal, in Hartz's view, shunned Marxist radicalism in favor of pragmatic reform.

Hartz saw American politics as a system wherein conflict was contained and consensus inevitably prevailed. This chapter has portrayed some of the same actors and issues analyzed by Hartz—small property owners and large property owners talking about rights and government power. But the findings here have been at odds with Hartz's view. Homeowners, through their political activity, did not discover that they shared values and assumptions in common with the owners of large corporations. Rather, individual homeowners learned that they had different interests compared to big business, and even compared to the community business leaders who owned restaurant franchises, real estate partnerships, and auto dealerships.

Common interests and a common program for small and large property owners do not inevitably arise because of some abstract law or cultural necessity. Creating agreement among property owners required direct activity by real actors—the community activists in Sherman Oaks and elsewhere in the San Fernando Valley, and the leaders of Citizens for Property Tax Relief and the United Organizations of Taxpayers. Homeowners tried many types of leftist affiliations before Howard Jarvis finally succeeded in forging a consensus between small residential property owners and community business leaders.

However, the tax protest movement might have taken a different course, perhaps lessening the tax burden on low- and moderate-income earners. Given the trajectory of the movement in the 1960s and early 1970s, the probusiness program of the tax revolt was an unexpected development that had, one might argue, unfortunate consequences. It was, in short, an accident. But even accidents require explanations and may have human causes.

Like a collapsing colonial farmhouse in Louis Hartz's storybook America, the coalition between small property and large property needed to be rebuilt periodically, almost continually if it were to stand. The tax reduction movement reconstructed the property owners' coalition one more time.

How this restoration was accomplished is the subject of the next two chapters. Howard Jarvis and other leaders in the United Organizations of Taxpayers mediated the conflict between homeowners and community business leaders by recruiting an important group—small business—to the tax revolt. Small businesses could be convinced to work side by side with homeowners in their community. Yet small business also advocated programs that ultimately benefited business in general, small and large.

Proposition 13 was the winning mixture of large business benefits, small business political activism, and the homeowners' crusading consumerism. The success of Proposition 13 sparked many similar movements and campaigns, one of which made Ronald Reagan president. For large business, there were tax and budget cuts; for small business, there was deregulation. For middle Americans, there was only the hope of Ronald Reagan's campaign rhetoric: it's morning in America.

6

Community Business Leaders: Bounded Power and Movement Alliances

After I arrived in Los Angeles in 1935, I was trying to decide what to do. . . . A little while later, after I had started to get a feel for California, I went out and looked at a piece of ground. . . . About 80,000 square feet was being offered. Part of it was a swamp, and the price was 17 cents a square foot. . . . I went back to my bank and they said, no, they didn't think it sounded like a good buy. . . . The man at the bank—a very distinguished white-haired banker—looked me right in the eye and said, "You might as well understand something: this town is never going west of La Brea." [Several million people live west of La Brea Avenue today.] . . . I walked past a store where they had rolls of linoleum in the window. It was on sale for 19 cents a square foot. I thought to myself, "This linoleum isn't very thick, but it costs two cents a square foot more than the land. . . . The land goes all the way through to China, and it's close to the beach. To hell with the bank."[1]

So the interest that every individual who was involved in real estate or in real property or in construction or development . . . would be in shifting the tax burden away from a direct levy on property. . . . I'm certain that a good many of these people wouldn't mind seeing the real property tax disappear altogether and have it replaced by a 100 percent levy on incomes of everyone making less than ten thousand a year. I think that would be ideal for them.[2]

These things ought not need to be done outside the Chamber [of Commerce].[3]

The broad linkage of enterprise and property, the cradle-condition of classic democracy, no longer exists in America. This is no society of small entrepreneurs—now they are one stratum among others: above them is the big money; below them, the alienated employee; before them, the fate of politically dependent relics; behind them, their world.[4]

As the Eisenhower presidency slowly expired, small business leaders of California's San Gabriel Valley—the white-collar world characterized by C. Wright Mills as America's rearguard—were indeed quite comfortable with the respectability and cautious optimism of chamber of commerce luncheons and sales presentations. But many of them showed an unexpected angry side when they supported, and then led, a movement to protest property taxes.

This angry side was a product of their dealings with unresponsive government. Although small businesses exerted considerable influence in their towns, their attempts to reduce their property taxes were dismissed by big city and big county government. Although leading small businesses in the community exercised some power, it was power on the decline, power whose bounds stretched no further than the confines of one community.

Through interactions with big government over the years—the tax protests in West Covina in 1957, battles over racial discrimination in housing, and a series of tax reduction initiatives in the 1960s and 1970s—community business leaders discovered their own bounded power and acted to overcome it. They gradually learned how to attract homeowners and citizens to support probusiness programs. Community business leaders discovered that promulgating antigovernment rhetoric, which reflected their own deeply felt concerns about government power, resonated among masses of indignant homeowners. Sidney Pink was one of the first to learn these political lessons.

The Largest Tax Protest in California

Apart from the stars and the legends, the entertainment industry in Los Angeles consists of the stagehand who neatly puts away the props, the accountant who adds up their cost, and the projectionist who wearily screens the night's last show. These thousands of ordinary persons have only a tangential association with celebrities and fleeting thoughts of fame.

In the 1950s, Sidney Pink had a modest role in the entertainment industry. He owned a movie theater in the community of West Covina, California, a suburban town where the population increased from four to fifty thousand during that decade. It was not easy to attract these residents to his establishment, however. Pink came close to ruin when the Fox west-coast chain planned to build a new theater and restaurant complex nearby, complete with a child-care center. He barely succeeded in getting the town government to block the proposal. Like other business owners who envisioned unparalleled opportunities in the boom towns of the San Gabriel Valley, Pink dabbled in real estate development, but without notable success.

His ticket to fame came in the unexpected form of a high property tax bill, much like the bills that shocked so many of his neighbors. Pink organized a rally of five thousand people in protest. Within one month, he became leader of the Citizens Committee for Fair Taxation, which spoke for dozens of tax protest groups that had arisen throughout Los Angeles. At another rally in December 1957, Pink shared the stage with a county supervisor, the chair of the state board of tax equalization, newscaster George Putnam, and actor Fess Parker, noted for his portrayals of frontiersmen.[5] That rally drew a crowd of six thousand, making it the largest tax protest gathering in the history of the county.

Attracting crowds produced not only fame for Sidney Pink but also a social movement of impressive proportions. During two and a half months in the winter of 1957–1958, a total of twenty thousand persons attended twenty-one different tax protest meetings. Many of these meetings were held in West Covina (four), Covina (four), Temple City (four), Glendora, and other towns in the San Gabriel Valley.

Who were these protesters who amassed in damp football stadiums and cramped auditoriums? How did they compare to the protesters of Alhambra in 1964? In some parts of the San Gabriel Valley, the communities were middle income like Alhambra. The relative affluence index was 1.12 in Covina and 1.16 in Temple City (compared to 1.00 for Alhambra).[6] Covina fired the first salvo in the tax rebellion of 1957. A gas station owner, an accountant, and two partners in a print shop formed the East San Gabriel Valley Taxpayers League. Their first meeting drew a crowd of over eight hundred. The leaders exhorted the crowd to action and warned that, "It is not a fight for the weak-hearted."[7] One week later, over one thousand protesters roared in approval when the leaders of the taxpayers league announced that an investigation of school expenditures would be the top priority. The league gathered signatures for a ballot initiative that would have reduced the tax rate for the elementary school district by 64 percent and the high school by 32 percent.

The adjacent town of West Covina also erupted in a tax protest with 7,325 attending mass meetings. Somewhat wealthier than Covina, West Covina could boast a relative affluence index of 1.30; the percentage of professional and managerial workers was 1.40 times that for the Los

Angeles area. Whereas the middle-income community of Covina tended toward militancy and drastic measures, the West Covina Citizens Committee for Fair Taxation attracted the support of community small business leaders and advocated a more moderate approach. The Committee for Fair Taxation criticized the league's proposed cuts as extreme. Instead, the committee favored cooperating with the superintendent of schools to reduce spending in an orderly fashion. One leader emphasized how the Committee for Fair Taxation was "not against the school board as such. I was a member of the school board."[8]

Many of the activists with the Committee for Fair Taxation represented the leading small businesses in West Covina. Those mentioned in newspaper accounts were Sidney Pink, the West Covina theater owner; Art Jett, a prominent real estate developer; J. Raymond Nehmans, a local contractor; and J. D. Brown, a town council member and a supervisor for a road construction firm. Other West Covina business leaders helping the committee included a large landowner who had been mayor, an orange grove owner who became a real estate developer, a property owner who headed an insurance agency, and the attorney for the developer who built the first large shopping center in West Covina. In addition, two prominent realtors in nearby Covina strongly supported the committee.

Not only individual West Covina commercial leaders, but also business firms and organizations assisted the Committee for Fair Taxation. Real estate companies were particularly opposed to high property taxes, which discouraged sales of homes. The Covina Valley Board of Realtors and the West Covina Chamber of Commerce donated money. Such contributions were to be expected, given that members of the Committee for Fair Taxation had been instrumental in founding both the realty board and the local chamber in the first place. According to Art Jett, 90 percent of the businesses in West Covina supported the committee.

Assistance from community business leaders enabled the Committee for Fair Taxation to become the leading tax protest group in the county. The East San Gabriel Valley Taxpayers League had been the first to organize and, initially, the West Covina committee briefly considered themselves a chapter of the league. But then, the West Covinians organized the Committee for Fair Taxation as a separate organization, which held a rally of 1,500 (compared to the 800 to 1,000 attending the league's events), and then a valleywide meeting of 5,000. A week later, representatives from thirty-six tax protest groups selected the West Covina Committee for Fair Taxation as its executive committee. Sidney Pink became the president of the Los Angeles County Citizens for Fair Taxation, which claimed to represent two million taxpayers. Pink was charged with coordinating the activities of other groups, raising money, promoting an initiative to recall the assessor, and organizing a large rally that would draw people from throughout the metropolis.

But where that rally was held, turned success into failure. The setting was the 100,000-seat Coliseum, the site of the 1932 and 1984 Olympics, which made the 6,000-strong rally seem underattended to the point of embarrassment. One month later, the protests had ceased. The Covina Valley had arisen in protest, but it would not arise again. In 1964, 1966, and throughout the 1970s, other communities would lead the fight against high property taxes.

Why did the protest of 1957 fail? Part of the explanation was the hollow echo from the 90,000 empty seats in the Coliseum that chilly December night. But even if the rally had been better staged, the West Covina protest still would have suffered from inherent limits to the power of the small business owners in the community that led the movement.

Interpretations: Discovering the Bounds of Power

Small business leaders played a key role in tax protests and in other civic issues in their communities. In metropolitan Los Angeles, towns and communities typically are inhabited by 10,000 to 150,000 residents, usually around 50,000. Community business leaders are found on a town's chamber of commerce, realty board, Rotary and Kiwanis Clubs, and businessmen's associations and usually own or manage businesses that hire some paid employees but less than about 50. Their enterprises are larger than those of the self-employed, who usually hire no workers and rely on the labor of family members. But community business leaders are still small business men and women when compared to the Fortune 500.[9] The top executives of large enterprises—the Bank of America, Atlantic Richfield Company, Southern California Edison, the Los Angeles Times Company, and Hughes Aircraft—are less concerned with town and community politics and are more active in the higher circles of government.

Community business leaders typically own or manage establishments whose success depends on growth in the town—an increase in population and the development of the highest and best use of land. Obviously, real estate developers and brokers, landowners, apartment owners, and officers in the branches of savings and loan banks are interested in new construction and growth. Other community business leaders own or manage retail outlets that mainly attract customers who live or work nearby. Small businesses also become interested in community leadership when they cannot relocate easily. A community newspaper, small law firm, or medical practice depends on its contacts in the community; a car dealership is tied to its large display lots and the land beneath them.

When the old landowners, real estate developers, and business proprietors walked into West Covina's city hall, they expected to be greeted with a snappy, "Yes, sir," at the door and a smile and a handshake in the upstairs offices. The leaders of small business in a community did not suffer from the generalized unresponsiveness experienced by tax protesters in communities like Covina and Alhambra, where town government did not respond. If community business leaders ventured into the Los Angeles County Hall of Administration or the state capital in Sacramento, however, they could easily be mistaken for tourists. At the metropolitan and state levels of government, community business leaders lacked political influence. They possessed only bounded power, bounds that were clearly revealed during the tax protests of 1957. Although they received support from their town government, they were brushed aside by county government.

The community business leaders in the Citizens Committee for Fair Taxation must have seemed like a formidable group to West Covina government officials. The town council unanimously voted to urge all taxpayers to attend a tax protest rally. A former mayor and town council member, the town engineer, and the town clerk were active members of the Committee for Fair Taxation. This support contrasts with the discouragement that the politicians of Alhambra heaped upon the protesters of 1964.[10]

Although the elected officials of West Covina supported the protest, they did not have the power to mitigate the problem of excessive property taxes, caused by decisions at higher levels of government. The power to assess property and collect taxes was vested at the county level. The county assessor did not answer to politicians from the towns but rather was elected in a countywide ballot. Assessment procedures were specified by state law and were enforced by the State Board of Equalization. Decisions on the county budget were made by five supervisors, each of whom represented an immense constituency of over a million persons, compared to the fifty thousand residents of West Covina. Given the much larger size of the constituencies at higher levels of government, county officials were not impressed with the West Covinians who had mobilized to protest their taxes. The same was true for officials of the City of Los Angeles, whose mayor represented a population of two and a half million.

Indeed, county and city leaders went on record as not favoring the great tax protest of 1957. County Supervisor Herbert C. Legg, in the words of one major newspaper, gave the "kiss off" to the protest when he stated that, "People will forget about this whole thing in sixty days." County Assessor Quinn was quoted as saying, "If you think taxes are high now, wait till next year." Quinn met with the family of protest leader Art Jett, but Quinn only hugged their little girl and then "buzz[ed] us off." As Jett recounted, "Quinn was a master at quieting things down. . . . You could go in there so mad and he'd look at you, 'Art, I'm so happy to see you.' "[11]

The tax protests of 1957 produced few tangible concessions. County officials adopted a hiring freeze, which only lasted sixty days. Officials drafted proposals for tax reform and discussed eliminating chauffeur-driven limousines for the Board of Supervisors. One lone supervisor suggested amending the state constitution to limit property taxes. This was the method that Howard Jarvis would successfully use twenty-one years later, but its time had not yet come.

County and city officials ultimately did nothing to actually reduce property taxes; they only established committees to discuss budgets. The Los Angeles City Council appointed Bradford Trenham to head two committees to study reducing taxes. The County Board of Supervisors appointed William Pixley to chair a committee to review the budget. Although both individuals were leaders of taxpayers groups, both had publicly criticized the tax protesters and had defended the assessor. Trenham had been head of the California Taxpayers Association, whose board of directors was composed of executives from the top corporations listed in the *Fortune* magazine directories. No individual associated with a tax protest was appointed to any committee. It was business as usual at big government, with "no sale" for the West Covina small businesses who dared to complain about their taxes.[12]

The power of community business leaders was bounded and did not extend to either the political or the economic institutions at the city, county, or regional level. The leaders of the Citizens Committee for Fair Taxation had held offices in their town's realty board. Yet, higher-level realty boards would not give support. Art Jett presented a proposal to the Los Angeles County Council of Real Estate Boards to recall Supervisor Legg for his unresponsiveness to taxpayers' demands. The county realty board did not approve and instead passed a general resolution that real estate boards should take the leadership in supporting economy in government. Jett also took his proposal to the realty boards for the City of Los Angeles and the state of California but had no success. Jett realized that the problem was the unresponsiveness of institutions that covered large constituencies. This was the same problem that had earlier motivated Jett and other West Covina realtors to break away and form the Covina Valley Realty Board, arguing that they lacked sufficient representation in the San Gabriel Valley Board.

Another West Covina realtor, John Hiatt, favored decentralization of county government power. He suggested that the power to assess and tax property should be taken from county officials and should be placed in a council, which would be elected by districts rather than at large. The proposal, however, needed support from "big business and the Los Angeles Chamber of Commerce and he couldn't get that support."[13] Thus, unable to build alliances with business groups that had a wider geographical scope, the commercial leaders in West Covina could only speak in the name of businesses in that town. The tax protesters of 1957, like those of 1964, began with grievances about the issue of taxes. They soon learned about the political issues of the unresponsiveness of government and other institutions.

Interpretations: Art Jett Discovers His Declining Power

The business leaders in West Covina gradually experienced another limit to their power, a limit even on their home domain in West Covina. Over the years, they felt their influence over town government diminish, as town managers strengthened their executive powers, expanded their budgets, developed their own political constituency, and devised more stringent regulations over business. The career of Art Jett illustrates an extreme case of how the power of government can circumscribe the power of business leaders in a community.

Jett was one of the "barn boys," a social club composed of the old landowners and business proprietors in the Covina Valley. Between their fishing expeditions and golf games, they met periodically in their clubhouse, a converted barn on a hobby farm. Like the other barn boys, Jett was at the height of his power in the late 1950s. By then, Jett had built the first large office building in West Covina and had founded the chamber of commerce and the realty board in the Covina Valley.

Jett and the other developers of West Covina had worked to make their town live up to its motto: a city of beautiful homes. In the short run, they succeeded, as thousands streamed into West Covina to purchase the homes that Jett built. The new arrivals were just as affluent as Jett but were a different type of middle class. Whereas the barn boys took pride in their fathers who had been farmers on the land, the new arrivals boasted of their professional credentials. Many upper-middle-class professionals settled in West Covina because they wanted to live in an attractive bedroom community, like Beverly Hills or San Marino, but a bit more affordable. On the one hand, the barn boys saw the professionals as "highly intellectual . . . do-gooders—[people who] thought they could change everything overnight and [thought] everything was being done incorrectly."[14] On the other hand, according to profession-als, the barn boys were a closed clique who stuck to their old, vested interests.

The contrasting values and styles of life between the professionals and the barn boys led to conflicts over government policy. After developers proposed expanding the shopping centers in two residential neighbor-hoods, the affected homeowners coalesced to oppose the plans. Home-owners groups mobilized hundreds to attend planning commission and city council meetings. Homeowners hired their own attorneys and even-tually elected two sympathetic representatives to the town council.

In the early 1960s, the political power in West Covina shifted from the barn boys to a progressive town manager, George Aiassi. Like the barn boys, Aiassi wanted growth. But whereas the barn boys wanted commer-cial development at the initiative of the private sector, Aiassi wanted growth to be regulated by the government. Aiassi stood for a larger city hall, more public works, and larger and more professional city depart-ments. In 1964, Aiassi consolidated his power when voters approved an initiative requiring at least a four-to-one town council vote to dismiss the town manager. Through the years, Aiassi maintained a working major-ity on the council due to support from the progressive West Covina Homeowners Federation, based in upper-middle-class areas. Aiassi held the town manager position until he retired.

Jett's problems began as soon as the town manager and the progres-sives on the town council increased their influence. The progressives on the council asked Jett to support their candidates. When Jett refused, they told him, "Art, you know you're a real estate developer and you need help." According to Jett, one of Aiassi's allies "told me that I'd never get anything zoned in the city of West Covina as long as he had anything to do with it." The pro-Aiassi majority carried out their threat and began to deny Jett building permits and zoning so that he could no longer build on the land he owned. The city manager initiated a civic center ordinance that prevented Jett from developing some choice property.

> That way they could control everything that I wanted to do. [T]hey wanted to make me bring in a sixteen-inch water pipe, down there two miles. . . . That would've cost me fifty thousand dollars. . . . When I finally built that building where the Wells Fargo bank is now, they made me bring in samples of all the different materials; bring it in a box, the tile and the wood and the cement; they made me put in colored sidewalks and a thirty-foot sidewalk. . . . Seventh and Broadway's [in the Los Angeles central business district] only a twenty-foot sidewalk.

Jett then spent ten thousand dollars to hire an attorney; he filed suit against the city, won, but later lost on appeal. His attorney cautioned,

"That's just a start. The city councilmen, they're spending taxpayers' money and they don't care if they spend a million dollars to fight you."

Jett gave up his lawsuit and sold his real estate business and all his land. If he could have continued to build, he might have become a multimillionaire. Jett now lives in a modest mobile home. Believing that personal rivalries and political in-fighting sealed his fate, he now says, "I honestly think these fellows were jealous of me because I was making money. . . . I know it was politics. . . . I was Republican and they were Democrat, and they fought everything that I wanted to do."[15]

In some ways Jett's case is not typical. Most leading business owners in communities are slightly less successful in their prime and somewhat more comfortable in their retirement. In other respects, however, Jett's case is symptomatic. Small business owners were constantly concerned with the twin specters of their own failure and government intervention. During Jett's lifetime, there was an inexorable decline in the political power of the barn boys—the land and business owners whose fortunes and horizons were bounded by the low range of hills that surround the Covina Valley.

As the owner of a clothing shop on Workman Avenue became a buyer for the May Company department store in the Eastland Shopping Center, she could no longer reach into the cash register to make a political contribution. As the president of the local savings and loan association merged his institution with the Bank of America and became a deputy to the assistant vice-president, he could no longer use his title in political endorsements. Any political stands had to be cleared with the heads of the bank's public affairs and legal divisions, who cared more about Seoul, Korea, than West Covina, and joined the University Club rather than the barn boys.

In short, the barn boys and other community business leaders faced a situation where their political power was bounded in scope and declining over time. The growth of the metropolitan economy and the rise of big government provided the terrain where protest movements had to operate. But the spark that gave life to a movement was the desire to contest that terrain, to challenge the limits, and to expand power and participation in political life.

For years, community business leaders watched as even the best-run stores and restaurants on main street nevertheless lost customers to Sears and McDonald's. They remembered an era when being a small business owner gave one a sense of independence, pride, and power—when one's hard work, honesty, character, and entrepreneurial talent were rewarded with success. They watched anxiously as the downtown skyline of corporate headquarters and government offices grew year by year. They shook their heads as success seemed to come more and more from connections to the politicians or the large banks.[16] And when the hand of big government reached back into the communities to collect high tax bills in 1957, that was enough for Art Jett.

It took decades for business men and women to follow the lead of Art Jett and try to reclaim power for the small businesses in communities. In 1957, although business leaders in the Covina Valley followed Jett, community business leaders elsewhere in the Los Angeles metropolis did not. The protests of 1957 failed. But the tax revolt would succeed as community business leaders in Jett's position found ways to increase their political involvement.

Community Business Leaders as Movement Activists

Many community business leaders became interested in politics because of specific government decisions that directly affected their enterprises. Restaurants wanted licenses; real estate developers sought zoning changes; and apartment owners needed the tax assessments on their buildings reduced. Construction companies could be counted on to give donations to the campaigns of incumbent town council members, who voted on planning matters.[17] But for the tax revolt to succeed, community business leaders needed to become involved in a different type of politics—not the politics of individual zoning cases but the politics of public issues—not handled by the friendly Republican party candidate but rather fought by an angry protest movement.

For community business leaders, to join Art Jett and become a tax protest activist was to take a step into the unknown. It was a step that angered one's contacts at city hall, the government officials eager for more tax revenues. It was a step that violated one's instincts to avoid controversy and adverse publicity. Yet in the 1960s and 1970s, community business leaders discovered that this was a step that had to be taken. First to come to this realization were community business leaders who dealt with the land—real estate brokers, developers, and apartment owners. Property-related businesses, of course, had a major interest in lowering the property tax: "Anything that holds down the property tax improves the value of land and real estate."[18] But the issue that first brought them into political activism was not taxes but rather race.

Proposition 14: November 1964

The issue of open housing taught many land-related community businesses that it was sometimes necessary to mobilize homeowners and citizens into a militant, issue-oriented campaign to fight the government.[19] Real estate businesses saw open housing as a crucial showdown.

The controversy over open housing in California began in January 1963, when the Berkeley City Council passed an ordinance that outlawed racial discrimination in the selling or renting of housing. Backed by the Berkeley realty board, local boards throughout the state, and the California Real Estate Association, the opponents of open housing gathered enough signatures to hold a citywide referendum on the ordinance. At the next election, voters defeated the measure and elected a mayor and two city council members who had opposed open housing.[20]

The events in Berkeley were a rehearsal for a statewide controversy over open-housing legislation. Soon after the Berkeley referendum, the California state legislature passed the Rumford Act, which sought to prevent property owners from discriminating against buyers or tenants on the basis of race. The act applied to homes financed with FHA, VA, or Cal-Vet loans, and to apartment houses of five units or more. In a departure from previous fair-housing legislation, the enforcement of the Rumford Act was delegated to the state's fair employment practices commission, which could undertake a conciliation process, hold an open hearing, and initiate court action that could lead to a $500 fine.

The opponents of open housing applied what they had learned in Berkeley—that they could overturn government policies by mobilizing white homeowners and community real estate leaders. To block the Rumford Act at the state level, the California Real Estate Association, the California Apartment House Owners Association, and the California Home Builders sponsored Proposition 14, an initiative that would amend the state constitution to guarantee property owners the right to refuse to sell or rent property to any person. Local realty boards gathered most of the one million signatures in support of the initiative. The Apartment Association of San Fernando Valley was founded by real estate broker Amelia Justice (no relation to Sojourner Truth) to campaign for Proposition 14. The initiative passed with 65 percent of the vote.[21]

In other localities, a similar coalition of white homeowners and leaders of real estate businesses defeated open-housing legislation. In 1964, the Greater Detroit Homeowners Council placed an initiative on the ballot which gave homeowners the right to rent or sell to any person the owner chose. The initiative's author, Thomas Poindexter, copied much of it from a model ordinance provided by the National Association of Real Estate Brokers. The initiative passed with 55 percent of the vote. Between 1963 and 1968, opponents of integration in ten cities used the referendum to resist open housing. The opponents of fair housing succeeded in all cases, winning between 53 and 75 percent of the votes.[22]

Philip Watson and the Limits of Community Business Leaders

The campaigns against open housing taught landed businesses in communities that it was possible to organize political movements that could undercut politicians and their policies. Land-related community businesses in California would mobilize a protest movement as a last resort, not as a first choice, to lower their property taxes. They were accustomed to giving donations to professional campaign managers rather than engaging in messy controversies directly. Their first tactic to reduce their property taxes was to work with Philip Watson, who wanted to become assessor of Los Angeles County.

Watson's original backers were a group of shopping center owners:

> [I]n the fifties a number of the shopping centers . . . had been taxed, assessed in a particular fashion, and didn't like it and went to court. . . . I think there were a half dozen of them. . . . We got called into the case in 1958. . . . Philip Watson . . . was employed by this group as their . . . coordinator of this tax activity. . . . [W]e won the case in the trial court. . . . The county refunded a fairly substantial amount of money to the shopping centers. . . . The thing you have to keep sight of in an assessment valuation case is that once you get the value established, it's really established for a long time to come. . . . When stretched out over a prospective period of time of ownership . . . [it] can mean a large amount of money.[23]

The executive committee of Watson's campaign in 1962 consisted of a shopping center owner, two law partners who had represented the owners, another attorney, and one partner in a public relations firm. Together they recruited supporters, including a movie producer, commercial property developers, and owners of construction companies, to lend their names and contribute money to the campaign. Their greatest asset turned out to be the candidate himself:

> Phil [Watson] had this kind of a personality—where he would walk into a casserole supper given by the First Street, Second Avenue chamber of commerce. There would be the clattering of dishes . . . [interviewee imitates toastmaster:] "Here's this fellow who's running for what is it, assessor, whatever that is, and he wants to take a couple minutes of our time while we're having our dessert and before the main speaker." . . . And this nice young man with a neatly pressed suit and wearing his tie would come in and would start talking. And the first thing you know, the place was quiet; everybody was listening. And when he got through and thanked everyone nicely, rousing ovation! I saw that happen I don't know how many times. What it is that he had, I don't know, but he had it. And he'd go on to the next one. And he did that all over the county.[24]

His popularity at chambers of commerce assured, Watson won the home-owner's vote with a bold pledge.

> He eliminated . . . the appraisers actually going out appraising personal property in the home. . . . That was one of the key things that got Phil Watson elected when he was first elected to office, was to get rid of the snoopers. . . . People just resented the knock at the door and, "I'm going to place a value on your personal property and that's going to raise your taxes." Phil Watson used that I'm sure, to get elected. "Vote for me and I'll get rid of the snoopers."[25]

Watson easily defeated the incumbent assessor. His financial backers and his campaign executive committee wanted to lock in their good fortune, once and for all, with an initiative that would limit the property tax rate statewide to 2 percent.

> It was out of those shopping center activities and really the persistence of one man [Bill, last name withheld] . . . that a movement got going to develop some tax reform. . . . He owned shopping centers and used to be in the lumber business. . . .
> [He] always had in mind the . . . limitation of taxes. . . . Property tax limitation was enshrined as something that just had to be done, in order to safeguard property owners. Part of it came out of his own experience in the thirties when he saw so much property sold for taxes. . . . There was just an enormous amount of property let go . . . particularly back then. Forty dollars to meet the tax bill was a month's pay and you just didn't have it. . . . Bill was one of the people who would buy property at the tax sales. . . . [H]e held onto it and suddenly it was Wilshire and Western [where there is high-rise development]. . . . So he was concerned genuinely.[26]

Watson tried to persuade the state legislature to place the 2-percent referendum on the ballot. But soon, Assessor Watson had the unpleasant duty of mailing out notices of increased assessments, which sometimes provoked taxpayers to call his office and shout a stream of obscenities. Then came the Alhambra outburst of 1964, the countywide tax strike of 1966, and Jarvis's initiative in 1968 to abolish the property tax. Watson's keen political instincts told him to be part of the solution and not part of the problem.

In 1968, Watson decided to place a tax limit proposal on the ballot by collecting signatures, instead of waiting for the state legislature. Watson courageously appeared at meetings of irate taxpayers, asking them to channel their anger into gathering signatures for his initiative. Few protesters did, however. Watson tried to work through an apartment owners association, getting apartment managers to obtain signatures from tenants, but with little success. Watson obtained most of his signatures from paid collectors; Robinson and Company, a public relations firm, came up with the signatures but also sent a bill for $270,000. When Watson made only a partial payment, the firm sued for $2 million in damages, charging that Watson had intended to defraud. Watson turned to his campaign financiers for a bailout.[27] Of the contributions in support of the 1968 initiative (see table 4), 80 percent were $1,000 or more in size. Most of these large donations came from community business leaders who dealt with land—real estate agents and boards, apartment owners, farmers, builders (such as Buckeye Realty and Management Corporation), and developers (the Irvine Company, Macco Realty, and Newhall Land and Farming).

Despite support from landed businesses that were highly influential in community politics, Watson was unable to secure the support of larger corporations and statewide business leaders. Opposing the Watson initiative were most major business groups, including the California Chamber of Commerce, the California Investment Bankers Association, and the powerful California Taxpayers' Association, whose board of directors mainly consisted of executives from the large corporations listed in the *Fortune* magazine directory. The shopping center owners and their attorneys had run up to the bounds of their own power.

Watson could only succeed if there were strong, organized support from homeowners, grass-roots activists, and voters. Such popular support was difficult to obtain because of Watson's backing from landed interests. Watson's opponents successfully tagged his initiative as the "landlord's tax trap" and "a big deal for the fat cats." One prominent opponent of the initiative charged that "[Watson's] . . . 'spontaneous effort' is now being revealed as a high-paid effort by professional circulators and promoters getting as much as 50 cents a name. . . . The big corporations are giving the money. . . . Are they really interested in little homeowners? . . . The little homeowner is going to be stuck with other taxes [if Proposition 9 passes]."[28] Watson's 1968 initiative went down to defeat.

Local landed businesses were also the major backers of Watson's second attempt to pass a property tax reduction initiative in 1972. Small- and medium-sized landed businesses won the backing of some large propertied interests and statewide realty groups. This coalition was a classic special interest group, different-sized firms organized around a trade or a sector of the economy. Real estate boards donated $260,000 and provided speakers, ads, and telephone banks. The California Farm Bureau Federation contributed $200,000, another sizable portion of the $1.04 million total for the campaign. These were the days before cam-

Table 4   Campaign Contributions for Tax Limitation Initiatives (in thousands of dollars)

	1 Yes Prop. 9 1968 (Watson)		2 Yes Prop. 13 June, 1978 (Jarvis–Gann)		3 No Prop. 13		4 For all campaigns June 1978	
	Contributions of $1,000 OR MORE						$500 OR MORE	
Business								
Real estate*	$76	(47%)	71.	(38%)	39	(3%)	480.	(4%)
Agriculture & ranches	0	(0%)	9.	(5%)	0	(0%)	513.	(4%)
Other corps. incl. financial, utilities, law firms	48	(30%)	44.	(24%)	613.	(40%)	6,354.	(48%)
Labor, public-employee orgs., professional, educational	0		0		820.	(54%)	1,845.	(14%)
Political orgs.	0		22.	(12%)	7.	(0%)	776.	(6%)
Individuals	37	(23%)	40.	(21%)	35.	(2%)	1,700.	(13%)
Health	0		0		0		580.	(4%)
Miscellaneous	0		0		0		987.	(7%)
SUBTOTAL	$161.	(100%)	186.	(100%)	1,514	(99%)	13,235.	(100%)
SIZE OF CONTRIBUTIONS (thousands of dollars)								
$1,000 or more	$161.	(80%)	186.	(8%)	1,513.	(71%)		
999 or less	41.	(20%)	2,093	(92%)	607.	(29%)		
TOTAL CONTRIBUTIONS	$202.	(100%)	2,279.	(100%)	2,120.	(100%)		

Source: Clarence Lo, "Mobilizing the Tax Revolt," *Research in Social Movements, Conflict, and Change* 6 (1984), 312.

Note: All figures include loans and independent direct expenditures.
*Real estate includes boards, brokers, apartment owners, construction (U.S. private sector), developers, hotels, industrial parks, parking lots, shopping centers.

paign finance reform, when special interests routinely wrote six-digit checks. The campaign director for the 1972 Watson initiative was James Udall, who had served as the president of the National Association of Real Estate Boards and also as the head of the Apartment Association of Los Angeles County.

Although Watson's supporters had organized themselves into a formidable interest group, they were stymied by other even more powerful business interest groups. Watson's 1972 initiative specified that the revenue lost from lower property taxes would be made up by increased taxes on insurance companies and liquor. The two industries contributed funds to defeat the proposition.[29]

The only force that could break the deadlock between squabbling business interest groups was organized grass-roots political pressure. A mobilization of the smallest real estate owners, homeowners, could force government to lower its tax take. But again, the involvement of large landed interests dampened grass-roots enthusiasm. "[Newhall Land and Farming?] Ah yes, they were supporters but they're not much help. They'd raise money for you but . . . I would imagine that if most of the California electorate, if they knew that the Newhall Land and Farming Company was on one side of an issue, they'd automatically be on the other. . . . They [Newhall] have kind of a reputation of being one step removed from robber baronhood."[30]

One large contributor to Watson's 1972 initiative was a real estate developer, a genius at lobbying and political negotiation who literally talked his way into millions of dollars.

Probably the biggest single backer of it was a man by the name of Ben Weingart. . . . As a matter of fact, the offices that we had . . . were in a building owned by Ben Weingart. . . . Weingart was one of the biggest property owners in southern California and in the entire state. His various enterprises control millions and millions of dollars worth of real estate. . . . I really admire him. He came to this county, he came to southern California a penniless immigrant, and died one of the wealthiest and most powerful men. . . .

Ben Weingart was a very shrewd manipulator and operator. . . . Barrington Plaza . . . was one of his major financial coups, . . . one of the largest high-rise apartment complexes in Los Angeles at the time. He was excellent in manipulating the political process in that way, but that's altogether a different kind of thing from building popular support for either tax reform, or tax . . . loopholes. So in that sense he would be willing to back someone else but I doubt that he would be in a position to stimulate or lead that kind of activity himself. He wouldn't be a Howard Jarvis type.[31]

If taxes were to be lowered at this critical juncture, what was needed was skill at a different type of politics—the mobilization of widespread citizen activism.

After 1972, Watson never succeeded in gathering enough signatures to place a tax reduction measure on the ballot. A year before the passage of Proposition 13, Watson's career as a tax fighter abruptly ended, along with his job as county assessor. Watson retired amid an impending city council investigation of corruption in his office.

Watson would not be the champion who would unite community business leaders with the popular base needed to halt the increasing spiral of property taxes and government spending. But through Watson's campaigns, community business leaders had increased their skills in direct, grass-roots political action—organizing phone banks to identify supporters, staging rallies, driving voters to the polls, and doing publicity work at the community level. For example, "Many local smaller newspapers . . . are dependent heavily on real estate advertising. . . . So if your friendly local real estate agent dropped in with a press release that he'd like to see appear in the paper . . . the little tiny dailies would circulate them. . . . The editor of the paper, and the publisher and the local real estate people are all kind of a tightly knit group."[32] The political power of realtors stemmed from their extensive contacts in the community, and also from their sheer numbers. In California around the time of Proposition 13, about 365,000 persons held real estate licenses. If all of these realtors attended a Beach Boys concert in the woods, a la Woodstock, that gathering would instantly become the sixth-largest city in California.

Real estate agents walked the precincts for the 1972 tax reduction initiative, visiting homes and pitching their campaign message. "Politics is working with people. Realtors know how to do this and get a message across. After all, they're salespeople, organizers. . . ."

> Realtors are a grass-roots organization because we go right down into the neighborhoods, the block, and that's where we work. A basic principle in real estate is the farm system. Real estate materials say a sales person shall have a particular area where they are known and where they work and they call regularly on the people. They are "farming," as the book says. And so they're pretty much aware of what the public is feeling.[33]

By the mid-1970s, there had been a definite increase in the political activity of real estate businesses.[34] Now, the tactic of choice was a community-based mobilization of not only businesses but of homeowners and other citizens. Robert Roumiguiere, a realtor in suburban Marin County (in northern California), worked to set a limit on county spending and property taxes. He formed a coalition, including Home and School Associations, homeowners groups, and taxpayers organizations. Based on his experiences, Roumiguiere devised a plan that was introduced at special seminars held in 1977 at San Francisco and Los Angeles, sponsored by the Local Government Relations Committee of the California Association of Realtors.[35] In order to get their taxes lowered, community business leaders were moving toward a major commitment to grass-roots politics. Were the angry tax protesters moving toward working with the businesses in their communities?

Call the United Organizations of Taxpayers

It took decades to tame militant tax protesters, until they could become political partners with community business leaders. Just as community business leaders themselves had to undergo a long process of comprehending the importance of political involvement, making mistakes, and then learning new forms of activism, so tax protest groups also had to undergo a major transformation. Perhaps the most important change was in the leadership of the principal coalition of homeowners groups. This change can best be highlighted by examining the succession of leaders of the United Organizations of Taxpayers (UO), a statewide coalition of homeowners groups, neighborhood associations, and individual members. The UO was the group that finally succeeded in placing Proposition 13 on the ballot and then winning at the polls.

Howard Jarvis eventually became the state chairman of the United Organizations. He insisted on the program that became Proposition 13— a rollback and a limit on property assessments, and a limit of 1 percent on tax rates, all of which would apply to business as well as residential property. In its early years, however, the United Organizations was an arena where many leaders competed, promoting different redistributive programs for tax reduction. Harry Crown, Milton Rubin, and James Christo were important leaders between 1966 and 1971, the formative period for the United Organizations of Taxpayers. As with other activists, the programs that they advocated were a product of the political process they experienced. Their initial protests yielded only a stony unresponsiveness from politicians and business leaders. Their resulting anger led them to undertake militant actions such as the tax strikes and demonstrations. Even though some of the leaders were themselves small business owners, they also expressed the antibusiness sentiments common in the middle-income communities that they represented.[36]

The Businessman as Antibusiness Crusader

Harry Crown was quietly reading his newspaper after dinner in 1966 when his wife asked whether he was going to the tax protest meeting. Startled, Crown looked up from his paper and asked, "What are you talking about?"

"Have you seen your tax bill? It's three thousand dollars higher."[37]

Crown rushed to a packed meeting of angry homeowners, who were glowering at the deputy to their representative on the Los Angeles City Council. Crown captured the spirit of the protest when he gave an impassioned speech, telling what he thought of the unfortunate deputy and all the other politicians, who were "a bunch of parasites." Homeowners at that meeting formed the San Fernando Valley Tax Protest League, later called the San Fernando Valley Property Owners' Association. Crown was elected president, because "I got up and talked to a councilman the way they always wanted to. . . . I told them what I felt about the council for the outraged community. It just rang a bell."

Crown accused the politicians of failing in their job of representing the people. Crown was angered by one elected official in particular, Assessor Philip Watson, who the shopping center owners and the chamber of commerce crowd had put into office. Crown alleged that Watson was assessing properties unequally. Crusading to remove Watson from office, Crown put together a slide show entitled "Watson's Wasteland," which showed how similar properties in the same neighborhood were assessed at widely different rates. "We found that all these huge modern buildings on Devonshire [Street] were assessed at almost nothing. . . . Taxes on the other side of . . . [a] street were one-quarter taxes on this side of the street." Watson was reducing the assessments for his acquaintances and for big business, alleged Crown. The assessor

never lean[s] on big property owners downtown. . . . [Their corporate headquarters] back east looked askance that they have enormous tax bills out of proportion [to] what they pay out of Detroit, Chicago, or elsewhere. So they expect their managers out here to make payoffs to the proper people. So they . . . buy the tables at these fund raising meetings for councilmen, supervisors, county assessors . . . and of course they're treated gently. They can go to the county assessor and say, "Look, we got a $100 million plant out here where we can't afford to operate here because our tax bill is way out of scale. . . ." Now all . . . [the assessor has] to do is to raise the assessment on $5 million [worth of] single-family home people and they don't have to raise the assessment of Continental Can.

Crown presented his slide show to a committee of the state legislature and to a meeting where assessor Watson was present. Crown had the satisfaction of seeing Watson at the moment he "couldn't stand it and got up and walked out." Crown Prince Hamlet would have approved.

Although Crown never hesitated to protest against the lenient assessments on big business property, he also took some steps to build alliances with other businesses, particularly those of a smaller scale. Crown owned a medium-sized engineering and manufacturing firm and campaigned for lower property taxes among his acquaintances in machine shops and other small companies. The publisher of a community newspaper and the head of one large land development and farming company supported Crown's efforts. In addition, Crown gave his presentation about Watson to the San Fernando Valley Apartment Owners Association. Soon, Crown was the association's director for tax policy. The apartment association, founded in 1964 to oppose the Rumford fair-housing law, was led by Ed Hankins, a carpet store owner who had a flair for political action. Hankins led a demonstration of twenty people clad only in barrels with signs reading, "Taxes stripped me." A start had been made in building an alliance between homeowners protests and community business leaders.[38]

The Businessman as Militant

In 1940, Milton Rubin bought a house for seven thousand dollars in a comfortable, middle-class community west of downtown Los Angeles. What first made Milton Rubin a community activist was not the issue of higher taxes but the problems of land use and corporate power. In 1957, an oil company wanted to drill a well right in the middle of his residential neighborhood. The company began contacting the neighbors, offering to pay for the oil under their homes. Angry homeowners crowded into meetings of their neighborhood group, the Beverly–Wilshire Homes Association, and elected Rubin president. The association fought the oil company for six years until the drilling project was finally abandoned.

Rubin's house, located near the high-rise development of Wilshire Boulevard, turned out to be a fine investment. As the value of Rubin's property appreciated over the years, his property tax bill climbed as well. His first tax bill was $200. In 1957, the year that Sidney Pink addressed the rally at the Coliseum, Rubin's bill jumped to $369. As taxes climbed inevitably upward, Rubin and a number of community activists—including Michael Rubino from Alhambra, Harry Crown from the San Fernando Valley, James Earle Christo from Bellflower, and Leona Magdison and Howard Jarvis from the Beverly–Wilshire community—

formed the United Organizations of Taxpayers. Rubin was chosen as the UO's president. The group wrote letters to the County Board of Supervisors, held demonstrations at the county offices and, when they had the opportunity, harangued the supervisors.

Government officials were unresponsive, however, to the plight of the homeowners. As Rubin recalled, it took less than a year for it to dawn on them that the supervisors weren't going to respond: "When you saw the results of two or three demonstrations and you saw the results of your conversations . . . and you go down and do speaking yourself . . . [you] realiz[e] that it is falling on deaf ears. . . . They're saying to themselves, 'It'll blow over; don't worry about it, you know, just a few people who are complaining and we've had those before over the years and they fade away. So we'll not do anything and it'll fade away too.' But it didn't fade away."[39]

In 1966, Rubin's tax bill jumped again, this time to $757. Over 17,000 Los Angeles county residents filed appeals with the assessments appeals board, the highest number ever to do so. Rubin issued a call for a tax strike, urging homeowners to refuse to pay their tax bills. Rubin declared: "We will continue our 'war' until all tax injustices have been corrected." Rubin traveled throughout Los Angeles, speaking at school auditoriums and urging homeowners to defy the government. On December 6, 1966, he led a group of 200 demonstrators who shouted, waved placards, invaded a County Board of Supervisors meeting, and protested in behalf of 75,000 citizens who had pledged to refuse to pay property taxes.[40] Rubin proclaimed that if the supervisors did not lower assessments and reduce spending, the United Organizations would launch a recall: "[S]o help me, we'll start a campaign against you. We'll target you as opposing us and every property owners association in the . . . county will be notified that you are approving of this excessive taxation and not doing a goddamn thing about it. And if you're not going to do anything about it, we . . . will do something about it. We'll run somebody against you."

But the organizers of the tax strike found that they were not half a million strong, as they had first envisioned. Despite reassurances to the contrary, homeowners feared that they would immediately lose their homes if they failed to pay their taxes. Furthermore, Rubin found that "in those groups . . . there would be wealthy people who wouldn't give a damn. Oh, what the hell, you know, two thousand dollars a year tax, that won't bother me a bit. So they walk out" of the protest meetings. Only years later would the homeowners in upper-middle-class neighborhoods walk back in with their six thousand dollar tax bills. In the 1960s Rubin's group tried and got some influential people to participate. It was still not enough, however. "[T]oo many of them were afraid to buck city hall and be recognized as part of the opposition. . . . So we really couldn't get any real influential people."

[Question: You pursued their support overtly? Did you covertly?] Yes . . . some of the large property owners covertly would contribute monies to the group, but very little personal time. You know, they give you their blessings, but don't include me. . . . Don't put me on your list.

Realtors did not play an active role in the early campaigns of the United Organizations, as they would later. Forging an alliance between homeowners and businesses proved to be a difficult task, particularly in the Beverly–Wilshire neighborhood, where the relative affluence index in the census tracts ranged from 1.03 to 1.18. In this middle-income neighborhood, residents fought oil companies and real estate developers and promoted militant tactics such as the tax strike.

Later, Rubin turned his attention to limiting and regulating the construction of high-rise office buildings near his neighborhood. In 1976, Rubin's property tax bill just about doubled, from $924 to $1,803. Although no longer a leader of the tax reduction movement, Rubin helped in the effort to pass Proposition 13, which reduced his tax bill to just $607 a year.

The earlier efforts of Milton Rubin and the Beverly–Wilshire Homes Association contributed to the building of a grass-roots movement that made Proposition 13 possible. Leona Magdison, a leader of the Beverly–Wilshire association, communicated with homeowners groups throughout the state, served as the secretary for the United Organizations, and hosted the UO directors' meetings in her home, which soon became the headquarters for the UO volunteers. Howard Jarvis, who lived in the neighborhood, got involved in UO when he provided some legal advice to the fledgling group.

The Shopkeepers Whirl with Earle

In the town of Bellflower, just another middle-income community in the sprawl between downtown Los Angeles and Orange County, James Earle Christo was the proprietor of a tuxedo rental shop with the motto "Whirl with Earle."[41] At first, Christo's tax protest activity led him to speak of the unresponsiveness of government, to suspect a conspiracy of powerful politicians and businesses, and to argue that big business should be taxed.

Beginning his tax-fighting career in 1959, Christo and the Taxpayers Association of Bellflower successfully blocked the imposition of a property tax in the town and then opposed spending tax money on a new city hall and other urban redevelopment projects. In 1965, Christo helped to form the United Organizations and was elected to a number of leadership positions through the years. Christo saw taxpayers as victims of a conspiracy of the powerful. "Forces" in Sacramento, for example, were blocking an initiative campaign to limit property taxes:

> These so called "forces" must remain anonymous. . . . We cannot name names because we do not know exactly who is behind the technical roadblocks being thrown up to keep this Jarvis Amendment off the ballot. . . . Powerful groups such as the oil, insurance, banks and certain categories of privileged landowners are, of course, behind the scenes calling the shots for the people who are trying to keep our amendment off the ballot.[42]

The businesses leading this alleged conspiracy were precisely the ones that Christo wanted to tax in order to pay for the homeowners' tax relief. Banks, according to Christo, were "notorious tax dodgers which, quite legally, shift most of their taxes to the shoulders of little people." Christo argued that if a bank owned a mortgage amounting to 80 percent of the value of a home, the bank should pay 80 percent of the property tax bill. When Christo was president of the United Organizations, he advocated such a plan, which would thereby "cut down the burden of the little 'homeowner' who actually owns [only] an equity or part interest."[43]

Christo condemned the $11 million worth of tax advantages accorded to insurance companies. "The big insurance companies are permitted to deduct all local taxes on their main office buildings from the total owed to the state. While these deductions are permitted year after year, great political fanfare is made of the fact that homeowners receive only a measly $750 exemption off their total assessed valuation." Christo also forcefully advocated a $2 billion tax on oil companies in order to balance property tax cuts for homeowners. Christo's proposals received the support of the board of directors of the United Organizations, which publicized them with the slogan, "Tax big oil."[44]

With all of the militant talk about taxing business, the United Organizations obtained only limited support from businesses between 1966 and 1971. The UO's first initiative drive in 1968 to abolish all property taxes entirely smacked of extremist ideology and was too drastic for community business leaders. "We never got support from realtors until Prop. 13 came along. [Question: Support for abolishing the property tax? Christo:] No, we never got their support on that."[45] In 1971, Christo lamented, "Many real estate dealers, I am sorry to say, seem to oppose us even though a 50-percent cut in property revenues would certainly boom the real estate and home market."[46]

Later in the 1970s, the United Organizations and Christo began to take a different approach to tax reduction. Christo concluded that

all previous petitions that were sent out, were sent out in behalf of the homeowner, and in doing so you alienated the businesses away from you. . . . [B]usiness is not going to stand still and allow [itself] to take the burden of homeowners' savings on their shoulders. . . . By also including business on a [tax limit of] one percent of market value—sure we did it because small mom and pop businesses supported us. See, I made a couple of radio speeches and directed us to small businesses. I expected the mamma and papa stores to support us one hundred percent. They did.

[Question: What about 13? Do you think it would have failed if you didn't include business? Christo:] Yeah, I think so, yes. Business would have lined up against us.

Christo and other United Organizations leaders had come to agree not to increase taxes on business but rather to lower them. This stand helped to increase support from community business leaders, especially those who deal with the land. Forging the alliance with the landed business community was Howard Jarvis's major contribution.

Howard Jarvis and the Emerging Alliance Between Homeowners and Community Businesses

Howard Jarvis in 1971 seemed to be a radical, antiestablishment champion of the homeowner. He attacked tax-exempt foundations and trusts; he proposed taxes on oil corporations and insurance company headquarters; he was the defender of the average homeowner unable to take advantage of tax loopholes. Jarvis claimed that "there are 18,000 charitable trusts in California which are tax exempt and there are, at last count, some 66,000 tax-exempt organizations, including foundations. Many of these own a great deal of land," amounting to some $16 billion, which should "begin to pay a fair share of taxes. . . . [T]he property owner without enough influence pays most of the property taxes." In 1971 Jarvis authored an initiative that would have levied taxes on all previously exempt property. Any exemptions would need approval by a two-thirds vote of each chamber of the state legislature.[47]

Although Jarvis grew famous because of this populist political persona, Jarvis had spent his working career as a business owner and his political life as a conservative Republican. This helped him to obtain support from community business leaders, leading to the triumph of Proposition 13.

Jarvis's probusiness views stemmed from his colorful career as an entrepreneur. In 1925 he borrowed money to buy a small-town newspaper in Utah. In five years, Jarvis owned a chain of eleven papers with a combined circulation of 30,000 and was making around $35,000 a year. Jarvis was proud to be a probusiness conservative. Since the 1920s he had been active in the right wing of the Republican party. He traveled on Herbert Hoover's campaign train in 1932 and stood on the platform with a pillow to block the rotten eggs and tomatoes that the Depression-struck partisans hurled at the incumbent president.

Despite the fact that Jarvis received government contracts during World War II, he concluded that the government was the adversary of business. It was the government that requisitioned his stock of latex during World War II, putting an end to his typewriter pad company even though the latex was never used later.

> After the war somebody from the War Production Board gave me a tip that if I wanted to see my latex, he could tell me where it was. Just out of curiosity, I went. The latex was stored in a warehouse on Santa Fe Avenue near downtown Los Angeles. I knew it was mine because we were the only place in Los Angeles that used that much latex. Latex is a liquid. It came in barrels and looks like milk. But after sitting in that warehouse for a few years, my latex was just like a big ball of mush. All the water had evaporated out of it. And it took me about three or four years before the Government paid for it.[48]

During the Korean War, the government set a fixed retail price for flatirons which didn't allow Jarvis to make enough profit; Jarvis avoided the price controls by shipping his irons to Mexico and then back again. Then, government controls made nickel chromium wire unavailable for civilian uses and forced Jarvis's gas heater company to close.

Jarvis's wartime business experience convinced him of the evils of government regulation; Jarvis's business partner during World War II, an engineer named James A. McDonald, taught him a lesson about taxes. Jarvis recounts:

> Then one day the IRS called me and said, "Mr. Jarvis, Mr. McDonald is going to be in our office tomorrow at ten o'clock to discuss his tax situation, and we thought you might want to be there." I hadn't seen Mac for a few years, so I decided to go.
> At 10:00 we were all there, these Internal Revenue agents in their pinstripe suits, and me. And no Mac. A few minutes late, in breezes Mac, all 4'9" of him. There were some preliminaries, and then one of the agents said, "Mr. McDonald, you owe $42,366.79, and we'd like to know what you intend to do about it."
> Mac said, "I'm not going to do anything about it. . . . I'll make it clear

for you. All you guys can go fly a kite, because I'm not going to do a damned thing about these taxes you say I owe. . . ."

And he got up and walked out.

That was the first time I saw a real tax revolt.[49]

While he was living in California, Jarvis served as Republican party precinct chairman and president of the Republican Assembly in Los Angeles County. Jarvis happened to be serving on a committee in 1946 which ran newspaper ads in the hope of recruiting candidates to run on the Republican ticket. For the congressional race in Whittier, the ad was answered by a young sailor, Richard Nixon. In the 1960 presidential election, Jarvis was a campaign director for Nixon in eleven western states, as well as director of the campaigns of state legislators in southern California. Jarvis ran in a primary election "as a conservative" in 1962, hoping to unseat Republican Senator Thomas Kuchel, who Jarvis thought was cooperating too much with the Democrats. Meanwhile, he had started several companies to manufacture car coolers, garbage disposers, and aircraft parts. At their peak, Jarvis's companies employed several thousand people; when he sold them to retire, he netted about $750,000.

With his background in business and conservative politics, Jarvis's inclination when he became active in the tax revolt in the 1960s was to recruit small- and medium-sized businesses. By 1971 Jarvis had gained some support from apartment owners. Charles Reynolds, the tax chairman for the Orange County Apartment House Association, confirmed that his group had gathered signatures for a Jarvis initiative in 1971. This initiative was also endorsed by the California Apartment House Owners Association.

In 1972, Jarvis became the executive director of the Apartment House Association of Los Angeles County. When he took over the association, it had 1,100 members; when he left in 1979, membership had risen to 5,000 owners, accounting for more than 50,000 units. As executive director, Jarvis engaged in much political activity, lobbying the state legislature against rent control. He fought against a Los Angeles City Council bill requiring the demolition of brick apartment buildings due to earthquake danger and against another bill that would have instituted garbage collection fees for large apartment buildings. During one of his drives to place a tax reduction initiative on the ballot, one newspaper announced that petitions were available at 551 South Oxford Avenue in Los Angeles, the headquarters of the Apartment Association.[50]

Jarvis also believed that property tax cuts would produce a building boom and spur business growth throughout California. Property tax cuts would be good for apartment owners and business in general. "[W]e wanted to give a tax break to business as well as to everybody else. The people in California who hire other people are in business. We were losing dozens of companies and thousands of jobs every year because business taxes were too high. And the property tax was one main reason."[51]

Jarvis's work at the apartment association, combined with his position as state chair of the United Organizations of Taxpayers, placed him in a unique position to bring homeowners and community business leaders together. In 1976, one more wave of taxpayer protest gave Jarvis a unique opportunity to make that coalition between homeowners and business into a political force that could not be ignored. Jarvis himself had an appeal that captivated audiences of middle-income homeowners. In the town of Glendale (relative affluence index 1.07), Jarvis could emphasize the popular side of the tax revolt and raise the theme of unresponsive government power: "We are getting no relief from our legislators in Sacramento. . . . We want one million signatures on petitions by Christmas to shake the teeth of the politicians in Sacramento." One way that citizens could regain power over government was "not to give them the money in the first place." Jarvis urged homeowners to refuse to pay their property tax bills. "[T]his is the only action property owners can take in 1976 to protect themselves against the power of government to continue to levy extortionate property taxes." To this audience, Jarvis emphasized the apparently egalitarian features of his proposal. "There are no loopholes, no corruption. Everyone pays his share, 1 per cent." The initiative would restore taxes on much previously exempt property.[52]

But the tax revolt would triumph not because of the support from Glendale or Alhambra or Covina, but because a very different type of community slowly began to stir.

The Support of Community Business Leaders and the Upper-Middle Class

The road to success for Howard Jarvis and Proposition 13 was difficult indeed. The route to his boisterous election night celebration at the Biltmore Hotel wound by the obscure American Legion meeting halls of Glendale and the elementary school auditoriums with seats too small to accommodate homeowning consumers suffering from high tax bills, excess calories, and late middle age. The route went by the signature-gathering tables in front of the prosaic Safeway grocery in Lakewood. This route took three decades to traverse. During the first decade, fiscal years 1949 to 1958, the road was traveled by others—Sidney Pink and the Citizens for Fair Taxation, who gathered 153,000 petition signatures before fading into history (see table 5). In the second decade, Michael Rubino pushed forward, gathering 200,000 protest signatures. It was during this decade that Howard Jarvis began his journey with a right-

Table 5   Tax Protest Petitions in California

First decade *Fiscal 1949–1958*	Second decade *Fiscal 1959–1968*	Third decade *Fiscal 1969–1978*
1958: 153,000 signatures to recall assessor JARVIS PETITIONS:	1965: 200,000	1977: 240,000; "Brown Bag" campaign
	1967: 100,000 to abolish property taxes (100,000 in L.A.)	1972: 461,000 (273,000 in L.A.) 1976: 489,000 (419,000 in L.A.) 1977: 498,000 (361,000 in L.A.) 1978: 1,250,000 + 250,000 (739,000 in L.A.) PROPOSITION 13

ward rather than a forward step. On an initiative to abolish the property tax entirely, he gathered but 100,000 signatures.

The third decade (fiscal 1969 to 1978) marked the rise and triumph of the tax revolt. In fiscal 1972, Jarvis submitted over four times as many signatures as he had earlier, although the number was still insufficient to qualify a ballot initiative. Then, in rapid succession, Jarvis gathered 489,000, 498,000, and then 1.5 million signatures, the last number placing Proposition 13 on the ballot. For each of these campaigns, the county providing the most signatures—in two cases, practically all of the signatures—was Los Angeles. The signatures gathered in Los Angeles County for ballot initiatives increased from zero in the first decade, to 100,000 in the second, to 1.8 million in the third (see table 6, row 1).

Proposition 13 was placed on the ballot by thousands of citizen volunteers who attended protest meetings, joined homeowners groups, and then gathered signatures in shopping centers—one last tidal wave of citizen activism against high property taxes. What was unique about this third wave was not so much the strength of the underlying grievances, nor the sheer numbers of citizens. What was unique was the social class of communities involved.

The third wave of protest originated in the increased assessments of fiscal 1977, up 16 percent countywide. This was high but not the highest; the record was in fiscal 1958 with its 17-percent increase. During the third decade, the average yearly increase in assessments was high, 6.6

Table 6   Three Decades of the Tax Revolt

	First decade: fiscal 1949–1958	Second decade: fiscal 1959–1968	Third decade: fiscal 1969–1978
1. Initiative signatures gathered in L.A. County	0	100,000	1,792,000
2. Average yearly increase in assessed valuation, L.A. County	12.6%	7.1%	6.6%
3. Increase in value of land	7.0%	12.6%	7.9%
. . . .			
4. Number attending tax protest events	20,550 (100%)	6,050 (100%)	21,735 (100%)
5. Number from upper-middle-class communities (relative affluence index at least 1.30)	8,025 (39%)	0 (0%)	10,450 (48%)
6. Number from middle-income communities	12,525 (61%)	6,050 (100%)	11,285 (52%)
. . . .			
7. Weighted average, relative affluence indexes of protesting communities	1.24	1.02	1.29

percent, but not as high as the increases in the first and second decades (row 2 in table 6). This greater increase in the first two decades might have been caused by the construction of new buildings rather than increased taxes on existing property. To partially correct for this possibility, one can consider the increase in the assessments on land only. Land assessments increased 7.9 percent in the third decade, but even more in the second (row 3 in table 6). The increased tax bills of the third decade cannot be a complete explanation for the final triumph of the tax revolt, because comparable or greater plights existed earlier.

The third wave of tax protest in fiscal 1969–1978 swept thousands of citizens into political activism—impressive, but again, hardly unique. Although 16,581 persons filed formal appeals of their tax assessments in fiscal 1977 (third decade), the peak number of appeals per year occurred during the second decade. Although 21,735 people attended tax protest events in the third decade when the tax revolt succeeded, an equally impressive 20,550 attended in the first decade. And whereas 17,040 attended events during one year in the third decade, this number was exceeded in the first decade. Despite the high numbers of protesting taxpayers in the 1970s, there were comparable or greater numbers in earlier decades.

Thus, a sharp increase in taxes and a large number of people participating are two general factors that contributed to the rise of the tax revolt.[53] But these two factors cannot explain why the tax revolt succeeded in the third decade (fiscal 1969–1978) and failed in earlier decades. In those first two decades, grievances and popular participation also ran high. What was unique about the third wave of protest was that it had struck a different type of community—upper-middle-class communities.

As the tax revolt was close to triumph during the third decade, homeowners in upper-middle-class communities were joining. Reported attendance at protest events in upper-middle-class communities went from 8,025 in the first decade and zero in the second, to 10,450 in the third. In clearly upper-middle-class communities with affluence indexes of 1.4 or above, there was a more pronounced trend.[54] Only 700 from clearly upper-middle-class communities participated in the first decade and none in the second; 6,750 attended events in the third decade, when the tax revolt succeeded (table 7).

The spread of the tax revolt to upper-middle-class communities is what made the last decade of the tax revolt so different from the first two. Upper-middle-class communities in the 1970s provided the common ground where homeowners and community business leaders could build a political alliance. By then, community business leaders had seen the limitations of working through politicians and had become more

Table 7   Protest Attendance in Affluent Communities by Decade

	Fiscal 1949–1958	*Fiscal 1959–1968*	*Fiscal 1969–1978*
Attendance in communities, relative affluence index at least 1.4	700 (3%)	0	6,750 (31%)
Attendance in other communities	19,850 (97%)	0	14,985 (69%)
Total:	20,550 (100%)	6,050 (100%)	21,735 (100%)

involved in grass-roots campaigning on the issues. At the same time, the leadership of the major coalition of homeowners groups, the United Organizations of Taxpayers, had dropped the antibusiness planks in its program and was trying to recruit support from the business community.

Thus, community business leaders and the UO had new political strategies that provided a spark. The tinder was the upper-middle-class communities that burst into fiery protest in the last decade of the tax revolt. In that third decade (fiscal 1969–1978) there were seven instances where newspapers confirmed that business leaders in upper-middle-class communities supported a sequence of tax protests. (In the first decade there were two; and in the second decade, none. There are approximately twenty upper-middle-class communities in Los Angeles County.)

In the 1970s in the town of La Canada, a community with a relative affluence index of 1.80, the principal leader of the Foothill Property Taxpayers Association was a business owner. The presidents of three boards of realtors in the area helped to organize the association's meetings. These businessmen and realty-board presidents vented their feelings of bounded power. They described how their elected officials had betrayed their trust; they advocated the recall of county supervisors. Similarly, in Manhattan Beach during 1975, real estate broker Jim Walker was the founder and president of Homeowners Under Rapacious Taxation (HURT). HURT organized several packed meetings of angry homeowners. The South Bay Board of Realtors offered to assist beach area homeowners in preparing appeals of their property tax bills.

The alliance between economic leaders and homeowners in upper-middle-class communities made the tax protests of the 1970s so different from those in earlier decades. As I will argue in the next chapter, it was the spread of the tax revolt to upper-middle-class communities that eventually made the movement a success. In upper-middle-class communities, business leaders organized meetings, planned activities, voiced their public support, and contributed money, office space, and phone banks to the movement.

In the San Fernando Valley, communities such as Sherman Oaks and Woodland Hills provided ideal conditions for the upper-middle class and community businesses to unite and promote the tax revolt. The Valley also was the crucible where the upper-middle class joined with middle-income Americans. The valley protests of 1976 drew strong support from communities in each of the ranges of affluence (5,960 from middle-income and 6,100 from upper-middle class). The different groups of small property owners—the community business leaders, the upper-middle-class homeowners, and the middle-income homeowners, came together around common beliefs about the unresponsive power of government. This was the coalition that could put Proposition 13 on the ballot and win.

7

Frustrated Advantage in Upper-Middle-Class Communities

You can't believe the sinking feeling when you get a communication in the mail that says your [property] tax is going to be up to $6,000 . . . because right away you already know what your budget is. . . . I wouldn't be living in my home now at all because from $6,000 I could be up to $12,000 now—that's mind boggling. . . . I'm sitting in a home that's appreciated in value like all of the homes up there. . . . It's my home, I lived there twenty years, I lived in every room in that house. . . . I notice that a lot of my neighbors are moving away but they're going into condominiums and many of them [are] moving out of the state. I'm not quite ready for condominium living yet.[1]

[D]on't take a mink coat away from a woman. Don't give it to her if you're going to take it away, because she'll never be the same and she might kill you in the process.[2]

[A]round the time I started becoming interested in tax fighting, the value of my house had been doubled. . . . And finally when it doubled again, then I had enough. Then I was an active tax fighter. . . . I couldn't see sitting here worrying about making a dollar when some guy downtown was planning to take it away from me. . . .

The Civic Center . . . should be split up in a city that's spread out as large as ours . . . so that it serves the public better. There ought to be . . . a kind of smaller civic center serving the Valley. . . . But [there is] no need to centralize it downtown. I find no reason to go downtown. It's disgusting to go downtown.[3]

For the one million residents of the San Fernando Valley, this is "The Valley." It is a 200-square-mile suburban sprawl of freeways and boulevards, two-car garages, and large backyards. The shopping centers range from the bustle and the lines of the North Hollywood K-Mart to the quiet elegance of the Woodland Hills Promenade.

Valley dwellers say that the quintessential intersection here is the corner of Sepulveda and Ventura Boulevards. North, one sees a gentle incline through the Valley, leading to distant foothills and the quaint mission of San Fernando. South, one can gaze up to the Sepulveda pass, the gateway through which hundreds of thousands of motorists squeeze on their way to work. East and west one can look past savings and loan buildings and Cadillac dealerships to an endless main street of one-story store fronts. Every imaginable commodity is for sale. Does the shop "Light Fantasy" sell lamps, or soft-porn video cassettes? For sure, is there really any other way to live?

The black population, concentrated in a small industrialized area, comprised only 3 percent of the Valley's 1980 population. Then, Valley residents enjoyed a mean household income of $26,400, compared to $15,800 for the less fortunate one and a half million residents who lived in central Los Angeles and adjacent communities.

In the center of the Valley lie the middle-income communities of Van Nuys, Reseda, and North Hollywood, with their 1950s tract houses and repainted, modern apartments with built-in dishwashers. As these middle Americans look *south* *of* the *boulevard* (Ventura Boulevard), they think of the "SOB's," whose four-bedroom houses grace the shaded hillside streets of Sherman Oaks, Encino, and Tarzana. This zone of $50,000-plus family incomes (in 1987) rims the Valley. It includes Canoga Park and Chatsworth in the west and curves around to Northridge. These are the communities where one claims to live if, in reality, one lives anywhere nearby. Here, even the roadside refuse is exclusively Perrier water bottles, Yoplait yogurt containers, and Pepperidge Farms cookie bags.

The homes in this rim of affluence were the ones reassessed in the hot summer of 1976. While Los Angeles County assessments increased by 14 percent, Sherman Oaks and Encino increased 67 percent; Chatsworth, 64 percent; and for one unfortunate area of Northridge, 111 percent. One homeowner described what happened when she received a notice that her tax bill had increased 250 percent. "I forgot all about where I was and what I was doing and fixed, like tunnel vision, on the bill. . . . Inside, I got hysterical. . . . I was filled with fear and also with anger, and it was such a mix of emotions that I just stood there, and I think I vibrated for about ten minutes."[4]

In Northridge, Leah Hill talked to her neighbors, stood in front of a supermarket, and gathered a thousand signatures on a petition. She then hosted a meeting that led to the formation of Taxpayers United for Freedom (TUFF), a Valley-wide protest group. At a TUFF-sponsored rally later that month, three thousand protesters booed elected officials off the stage and cheered as activists repeatedly criticized politicians for not representing the taxpayers. Relatively unknown at the time, Howard Jarvis nevertheless drew the most enthusiastic response of the evening when he proclaimed, "This is the year that people take back their government from the politicians."[5] Activists in middle- and upper-middle-income communities denounced not only high taxes but also the politicians who did not care.

Upper-middle-class communities provided much of the support for the two groups that led the protests in the Valley, TUFF and the Sherman Oaks Homeowners Association. The property owners of Northridge and Encino provided TUFF with many members; the TUFF coordinator and the legal advisor were officers in the homeowners associations of Porter Ridge and Canoga Park, respectively.

Concerns about government unresponsiveness led some angry protesters to advocate militant tactics. But unlike activists in middle-income communities, those in upper-middle-class communities tended to discourage the militancy that did break out. A few taxpayers publicly burned their tax bills and encouraged others to refuse to pay their taxes. Some shouts of "Strike!" resounded at meetings. The tax strike, however, was not endorsed by TUFF or the Sherman Oaks Homeowners Association. TUFF emphasized that it would consider it only when all other tactics failed. TUFF pressured county officials to cut spending by five hundred million dollars. Instead, the county reduced spending by about ten million, making possible a token tax reduction of about seventy dollars for the average homeowner.

Even TUFF's positions were a little too militant for the leaders of the homeowners associations in Encino, Tarzana, and Woodland Hills, who warned their members that "we may not agree with their [TUFF's] more radical proposals."[6] The president of the Sherman Oaks Homeowners Association, Richard Close, did not recommend a tax strike either. He also discouraged the angry taxpayers who demanded a massive recall of government officials, beginning with the governor.

Rather than tax strikes or expressions of anger, the Sherman Oaks Homeowners emphasized lobbying the state legislature to change tax laws. The Sherman Oaks group gathered a quarter-million letters calling for a special session of the legislature to enact tax reform. The fifteen tons of letters, wrapped in brown bags, were delivered to Governor Jerry Brown. Brown met with the protesters for thirty-five minutes, established a task force to study tax reform, but did not convene the desired special session. As a year dragged by, the legislature continued its deadlock over tax relief bills and then recessed, without passing a tax bill.

The protesters of 1976 did not achieve immediate success. Their interactions with big government gave them a lingering sense of frustrated advantage. The affluent homeowners of the Valley, when they spoke, expected their clients, their patients, their vendors, and their secretaries to listen. The homeowners had approached the halls of government on a matter of deep concern. They were told to leave by the rear entrance. One legislator made the fine understatement, "It may well be the public has given up on the legislature and is turning their attention to the initiative."[7] The public did, with a vengeance.

Suburban homeowners, interested in reducing their property taxes and yet maintaining services to their own advantaged communities, decided that it was time to break away from big city and big county government—time to use their taxes to pay for their own amenities rather than inner-city welfare costs. Suburbanites organized movements to form independent cities and new counties, separate from the teeming poor of Los Angeles County. Through their political actions, upper-middle-class homeowners found common cause with small business leaders, who also sought to use their advantages in community life to battle big government. In Proposition 13, property owners in suburbia discovered a program that would redistribute outward, from the city to the suburbs, and upward, to business and the wealthy.

Interpretations About Unresponsive Government

In upper-middle-class communities, activists became frustrated about big governmental units, the City of Los Angeles, the county, and the state, which were unwilling to cut property taxes. Frustrations were aggravated when activists compared their relative powerlessness on the tax issue to the influence they had won on community growth issues.

For some land-use decisions, upper-middle-class communities did have some political influence, which middle-income communities totally lacked. For example, the Hillside Federation, a coalition of neighborhood groups in the exclusive Hollywood Hills and Santa Monica Mountains, got their members appointed to various governmental commissions.[8] On zoning matters, the federation had considerable power, helping the Beverly Glen Residents Association to stop a proposed condominium project. In the upper-middle-class community of Tarzana, named in honor of the character created by resident Edgar Rice Burroughs, homeowners were consulted on all zoning matters:

> We took part in the Hillside and Canyon Federation law suit to bring zoning into conformity. . . . We won that case. It was done through the Center for the Law and Public Interest, I think. . . . [W]e do now have a credibility and I think that's what's important. [Los Angeles City Council member Marvin Braude] . . . his office communicates all the time with us. I mean if there's a development coming in that's going to be asking for some kind of change we know about it right away, and then we can begin to function. And what we do is we check on the application: Is it appropriate? We have a community plan that several members of our board worked on when they had a citizens' advisory committee, and we check and see if it applies to the community plan properly. If it doesn't, we get busy. It has grown to the extent that now, the councilman's office suggests that these people come and see us before they put their application in.[9]

But all of the wealth, status, and influence of upper-middle-class communities could not halt skyrocketing property tax bills in the 1970s. In the upper-middle-class town of Manhattan Beach, a leader of a residents association contrasted the responsiveness of town government to the indifference of county government:

> On the local city level . . . I can go to . . . [town] government and the chances are if I've got a legitimate gripe I can get some action—they will hear it and I probably will get something done. . . . I think that most local people might take a complaint down to the . . . [town] government; [but] I don't think that they would bother [with] the county level, no. . . . I did talk to our county representatives at the time. . . . If you start talking to public officials, one of the problems . . . is that everybody agreed with you [that taxes were too high] but you never could really get any action. . . . You'd get bounced from one area to the other. . . . You simply were . . . wasting your time. You were getting verbal agreements, everyone was crying on the towel, but . . . action you weren't getting.[10]

People who were highly privileged compared to most Americans could still feel powerless and frustrated on the issue of property taxes. For example, a former director of the Tarzana Property Owners Association, who lived in a census tract where 57 percent of the work force were professionals and incomes ran 2.2 times that of greater Los Angeles, had an experience that convinced him that going through the established channels of government was futile. He recounted how he tried to complain about his tax bill but received only a lot of "double talk":

> I went to the local . . . [assessor's office] and was refused any recognition. There's no question about it, you don't get a break. . . . [S]o I went

downtown and appealed it by myself. After about four times like that . . .
I did get it reduced, but . . . the only year they reduced was for the year I
was screaming about. . . . I had been paying extra taxes for the previous
eight years. They said, "You have to file one [appeal] for each year."[11]

As individuals, then, upper-middle-class people could feel powerless
against the governmental bureaus of the County of Los Angeles. Even
when residents of upper-middle-class communities formed associations,
they could not obtain relief from the county assessor. A film editor for a
movie studio, who lived in a census tract where the relative affluence
index was 1.92, organized a tax protest meeting that attracted one thousand persons from the neighborhood. He led a delegation of six representatives who conveyed their grievances directly to the county assessor:

> Well, we got nowhere. . . . We were bucking city hall and there weren't
> enough of us to make an impression on them. . . . We went to the asses-
> sor's office and we got a flat . . . "This is our problem, not yours; . . .
> don't try to tell us how to run our business. . . ." As long as they had a
> penalty on non-payment of taxes, why, they didn't care whether we ob-
> jected or not because eventually they could seize the property. . . . We
> talked with [County Assessor] Quinn and explained our problem. . . .
> He's probably heard this problem from every other part of town too, so he
> just sat and listened to us and he didn't give us any satisfaction.[12]

Even when tax protest associations gained the support of elected
officials in an upper-middle-class town, they could not make any head-
way against higher levels of government—county and state—which held
the powers to tax and spend. As an activist in Manhattan Beach concluded, "A group like [the residents association here] . . . would have
some voices in the local [town] government here. . . . Now getting beyond that, no, unfortunately when you get into those areas you're talking about [interest] groups that expend money."[13]

A case in point is the tax protest that took place on the affluent Palos
Verdes peninsula, where 58 percent of the work force were professionals
and 74 percent of the people over twenty-five had attended one year of
college or more. (The relative affluence index was 2.16.) In 1976, homeowners groups had just succeeded in forming their own new town, Rancho Palos Verdes, but nevertheless had little voice in county government:

> [S]o we had local government and we could go down and talk to the
> people. . . . So you walked into the city [town] council meeting and you
> knew the people . . . and you had a feeling that we can get things done
> here. . . .
> [Question: What about one step up, on the county and state level?]
> That's where it goes to nothing in one jump. . . . The further government

gets from you as an individual, the worse it gets. The next step is the county, and the county is, in my estimation—I just feel that they're all bought off down there. . . . We were talking to the County Board of Supervisors. You know, they have those deals where you can go in and you're on the agenda for five minutes. . . . There were about five of us that went down and each of us got up and sort of gave a squirt transmission of about one minute and thirteen seconds. . . . You don't normally get much feedback from them.[14]

County government gave the homeowners groups similar treatment even when the homeowners were protesting taxes that had doubled over the past three years. Three mayors from the peninsula organized two busloads of town officials and residents to lobby the county supervisors to reject a proposed tax rate increase in 1976. Supervisor James Hayes, who represented the area, was not present when the delegation testified. One town mayor, Gunther Buerk, could not obtain the record of supervisors' votes on the budget and could not even get Hayes to return telephone calls. After learning that Hayes had voted in favor of the tax increase, Buerk concluded, "Supervisor Hayes did not seem to think it necessary . . . [to call]. I am very disappointed that we have this type of representation when we do not have some kind of accountability [and] not even the voting record."

Hayes later responded, but only by forming a citizens' advisory panel, which he claimed would "provide the perfect vehicle for community participation. . . . There's a lot of criticism about county government being unresponsive to the people in the community."[15] How right Hayes was. Angry peninsula residents demanded a recall of Hayes and then campaigned for South Bay communities to secede from Los Angeles County.

As property taxes continued to rise, peninsula homeowners continually fought the county to reduce taxes and spending. "We would go down routinely on Tuesdays to the County Board of Supervisors especially in the summer months when the budget hearings were held. . . . I don't think we had any impact whatsoever on them. . . . So while we would get our material into the record, I would say we were not essentially convincing them."[16] Gunther Buerk concluded:

[R]eally, the county budget is something that you cannot very easily fight. You can go to those hearings and you really don't find out what's happening unless you do really a thorough research and really very carefully check into the details of the budget and understand what's going on, and it's not very easy for any outsider to understand what's going on. The budget is, first of all, a document that's that thick [indicates a thickness of several inches]. The way the accounting is done in it, the way those things are discussed lends itself very much to really decisions being made long before it actually goes to votes, and also even if votes are taken, you don't really understand what is voted on and what the consequences are. . . .

[I] suggested that they cut out of the budget . . . at least eighty or ninety million [dollars]. . . . That was the first time something ever like that had been proposed and of course that wasn't taken too serious[ly] by the supervisors because they were just doing business as usual. . . .

I think the supervisors at that time never quite understood how big the frustration of the people was. They never understood how serious a situation it really was and that the people were not really willing to stand that any longer. And so they did little things. . . . They cut a few dollars out of this and a few dollars out of that and then slapped themselves on their back and said how great they were in doing this. . . .

Sure, we talked to our representatives in Sacramento, and they, of course, gave us also lip service.[17]

Homeowners associations were disappointed when they attempted to reduce property taxes by influencing state-level politics. The director of the Brentwood Homeowners Association, a lawyer by profession, lived in an affluent census tract where 60 percent of the employed population worked in professional, technical, and managerial occupations and the relative affluence index was 2.54. The Brentwood homeowners were quite influential in community politics, as demonstrated by their ability to veto a proposed freeway and three condominium-conversion projects. The director of the homeowners association recounted his trip to the state capital as property taxes became a concern in 1975:

Believing in our legislature as we did, I went to Sacramento repeatedly to work with Mr. Willy Brown, Senator Behr . . . Howard Berman, and Paul Priolo . . . to do something about property taxes. . . . Unfortunately, they just weren't doing the job. . . . We spent quite a bit of money, but that is not the critical point. . . . [I was] received with a great deal of friendship and courtesy and [was] offered free lunches. . . .

Property taxes were the source of all gold to them in Sacramento. . . . Nothing would be accomplished because . . . the state employees' association and many other[s] . . . had such powerful lobbies and wanted these taxes. . . . [They] were contributing to the legislators' campaign funds. . . . I was surrounded by public employee associations and teacher associations that had 160 representatives present. I was the only one there in the state of California to speak on behalf of the homeowner. . . .

We did everything we could legitimately to try to do something about controlling taxes, and we would have been very satisfied if the legislature had come up with any . . . mildly effective solution. But they came up with no solution.

And that's why the initiative was forced upon us. . . . Our people are not disposed to act publicly. . . . We accepted it [Prop. 13] and supported it totally and very effectively as we will in any case when we're forced to the wall as we were there. . . . Proposition 13 eclipsed everything in a way that I've never seen [on] any other issue.[18]

One activist who had tried to discuss tax issues with a state senator and a state representative concluded, "Anyone who seemed to be associated with the government was completely opposed to Proposition 13 and its objectives. I found so little cooperation on the part of anyone in government. We were received cordially and they would listen to our story, but they would do nothing." As another activist in the upper-middle-class community of Agoura concluded, "I could show you a bunch of [state legislature] bills . . . on this computer. Next to the bill number there are names of people that have requested or have indicated a problem. . . . You might find one out of ten that's actually instituted by a local homeowners group for the benefit of some local service, or some bad state law that . . . effects them locally. The rest is all special-interest legislation."[19]

What activists in upper-middle-class communities learned from their computer screens, protesters in middle-income communities had already learned by having doors slammed in their faces. The community groups that fought for tax reduction soon discovered they lacked the political power to gain relief from high property taxes. Political powerlessness became an important theme of the tax revolt, dramatized, for example, when protesters placed a row of empty chairs on a stage, reserved for politicians who had been invited but did not appear.[20]

Besides objecting to government unresponsiveness, tax activists took positive steps to increase citizen participation in goverment. The Sherman Oaks Homeowners Association and the Citizens for Property Tax Relief organized citizens' committees to examine government budgets and publicize their findings. The League of California Citizens and the Taxpayers' Congress, two tax and expenditure limitation groups, announced that one of their major goals was to prod local government to release more information to the public.

Advantages for Naught

Among the communities that erupted in tax protests in 1976, many were upper-middle class, with relative affluence indexes of 1.3 or more.[21] Several of the communities that led the protests of 1976 and the campaign for Proposition 13 had relative affluence indexes well above the 1.3 cutoff. The principal protest leaders from the San Fernando Valley and the Westside lived in census tracts where the relative affluence index ranged from 1.62 to 2.54. The 1976 median family income in these tracts varied from $25,000 to $48,800. (In 1987, an income range of equivalent standing would be approximately $49,000 to $77,000.) In these tracts, 48.0 to 76.7 percent of the work force was engaged in professional, managerial, and technical work; 50.2 to 77.0 percent of the population over age twenty-five had attended at least one year of college. The principal leaders from these affluent communities were themselves professionals, business owners, or high-level managers, or (in three cases) were married to people of similar standing or were retired.

Similarly, on the Palos Verdes peninsula, one activist described the people involved in Citizens for Property Tax Relief: "We had an economist, . . . legal counsel, . . . [and] many disciplined people from aerospace. We had . . . a graduate of Harvard in public health, . . . a college professor, . . . [someone] who runs a worldwide investment service, . . . an accountant, . . . the sales manager for Garrett AiResearch, . . . [and] an expert, very important to us, in computer technology. . . . We had people who were technically very disciplined and very competent."[22] The chairperson of Citizens for Property Tax Relief, James K. Lee, was president of a management consulting and computer-design company.

Upscale neighborhoods provided the leaders and organizations crucial to the success of the tax revolt. Here were concentrated individuals who exerted power and commanded prestige at their work situations. Their advantages in the job hierarchy led them to expect to have power and status outside their workplaces, especially in the communities where they lived. One activist described how his community involvement stemmed from his "I'm in control" attitude:

> I'm not afraid to sit down and do something. Like if I go into my community in Tarzana, and I find that across the street from my house a developer moves in . . . well I don't sit around and wait for that, I do something about it. I call the city councilman and have the zoning ordinance checked and so on. . . .
>
> So I've been doing this in my community, and people come to me and say that . . . the school board has decided to . . . have a lot of houses removed so that they can build a [day] care center for the school right alongside there. . . . And the next thing you know they're having a meeting at the school here to tell the people how beautiful it's going to be once they have this day care center, and these people are saying, "They're going to move us out?"
>
> So . . . what I did, I just went to the meeting and I sat there and here are two dozen people sitting there listening and you got a whole battery of people up front from the school board and the city engineering department and so on. I just walk up to the platform and ask, "Who are you? And I'd like your card, each one of you. . . . Identify yourselves." And I

turn around and I take over the meeting and tell the people assembled, "Look, I live on the next street and I don't know how this is coming about but whose house can we meet at Sunday to discuss this thing?" And [the officials] they're sitting there with their faces red and angered. . . .

And the net result of this is that after we have a meeting we drive a mile away and find a school that has a lot of room not in use, and we make a recommendation to the school board that they get off these peoples' backs and go down there and build their nursery. And the net result is that we killed it.

So it always takes a spark plug to move people.[23]

When this activist dealt with public officials, he thought himself superior in status and intelligence, but still without political power. In his view, most public officials

are what you might call socially illiterate. . . . I'd raise . . . [a] question at city council . . . so who would stand up? . . . [Names councilman who represents an inner-city district], paragon of intelligence. . . .

Here [where I live] you have a community that supplies forty percent or more of the city's tax revenues, and with our destinies guided by ex-janitors like . . . [the councilman named above] and a bunch of others who are political pork-barrel operators. . . .

Real stupid. These are the kind of people—it's really hopeless . . . unless you have enough clout or unless you meet somebody intelligent like the one intelligent guy on the whole council. . . . Go talk to the others and they're all political flunkies. . . . So we met a lot of resistance from political authorities. They were not the least bit sympathetic. . . .

I don't think that any of these people are any bigger than the next guy, and if you look at them eye level, peer level, none of them are any higher or any lower, they're all people.[24]

The solidly upper-middle-class suburbs throughout California were filled with people who had all of life's advantages except access to political power. In California in 1980, for example, 1.3 million families (21 percent of all families) earned above $35,000 a year, an income more than 1.6 times the median family income in both California and the Los Angeles metropolitan area. Over 3 million Californians were employed in professional, technical, managerial, or administrative jobs.

Although those with upper-middle-class occupations and incomes number in the millions, the politically influential number only in the thousands. One crude indication of political influence is the making of a significant campaign contribution. For example, for the June 1978 election (when Proposition 13 passed), about 140 individuals contributed more than $500 to campaigns for ballot initiatives or candidates in Cali-

fornia. Contributions from these politically influential individuals totaled $1.7 million. During the June 1978 campaign, about 320 businesses
contributed $5.1 million and 80 banks and insurance companies $1.3
million.[25] The few thousand individuals—top managers, owners, and
lobbyists—associated with these group contributions could expect to
have routine access to government decision makers. For individuals,
then, political influence is much more scarce than either occupational
status or wealth.[26]

Having little political influence with big government at the county and
state level, the upper-middle class developed an intense sense of its frustrated advantage. To resolve their grievances, affluent citizens sought to
contact government leaders but found no satisfaction. In upper-middle-
class communities, the activists' own experiences of unresponsive government led them to develop viewpoints and rhetoric that resonated with the
activists from less affluent areas. Middle-income Americans also knew of
unresponsive government and even went further, to express a generalized
sense of powerlessness against many political and economic institutions
and leaders.

Together, activists from both upper-middle and middle-income communities thought that big government was unjust for increasing property
tax collections year after year. They felt that big government was unresponsive to their petitions. Together, they denounced the powers that
they deemed responsible for the tax burden—politicians, bureaucrats,
and established interest groups.

Unable to win by themselves, upper-middle-class homeowners drove
down from the scenic hills of the Palos Verdes peninsula, back through
the stoplights of Hawthorne Boulevard; down from their *Sunset* magazine homes in the Santa Monica Mountains, back to the unwashed
Toyota Tercels gridlocking Ventura Boulevard, back to where they
would have to live if their property tax bills rose any further. There, they
mingled with the K-Mart shoppers in the high school auditoriums of old
Van Nuys, perhaps sensing the subtle differences in bearing and in
taste—realizing just what it was that they had worked so hard to escape.
Joining the less affluent in mass meetings, the homeowners of Rolling
Hills Estates and Sherman Oaks eventually took the lead in organizing
and shaping the entire tax limitation movement.

How did these outside agitators from upper-middle-class communities affect the political direction of the tax revolt? Was this direction
different from the one sought by activists from middle-income communities? Even though the activists from middle-income and upper-middle-
class communities shared common grievances about unresponsive big
government, the two groups had different backgrounds and cultures that
produced suspicions and tensions. James Lee, the president of the engi-

neering firm who lived in the peninsula, described the difficulties of working with those from less affluent communities:

> I'm already different from them, and I'm not gonna try and remake myself. . . . Look at where we're from. Here we are from the peninsula. I go down to Gardena and I drive up in a brand new Cadillac. And I get out of that and I go down and talk to people who are making minimum wage, working in a factory, putting together little circuit boards. Now I go in there and what's their first inclination: . . . "What's he getting out of this?" If I can't stand up there and say, "I swear to God I'm not getting a damn thing out of it," . . . then I won't have credibility at all.[27]

Social Class and Tactics for the Tax Limitation Movement

One major difference was that the activists from upper-middle-class communities shied away from the militancy expressed by protesters in middle-income areas. As a leader from the Palos Verdes peninsula put it, "None of [us] . . . are the kind that will carry signs." Leaders in upper-middle-class communities discouraged militant or expressive actions, especially those that were illegal. Several of the leading tax activists in upper-middle-class communities were attorneys who headed the homeowners associations in Brentwood, Studio City, and Sherman Oaks; the president of the latter association closely monitored the activities of his tax-issues committee to be sure that they were "strictly legal." Activists in professional middle-class communities also opposed the tax strike and thus prevented the movement from focusing on this tactic as it did during 1966.[28] This antipathy extended to other actions that involved violating the law in any way:

> [The tax strike] was ill advised. We were against it. People tried to get us into it. . . . I told them what would happen. They would lose all their credibility. . . . [Homeowners] who had old-time mortages with six percent—by . . . failing to pay . . . [the bank] could foreclose . . . and . . . issue new mortgages at thirteen percent.
>
> [Some protesters] wanted . . . everybody in the community [to] drive downtown before the county building and blow your horn and flash your lights. And of course, that's silly. You antagonize more people. . . . [Y]ou jeopardize the safety of a lot of police officers and firemen. . . . There's a much more effective way to go about this.[29]

Thus, upper-middle-class communities put a damper on the tax strike and other expressive protests, and channeled efforts into gathering signatures on tax reduction initiatives. A former director of the property owners' association in Tarzana described why the initiative was a favored tactic: "[O]ne of the beauties of [Proposition] 13 was the fact that it used the constitutionality of the initiative to prevent violence or any one strong-headed individual who may be warped in his thinking. . . . It wasn't like the Boston Tea Party. . . . It happened by constitutional, legal means."[30]

When it came time to undertake specific activities to support tax-cutting initiatives, some activists in upper-middle-class communities dutifully stood in front of supermarkets soliciting signatures. Many who considered themselves professionals saw this as a monotonous task that was a little demeaning. They searched for roles in the movement where they could exercise leadership and utilize their expertise.

Because of their work, their experiences, and their culture, the upper-middle class was attracted to certain tactics. In their work, they rely on their skills in processing information and organizing people. It is the possession of these skills that differentiates the upper-middle class from middle-income earners and accounts for the higher incomes and prestige of the former. Some of the upper-middle class who participated in the tax limitation movement emphasized the importance of providing factual information. "The most effective strategy is to get one person who is very angry and mad and who is professional and who will sit down and work up all the facts and make a brief.[31] The presentations of carefully researched facts would lead to favorable media coverage:

> We looked at what the grass roots were doing and we said, "Hey, they don't have credible numbers." So you get people who know something's wrong but it's not printable in the press because . . . [it's] all value judgments. . . . [The grass roots] were very nice people but . . . not professional people; they were average working folks. . . . They need credible numbers because they don't have a story to last more than one or two news shots. And without the statistics the other side steam rolls them. They can't even tell when the other side is lying.[32]

One activist from an affluent community summarized another specialty of the upper-middle class—organization: "We tried to organize. . . . What we did was to send missionaries out to help other people organize. . . . Consulting was our specialty."[33]

Activists from upper-middle-class communities sought out others who would be committed to producing ballot-initiative fact sheets rather than militant protests. Unlike some protesters in middle-income communities who sought assistance from and then affiliated with right-wing political groups and charismatic leaders, protesters in upper-middle-class communities avoided anything that could be construed as extremism or demagoguery.

For example, the night before a major tax protest rally in Woodland Hills, the leaders of Taxpayers United for Freedom (TUFF) discovered that their chairperson was connected to the Libertarian party. That night, an emergency meeting of the TUFF steering committee voted to exclude all Libertarians from participating.[34] Leaders in affluent communities feared that ties to right-wing groups would lead to charges that the movement was irresponsible. Similarly, some upper-middle-class leaders had misgivings about the militant rhetoric of Howard Jarvis. One leader of an affluent homeowners group disliked Jarvis and his "mannerisms" and preferred to work with Paul Gann, the co-author of Proposition 13. The head of the Brentwood homeowners also had a closer relationship to Gann than to Jarvis.

Instead of seeking help from charismatic leaders or right-wing political groups, tax protesters in upper-middle-class communities in the 1970s increasingly turned to community business leaders. To a lesser degree, this had happened earlier; in West Covina in 1957 homeowners and community business leaders had worked together. The upgrading of the social base of the tax revolt simply accelerated this tendency.

The Naugahyde Handshake: Upper-Middle-Class Homeowners and Community Business

By 1970, soaring property values in affluent communities led to property tax bills that even the upper-middle class could not afford to pay. On the Palos Verdes peninsula, property tax assessments in 1976 increased 35 percent in Palos Verdes Estates and 23 percent in Rolling Hills, compared to a countywide increase of 14 percent. As a result, upper-middle-class communities joined the tax revolt, especially those at the high end of the upper-middle-class category. The West Covina activists in 1957 lived in census tracts where the relative affluence was 1.30; the 1976 activists in the San Fernando Valley, the Westside of Los Angeles, and the Palos Verdes peninsula lived in census tracts where the relative affluence index was higher (1.62 in Sherman Oaks and 2.54 in Brentwood).

When more upper-middle-class communities joined the tax revolt, they brought along the leading small businesses in their communities. Of the nine protests that generated large meetings in upper-middle-class communities during the decade before Prop. 13, community business leaders supported seven of the nine protests. These upscale communities played leading roles in the burgeoning tax revolt: Manhattan Beach, where real estate broker Jim Walker led a movement of affluent beach communities to secede from the inner-city areas of Los Angeles County; the Palos Verdes peninsula, where activists created a sophisticated campaign organization for Proposition 13; and Woodland Hills, Northridge, and Sherman Oaks, where homeowners and community businesses gathered half of the signatures required in the entire state to place Proposition 13 on the ballot. These activities, organized in suburban communities, were crucial to the success of the tax revolt. The unity between homeowners and community businesses greatly contributed to the grassroots politics that made Proposition 13 victorious.

Homeowners and the leaders of community small business formed an alliance because of their similar tactics to deal with their common obstacle, government unresponsiveness. Both groups, despite their resources, advantages, and standing in their communities, nevertheless lacked power with metropolitan- and state-level government—power that was needed to win a reduction in property taxes. Community business leaders possessed bounded power. Although they had significant influence in the politics of suburban towns, they could not affect the fiscal policies of county and state government. Homeowners in upper-middle-class communities were in a similar situation. Although they had the advantages of higher income, professional employment, and social status, their advantages were frustrated by the unresponsive politicians and bureaucratic agencies at the metropolitan and state levels.

Homeowners in upper-middle-class areas and community business leaders possessed similar resources—money, social connections, and skills in organization, communication, and leadership—and faced the common hindrance of big government. Tactical necessities drew homeowners and businesses together. But if the two groups were to lead a successful tax revolt, they needed to find common ground not only about means but also about ends. They needed to reach agreement over whose taxes would be cut and who would suffer; they needed to agree on a common program for tax reduction that would designate the specific interests that the movement would pursue. Proposition 13 embodied just such an agreement over interests. Taxes would be cut both for businesses and homeowners. Tax relief would not be targeted to low-income homeowners or renters. Those property owners who had the largest tax bills—those who owned large businesses and the most expensive houses—would gain the largest reductions.

Thus, the tax revolt succeeded when homeowners in upper-middle-class locales and the leading small businesses in those communities worked together and developed common interests. This mutual activity occurred mostly in upper-middle-class communities, because there some of the homeowners were themselves owners or managers of businesses in the area. The head of the Brentwood Homeowners Association described relations with the business leaders in his community: "Our community leaders are members of the Brentwood–San Vicente Chamber of Commerce . . . [who] are very closely related to the homeowners association because they own homes in this area. . . . In Proposition 13, they helped, yes, yes. . . . They approach their problems *pretty much the same* as we do."[35]

Of the thirteen major activists representing upper-middle-class homeowners in the San Fernando Valley and the Westside of Los Angeles, one was an owner of a business based in the community and one was a vice-president of a small business. Another activist distributed auto parts to repair shops and retail outlets in the area; two others were attorneys whose practices involved real estate or other businesses. Five out of the thirteen, in short, were themselves community business leaders.

But a majority, eight out of thirteen, were not. Why did other leaders of homeowners' protests—including an electrical engineer, a screenwriter, an attorney working for government, and a retired schoolteacher—who were not in business themselves nevertheless support a probusiness program? Some of these homeowners in upper-middle-class communities, and even an occasional small business owner, voiced antibusiness sentiments. An orthodontist from the Palos Verdes peninsula argued:

A lot of what the conservatives want I'm really not for either because a lot of conservatives feel that if business does anything it's O.K., and yet I consider what so many businesses want to do as far as protecting with import taxes and other special interests—you really find business today is enmeshed in lobbying with governments, and what they want is—they want special favors for themselves at the expense of the consumer and the marketplace.[36]

Of all the disagreements between homeowners and businesses in upper-middle-class communities, the most heated were over urban growth. On the Palos Verdes peninsula, homeowners formed an organization, Save Our Coastline, to limit new construction. Similarly, in the Westside of Los Angeles, homeowners groups fought developers and sought to preserve green areas, maintain restrictive zoning, and veto new apartments.[37] Immediately before the tax reduction campaigns of 1976, the Sherman Oaks Homeowners led a coalition of homeowners groups that raised one hundred thousand dollars and lobbied politicians to limit the number of flights at the Burbank airport. Local chambers of commerce favored more flights, hoping to increase business nearby the airport and spur economic growth for the entire San Fernando Valley. The issue of urban growth tended to divide the upper-middle-class homeowners and the community business leaders. However, upper-middle-class homeowners in the mid-1970s set aside their quarrels with business and steered the tax protest movement into an alliance with community business leaders.[38] How did the homeowners in upper-middle-class communities come to support a program that reduced taxes not only for themselves but also for business? What, precisely, made the approaches of the two groups "pretty much the same?"

The Preservation of Advantage

Even though activist homeowners and leading small businesses in affluent areas clashed over growth, the two groups nevertheless shared certain values. The upper-middle class, through its credentials and skills, seeks to maintain its higher pay and status and a variety of advantages over other workers. Consequently, activists in upper-middle-class communities tend to defend the notion that greater effort should be rewarded with more expensive consumer goods: "My basic philosophy [is] that if you have two people, and one works harder than the other, the guy that works harder is entitled to . . . make more, keep more, and live better. . . . I'm . . . I guess, strictly a capitalist if you want to call that being a capitalist. I think effort deserves reward."[39] Note that capitalism here is equated not to business growth or to large corporations but rather to inequality in the distribution of income. Government, however, sometimes erodes the returns of work:

> We actually penalize people for making money. . . . The government is not going to make you rich. The government is socially engineering things to level everyone . . . so that no one has more than anyone else. And this is not free enterprise, and it is not freedom at all.[40]

The proper role of government is to protect small property, the homes and possessions that are the fruits of labor. If, on the contrary, the government fails to protect property or acts to take property from the deserving, hard-working owner, government has violated its fundamental purpose. The large jumps in property tax bills year after year threatened to do precisely this and actually forced some to sell their property in order to pay tax bills. Drastic measures were in order:

> Everything that we have in this county flows from our right to own private property. When . . . [that] right . . . is taken, everything else, every other freedom falls behind it. . . . What the people . . . in authority at that time were doing was tantamount to divesting us *en masse* of our private property. . . . [What got people the maddest was] the greed of government and the careless way they spent the fruits of our labors.[41]

Upper-middle-class homeowners and community small businesses, in their own peculiar ways, agreed with the notion that government in America had a fundamental obligation to protect property. The homeowner thought of property as consumer property and felt that if the accountant went to night school and got his M.B.A., he was entitled to his condo and his BMW, without the burden of the property tax. The small business owner felt that the value of his enterprise was gained through entrepreneurial effort, and that he too was entitled to material rewards free from excessive taxation. When they both thought of property, they envisioned small property, not corporate fortunes of unimaginable scale, but property of a human scale that was the clear result of a person's lifetime of work. Small property was the magic meeting ground for the middle class, where business and consumer could stand proud and stand together.

This generalized consensus, though, was just the first step in forming a specific program for joint political action. A definition of common interests was formed during the tax protests in upper-middle-class communities in the 1970s. These times were marked by a convergence of views not only about wealth and property but also about how and where local government should spend the taxpayers' money.

I Got Mine, You Scat

Homeowners had many expectations about local government in addition to the principles that government should protect property and keep taxes low. They wanted government to be their active servant, servicing their consumer possessions. Presumptions about local government began at home.

"Our little area here when you came down Rocking Horse Road is a private street and has a homeowners association. And all these people have the responsibility of maintaining their own road and have deed restrictions on their property to make sure no views are blocked."[42] In upper-middle-class communities, homeowners wanted ornamental lights, entrance gates, and street signs to accent the fine qualities of their homes and enhance their property values. Sometimes these amenities were provided by a private homeowners group, which charged fees for landscaping and maintenance and took on the air of an exclusive club. When these services were provided by the government and paid through taxes, residents in upper-middle-class communities sought what they received at Neiman-Marcus—quality goods to gratify their own desires at a price that reflected the quality of the merchandise. Homeowners thought of themselves as consumers and in upper-middle-class communities they were luxury consumers. The city hall in their town was just another elegant shopping mall.

The consumers in upper-middle-class communities were unwilling to pay for goods that were never even delivered. They would be outraged to go to a restaurant and receive a bill for someone else's extravagant tastes in wine. But these consumer nightmares were standard fare at the boutique of local government. Activists from upper-middle-class communities argued that they were paying premium prices to the government: "We were assessed three times in five years. . . . And they seemed to always pick on the areas that they felt were the most affluent, and that was their assessment practice. It was very difficult on the people who were assessed too frequently."[43]

In upper-middle-class communities like the Palos Verdes peninsula, activists thought that they were paying the highest tax bills and that they deserved tax reduction the most.

> We really didn't think that the problem was the [tax on] lower-income people. . . . It was more the [tax] increases from $2,000 to $6,000 that were the big problems. I, at one time, was invited to a party where Governor [Jerry] Brown was there and we had a three-quarters of an hour debate, he and I, and everybody gathered around, on this issue. . . . Some things like this came out. . . . For low-income [earners], there was anyway [a benefit]. I recall on the property tax bill the first so-and-so many dollars are forgiven—homeowner's exemption or something like that. So there was . . . a relief for lower values where they pay . . . significantly less. But he could not understand—that somebody, let's say, who makes $40,000, $50,000 a year, lives in an area like this, and suddenly gets hit with a $6,000 tax bill—that something has to give. For some reason, people think that people who live in an area like this are all millionaires, and they're not. And if you have, let's say in 1977, a $40,000 income, then you're already above average of the people who live here. . . . If you subtract your federal taxes and state taxes that you pay—that may be $8,000 or something, maybe $9,000, then you pay the sales tax on all the things you buy, and when then suddenly something like $6,000 comes along, it doesn't work. And he did not understand that.[44]

Homeowners in upper-middle-class communities insisted that they, and not the less affluent, were being cheated the most by property taxes. Affluent activists objected that their high property taxes did not pay for amenities that would enhance their own properties but rather went for welfare and other social programs for the poor and recent immigrants:

> We were just being hung up to dry with our property taxes, and the largest portion of which was going down to the county. And it bore no relation to

flood control, street maintenance, or any of those things that related to property taxes which property taxes should go to. I mean, if they want to subsidize the welfare program and the health program of L.A. County and all their county hospitals and having all these people having children and all, if they want to do that it should be on a broader base. It shouldn't be just on your property. . . .

As soon as somebody came in from Mexico or off the boat had a baby, then they were entitled to welfare. So we not only were paying all of their health bills but we were paying all their welfare bills and it was coming off our property tax. It was madness. . . . Immigrants will come in and they can get a cheaper interest rate to start a business than a citizen can, and I think that's not right. Nobody should get a better deal than the people who are paying the taxes.[45]

The inner-city area was allegedly deriving all the benefits from the property tax; furthermore, the tax bills in poor communities were not increasing as they were on the peninsula:

[On the peninsula] any time anybody·sold a house, that whole census tract was reassessed, so we had a double whammy of not only being reassessed the most often of the whole L.A. County, but we were also having an increased tax rate the county was putting out. Since the rest of the county was not going up in value relative to what we were, they had to keep increasing the tax rate. So if you go, to like the central city, Bell, Hawaiian Gardens, all those areas, they were not having their property [assessments] increased because there were not substantial increases when the property changed hands, whereas on the coastline it was. . . . If you go down on Vermont and Broadway you'll see boarded-up windows. So all those were going down in value, and we were going up in value, and so they had to keep raising the tax rate because proportionately the rest of the county wasn't experiencing the increased property values that the coastline was. . . .

Phil Watson was the county assessor and he said that . . . we're not going to waste our time down in Lennox if property isn't changing. . . . So if a house [on the peninsula] would go during that time, with inflation and all, it was a question of how many days it was on the market. It was that high. And so we were just being killed.[46]

Many activists in upper-middle-class communities believed that they were being defrauded by the inner city and downtown big government: "Most of the subsidies go to inner-core cities . . . and it comes out of the county budget. So you had everything being sucked out of the suburbs. . . . It just got to an intolerable point."[47] These activists believed that property taxes should not be used to redistribute wealth or help the needy but rather should gratify those who paid the bills.

Action: Secession and County
Formation Movements

Activists in upper-middle-class communities wanted to use their property taxes to pay for their own amenities and not someone else's social programs to benefit the teeming millions of poor Los Angelinos. To avoid this rich man's burden, some affluent communities had constituted themselves as independent municipalities, separate from the City of Los Angeles. Beverly Hills had been the trendsetter, incorporating itself as a city in 1914. The City of Los Angeles fought back, seeking to engulf as many prosperous homeowners within its bounds as possible, and finally played the trump card of California politics—water rights. Through the daring of City Engineer William Mulholland, Los Angeles constructed a huge aqueduct from the Owens River, two hundred miles away, and used its stable supply of water to tempt communities to join the city. In a drought of 1923, the City of Los Angeles almost succeeded in annexing Beverly Hills, which maintained its independence due to the efforts of entertainment stars such as Will Rogers, Douglas Fairbanks, and Rudolph Valentino. The San Fernando Valley, however, succumbed to an offer of water that could not be refused. Towns such as San Marino and La Canada/Flintridge held on to their fiscal independence.

In 1975, residents formed the new town of Ranchos Palos Verdes, which together with the other independent towns on the Palos Verdes peninsula had achieved some fiscal control. Palos Verdes Estates taxed its residents 1.1 percent of assessed value and used the proceeds for amenities in the town.[48] The problem was that the County of Los Angeles was levying a tax rate of 4.5 percent—a tax that was widely seen as funding welfare mothers and illegal immigrants.

Around this time, one could almost hear the simultaneous click among legions of affluent suburbanites who hit upon the obvious solution—to form not only independent cities but entire new counties that would be separate from the impoverished millions of Los Angeles County. Here was a dramatic program—to secede and go it alone, to declare independence from unjust taxing power. It positively reverberated with cultural themes of rugged individualism in the American West and the patriotism of the Boston Tea Party and the American Revolution. Movements to form independent new counties built the alliances that sustained the tax revolt. Homeowners and community-based businesses united against the power of big government.

One of the largest movements for county formation was the Committee Investigating Valley Independence City/County (CIVICC), which sought to make the San Fernando Valley a separate city and county. CIVICC argued that the Valley had a sufficient tax base to fund all the necessary services for itself. The Valley secession movement almost triumphed when the town council of San Fernando, one of the few politically independent jurisdictions in the Valley, fell one vote short of passing a resolution that would have taken advantage of a legal loophole and would have annexed the entire San Fernando Valley.

In the mid-1970s, higher property taxes and increasing expenditures for the inner city caused many homeowners from upper-middle-class Valley communities to support the secession movement. They were joined by leaders of small business in the communities, who also wanted local government spending to benefit the Valley, rather than the central-city poor or the towering corporate headquarters downtown. "The original leadership [of the secessionist movement] were significant business people in the San Fernando Valley. Not big business, not General Motors. . . . It was land developers, some attorneys, substantial members of the chambers of commerce within the San Fernando Valley. . . . The guy who was head of the San Fernando Valley Board of Realtors . . . was one of the founders of . . . CIVICC. . . . Just call him . . . the Godfather. . . . He's also a . . . regional vice-president of the L.A. County Board of Realtors."[49]

The president of CIVICC, Steve Frank, was the public affairs officer for a medium-sized firm in the San Fernando Valley that made kitchen and ground-support equipment for airliners. Frank wanted economic growth in the Valley and argued that the controversial Burbank airport should be expanded (even though he lived under the flight path of another valley airport). Although Frank disagreed with homeowners groups on growth issues, he agreed with the homeowners who wanted to see their tax dollars spent in the Valley rather than downtown. Frank argued that for every dollar of city taxes paid in the Valley, only fifty cents was spent in the Valley; for every dollar of county taxes, only thirteen cents.

The city's and county's miserly spending in the Valley, according to Frank, made a dramatic contrast to its wasteful spending downtown. "You have an idea of how large the San Fernando Valley is. In 1977 from midnight to 6 A.M., the San Fernando Valley had a total of eight police cars at night. . . . Eight!" Meanwhile, millions of dollars had been spent on urban redevelopment projects, such as the stadium for the Los Angeles Dodgers and the high-rise apartments and condominiums on Bunker Hill adjacent to downtown:

You mean the ripoff of Bunker Hill? . . . The theft? . . . One of the causes, at least in the 70s, that got CIVICC together was rapid growth of these redevelopment agencies with their incremental financing. Incremental financing means those communities [like the Valley] that are not part of the redevelopment project wind up paying extra taxes to pay for it, whether we like it or not. . . . We want a dollar's worth of services for a dollar's worth of taxes.[50]

In other suburban communities, similar movements arose with the aim of breaking away from Los Angeles County. In 1975 and again in 1978, hundreds of people in the Santa Clarita Valley gathered signatures on petitions that would have established a separate Canyon County. The chair of the county formation committee, Dan Hon, was an attorney who was on the board of directors of the Canyon County Chamber of Commerce and the Newhall Business and Merchants Association. Hon argued that the goals of the movement were similar to CIVICC's—to reduce taxes and overcome powerlessness. County taxes collected in the Santa Clarita Valley exceeded the funds spent there by about ten million dollars. County formation was also "a fight for local control, a fight to bring government to the people. The gripe that you hear from the man in the street, and I consider myself one of those, is the lack of responsiveness of government. Unfortunately, our lives are being now governed by people that we cannot elect. We have a bureaucracy that just won't quit. It's huge." In a new county, "you would have the Board of Supervisors elected who lived in the area, who shopped in the area, and who would have to be responsive because everyone would know them by name. The supervisors of L.A. County, on the other hand, are anonymous."[51]

Similar arguments were raised in the South Bay area of Los Angeles County, where a secession movement was led by real estate broker Jim Walker. "The truth is, we've got three percent of the population paying six percent of the tax, and that's basically inequitable." According to Walker, much of their property tax payments went to county police and fire departments that the South Bay never utilized because the town governments in the area provided the services themselves. "The South Bay Committee . . . is committed to supporting the new county if there is in fact an actual tax savings."[52] Here again, homeowners in the suburbs discovered that they had a common interest with community business leaders who wanted to pay lower taxes. Both groups united around lowering taxes for homeowners and businesses in the suburbs, by calling for the suburbs to break away from the inner-city areas that drained the budgets of big government.

But throughout the 1970s, not a single community managed to secede, as the political leaders of Los Angeles County and the City of Los Angeles fought to keep their tax base intact. Despite the immediate failures, county-formation movements did leave two important legacies.

First was a pattern of cooperation between homeowners and businesses to reduce the taxes for both groups. Business leaders began to take an active interest in reducing the taxes not only on businesses but also on homes. Ernest Dynda started his community involvement as a director of the chambers of commerce in Agoura and Las Virgenes, defending business interests: "If you tax business too much, you put too much of an overhead on business up front, you're going to kill the goose that laid the golden egg."[53] Then, as Dynda saw the property tax bill on his own house rise from $500 to $2,400, he gathered signatures for Proposition 13 from the homeowners in the western fringe suburbs of Los Angeles County. (He later succeeded Howard Jarvis as the president of the United Organizations of Taxpayers.)

Meanwhile, homeowners were becoming more favorable to lowering taxes on business. In upper-middle-class communities, homeowners were rejecting proposals from middle-income communities to lower taxes on homeowners only and to let business pay the same or even higher rates. The leader of the homeowners group in Studio City described his constituency as "affluent." "All of our stuff would be high end . . . the upper twenty percent of the cost of houses." This activist opposed proposals to let business pay a higher tax rate than homeowners, posing the question himself: "Should there be a differential between commercial property and residential property? I don't think so. [Question: At the time of 13? Answer:] I don't see any reason for a differential."[54] Similarly, Jim Walker, leader of the South Bay secession movement and the Homeowners Under Rapacious Taxation in upper-middle-class Manhattan Beach, felt that taxes should be lowered for business and commercial property as well as for homeowners.

> Well, I've got some reservations about businesses being taxed any differently than our taxes. . . . Property should all be taxed the same. Businesses pay additional taxes through the Board of Equalization and other things, and they're carrying more than their fair share. . . . I don't think that just because you are a business you should be paying more than an adjacent property owner who is a residential user. And the notion that we're gonna all of a sudden be relieved from our responsibility to pay by passing it on to someone else is terribly odious to me. I don't think that that's right.[55]

The program of Proposition 13, tax cuts for both business and homeowners, would be the final expression of this unity of interests.

Overcoming the Bounds of Power: Constructing Territorial Alliances

The second legacy of county-formation movements was a widening circle of cooperation among towns and communities in areas the size of the San Fernando Valley or the South Bay. Building cooperation between communities was no easy task. Community business leaders seeking to sell condominiums or elegant dinners are competitors to their counterparts in nearby communities. Homeowners associations compete to put the ugly apartment building or the freeway off-ramp in someone else's backyard. Collective action to defend home-based consumption first encompasses one's immediate neighborhood. To reformulate Lenin, if the spontaneous consciousness of workers is the economism of trade unions, then the spontaneous consciousness of the besieged homeowner is the fragmentary localism of the neighborhood crime watch.

The tendency of homeowners to fragment was accelerated by government tax policy. All of the properties in Los Angeles County were not reassessed each year; those that were revalued did not increase by the same percentage. One neighborhood was hit with a 200-percent increase, whereas an adjoining neighborhood escaped reassessment for years. Such comparisons made provocative newspaper stories. The reassessment process, in short, pitted neighborhood against neighborhood.

In addition, communities compete with one another to offer advantages specific to a particular geographic place, such as good schools or an attractive environment. Residents then seek to make those benefits exclusive to themselves. One leader characterized this as the "lifeboat philosophy: I've got mine—you stay out."[56]

As a result, homeowners associations in a community were frequently suspicious of similar organizations elsewhere. Paul Gann's coordinator in southern California described how several associations in adjacent neighborhoods used the same meeting hall but never cooperated or met together until the campaign for Proposition 13. "I compare them [homeowners associations], unkindly I guess, to gangs . . . in south Los Angeles. They've all got their little turfs and they're very protective."[57]

County-formation movements succeeded in unifying the fractious community groups in major areas such as the South Bay and the San Fernando Valley. Community-based small businesses and upper-middleclass activists coordinated the activities of neighborhood groups (representing hundreds of people) and community groups (representing tens of thousands). From these groups leaders built area-wide organizations that could speak for hundreds of thousands. County-formation movements challenged the power of larger economic and political institutions at the metropolitan and statewide levels where constituents numbered into the millions and tens of millions. It was on this ground that the county-formation movements were defeated. But the coalitions of communities into areas would arise once again.

Tax protest activists then turned to another strategy to challenge big government at the metropolitan and state levels. "Secession and 13: they were tied together."[58] The campaign to put Proposition 13 on the ballot would continue the key alliance between community business and home-owners and would articulate a program of tax reductions for both. But the spatial form of the tax revolt would no longer divide geographical area from area. The success of the tax reduction movement depended upon building horizontal alliances among communities throughout California, as well as vertical alliances between middle-income and upper-middle-class homeowners and business leaders.

Action: The People's Campaign

Howard Jarvis and the United Organizations of Taxpayers worked hard in 1976 and 1977 gathering signatures in southern California. These efforts grew into a triumphant show of unity that culminated by placing Proposition 13 on the state ballot. The participants in tax protests hoped to recapture their power as citizens. By working for Proposition 13, activists could feel "that the public was actually running government rather than being run by government." Another activist described the exhilaration and camaraderie among the volunteers, whose work for Proposition 13 led them to realize that "they were the government."[59]

Homeowners in upper-middle-class communities took the lead in tax reduction activity and, in those communities, leading small businesses made major contributions. Acting together, they discovered that they had the people—along with the resources, the organization, and the skills—to halt the taxing and spending of big government. In Santa Monica's most upscale neighborhood, "The Santa Monica Homeowners Association was formed by businessmen. . . . That group was formed primarily for the people who were in real estate and business who were seeing escalations in their taxes."[60] In the San Fernando Valley, the tax protests of 1976 increased the cooperation between homeowners and businesses. At the first sign of discontent, the San Fernando Valley Board of Realtors placed newspaper advertisements containing a protest letter that could be sent to government officials. A vice-president of a community chamber of commerce served as the master of ceremonies for the first large tax protest meeting in 1976. The Round Table Council, composed of nineteen Valley chambers of commerce, harshly criticized the increased assessments on homes.

This pattern of cooperation between homeowners and business helped make the petition campaign a success. One tax protest group in the Valley, Taxpayers Watchdog, tapped the business community for donations: "We would go to someone like . . . [name withheld], [who] is a very influential

community leader, with raising money and so on. . . . He owns a Ford
dealership. We have a list of many small businessmen that we can go to
and will help us." The owner of a chain of muffler shops "gave us a
tremendous amount of help, both financial [and] physical, and he passed
literature for us; he got petitions signed. . . . The Chevrolet place . . .
they were a great help to us. . . . There were . . . printers . . . who contributed. . . . We had a certain kind of assistance . . . from the gentleman
who owns the Hughes [grocery] markets. . . . A lot of businesses were
more than eager to help us put petitions in their store, to sign."[61] Realty
boards "became part and parcel of the campaign":

> Local board[s] of realtors were very cooperative. . . . My job down here
> was to keep them supplied . . . [with] petitions. . . . They'd give the peti-
> tions to the salesmen who was [sic] going out and showing property. . . .
> And when it come to the question . . . that the person was going to ask
> when buying a home, . . . what the tax rate is . . . , and so that would give
> them [the realty agents] the opening sesame to bring this question up and
> they would get this person to sign the initiative. They [the agents] had
> them with them all of the time.
>
> One of the Red Carpet places . . . I went out there and they said, "We
> only have twenty salesmen here, but we do have a lot of people coming in.
> So do you have a sign I could put in the window?" . . . This was done in a
> lot of the real estate companies. . . . But later on . . . they begin to use
> this as an excuse to . . . interview [solicit] people who are willing to sell
> their home or trade it or buy a new one.[62]

The Sherman Oaks Homeowners Association, the affluent homeowners group that led tax protests in 1976, coordinated the signature gathering for Jarvis's initiatives in the entire San Fernando Valley and Westside
of Los Angeles. Thirty volunteers worked to direct the efforts of hundreds of signature collectors. The weekly meetings of the Sherman Oaks
Homeowners provided the opportunity for other homeowners groups to
obtain advice and coordinate their activities. In the San Fernando Valley
alone, residents gathered more than 250,000 signatures for Proposition
13, out of a total of 499,846 valid signatures needed in the entire state.
One out of every three adults in the Valley signed.

Down the coast, Virgil Elkins, the chair of the petition campaign in
Orange County, reported that the strongest support came from the affluent communities of Newport Beach and Laguna Hills.

> We had a lot of people come in on 13 that never showed up before. We
> had a lot of business people come forward. We had attorneys; we had
> bankers. There was one banker come [sic] in here one day . . . he had five
> banks, and he wanted a hundred petitions [blank forms]. . . . They had
> million-dollar homes down there and I don't know what kind of taxes they

were paying. In fact, my Newport cochairman down there was a multimillionaire and a retired industrialist.

[Question: Were any developers or real estate people involved? Answer: . . . In Proposition] 13? Oh, all kinds of them. Yeah, you take Red Carpet [Realtors], [Century] 21. . . . The Orange County Board of Realtors come forward . . . [and] got petitions, got their members to talk it up. . . . The realtors really worked on it, no question about that. . . . In fact . . . [the] Citizens United [the tax reduction group] first vice-president was a member of Red Carpet. He's the one who really got Red Carpet to go to bat for me here in Orange County. . . . Local industry and business down here, why they were for 13.[63]

Meanwhile Paul Gann was also organizing a network of volunteers who were gathering signatures, mainly in central and northern California. The owner of a novelty shop in Fresno was coordinating the efforts in the Central Valley: "What really put across Proposition 13 was the apartment owners' association. . . . [T]hey gave money and they had meetings and they got people to sign petitions and, really, I think that's what put it across." Paul Gann also thought that the support of community businesses was crucial. "I had chambers of commerce all over the State of California helping me, I had real estate people in every section of the State of California. In fact, they make the difference, believe me—small business and real estate. Those people . . . who were out there selling that property, were the people that had taken that petition [around]. And they obtained signatures and signatures and signatures." All told, Jarvis and Gann submitted 1,263,698 signatures to the California secretary of state; they had another 300,000 that could not be processed in time.[64]

To the Biltmore Hotel

With Proposition 13 on the ballot, suburban communities continued their revolt against the headquarters of big government in downtown Los Angeles and in Sacramento. In middle-income communities, actions to protest high property taxes became occasions to urge voters to support Proposition 13. In Glendale, more than seventy-five persons demonstrated with signs supporting Proposition 13. One elderly protester had been forced to sell her home because of high property taxes and found Howard Jarvis the perfect embodiment of her frustrations. "I'm all for Jarvis and I don't give a damn what happens to the system. I lived in Glendale for 40 years and I'm mad." The residents of Glendale and nearby communities—shouting, "Hey, hey, we won't pay," "Hey, hey, we can't pay," and "Taxation without representation is tyranny"—

marched to the branch office of the county assessor and dumped tea bags on the receptionist's desk.[65]

On the Palos Verdes peninsula, the Citizens for Property Tax Relief (CPTR) took a somewhat different approach, providing speakers, consultants, and fact sheets for the campaign for Proposition 13. Every month CPTR wrote the newsletter "Tax Facts," which detailed the sharp increases in local government spending, the latest extravagant government purchases, and the unflattering excuses of politicians. "With the bullet items and the two- or three-liners, people will read it. And they found it devastating." CPTR also created files of registered voters and their occupations and then used word processors to generate customized letters "addressing the issue from their point of view. What it means to them and their shop, so you can be lethal. . . . To a mechanic you say, Do you realize how much of your rent goes to property tax? Do you realize what it will be three years from now?"[66]

Valley residents formed an independent campaign committee, Californians for Proposition 13. Meeting at the good old Chevy dealership that had assisted them from the tax protests in 1976, they raised funds and organized campaign events. A week before the election, Steve Frank roped off his street and threw a block party in support of Proposition 13. One thousand people attended, including Howard Jarvis and a crowd of local media reporters. "Small business owners were really the backbone of the campaign." "The Apartment Association was deeply involved in Proposition 13. Howard Jarvis was the director of the Apartment Association of Los Angeles County and used that as one of his bases to raise money and to conduct the campaign. . . . They made large contributions; they solicited their membership for contributions."[67]

Indeed, the largest contribution to the campaign for Proposition 13 was $31,000 from the Apartment Association of Los Angeles. Earlier, a computerized mailing to apartment owners had yielded $120,000 in donations. Of the major contributors (larger than $1,000) to the campaign for Proposition 13, most ($80,000) came from real estate and agriculture.[68] In securing contributions from landed businesses, Jarvis did as well as Watson had done ($76,000) in an initiative campaign during 1968. (See table 4 in chap. 6). Jarvis had what Watson lacked, however—a grassroots movement. Most of the $2.3 million in support of Proposition 13 came in small donations from hundreds of thousands of homeowners. In the Yes on 13 campaign, contributions of less than $1,000 accounted for 92 percent of the funds (compared to only 20 percent for Watson and 29 percent for opponents of Proposition 13).

Although suburban homeowners had gained the support of community business leaders and especially small businesses dealing with land, no support was forthcoming from big business. Large corporations such as

Standard Oil of California, ARCO, the Bank of America, Dean Witter, Paine Webber, Ford, U.S. Steel, Bethlehem Steel, Kaiser Aluminum, Lockheed, Rockwell International, Bechtel, Hewlett-Packard, Crown-Zellerbach, Levi Strauss, Coca-Cola, Southern California Edison, and the Southern Pacific railroad made large contributions against Proposition 13. Although the campaign for Proposition 13 raised $124,000 in large (over $1,000) contributions from business, the No on 13 campaign raised $652,000 in large contributions from business. Although both the Yes on 13 and No on 13 campaigns each raised over $2 million, No on 13 mostly relied on big business and labor organizations. Jarvis tapped relatively small donors—small property owners who were at odds with big business, big labor, and big government.

Big business's opposition to Proposition 13 irked many small property owners. The Orange County coordinator for Prop. 13 condemned a big business group opposing 13: "They oppose everything that is for the people." Supporters of 13 picketed the downtown offices of the Bank of America because of its stand against the proposition.[69] A tax activist and business leader in the San Fernando Valley, himself the public affairs director for a medium-sized firm, spoke like a populist: "Big business works to create laws that help protect it. They support more regulation, and they can afford more regulation. Small business can't. . . . The best thing that happened to this state and this country was the passage of Proposition 13. It had nothing to do with taxes or economics. What Proposition 13 taught people is that you can go against government, you can go against big business, you can be a little guy on the block, and you can win."[70]

Election day was June 6, 1978. The realtors in La Canada and Flintridge had been talking up Proposition 13 with their sales prospects for weeks. Some 40 percent of the realtors in the town were making calls to remind people to vote today—and yes, houses would only get more expensive the longer one delayed buying. By late evening, the results were starting to come in. Ignored was the vote of the inner-city community of Compton—27 percent in favor of Prop. 13. On the Palos Verdes peninsula, "We carried 76 percent in our lowest turn-out precinct in the Prop. 13 election. We carried most by over 90 percent!"[71] Rolling Hills was 95 percent in favor; Palos Verdes Estates, 89 percent. In the San Fernando Valley communities of Van Nuys and Reseda, 73.8 percent cast ballots in favor; in Northridge and Sepulveda, 77.6 percent; in Canoga Park and Woodland Hills, 81.4 percent; and in Chatsworth and Valencia, 84.2 percent (compared to 64.8 percent statewide).[72] By nine o'clock Howard Jarvis was on his way to the Biltmore Hotel. By ten o'clock the generic-label Scotch was beginning to flow at the victory celebration.

Postmaterialism, Liberalism, and
Other Upper-Middle-Class Chimeras

The tax revolt in upper-middle-class communities, in short, had begun with a simple materialistic impulse, to spend money on family and consumer goods and not on increasing tax bills. Property taxes threatened to deprive even the most affluent of their prized material possession, their home. This materialistic impulse took direction as protesters aimed at redistributing money toward themselves[73] and away from the inner-city population of Los Angeles, away from welfare and other social programs of big city and county government. Goals were further refined as professionals in upper-middle-class communities joined with community business leaders in supporting a program of tax cuts for homeowners and businesses, enshrined in Proposition 13.

It is not surprising that community business leaders acted in self-interest, favoring tax cuts for themselves and taking their usual stand against government social programs. What is noteworthy is the reaction of the homeowners in upper-middle-class communities who were not business owners or top managers—who instead were college-educated professionals. The professionals' unabashed materialism, their stance against government programs, and their probusiness alliance in the late 1970s seemed to be a significant departure from their leftist political orientation a decade earlier.

In the 1960s, the public image of professionals was dominated by the lawyers who joined legal aid societies, the physicians active in the Medical Committee for Human Rights, the educators who spoke out for racial integration, and the students in elite universities who protested against the Vietnam War. Many a writer concluded that there had to be something about professionals or their work or training that generated critical views of society.

Ronald Inglehart concluded that professionals who had been raised in affluent families had come to reject the conservative values of economic expansion and materialism. Instead, they adopted "postmaterialist" values such as environmentalism, the quality of life, and personal development and expression. Inglehart further argued that postmaterialist values led to political leftism, an opposition to the establishment, and the advocacy of radical tactics. Similarly, Burnham argued that the liberal tendencies among professionals led them to advocate a more reform-minded and activist federal government. Other writers argued that a basic characteristic of professionals was their hostility not only to materialism but to business as well. Alvin Gouldner suggested that a "new class" of professionals was trying to win control of institutions and government policy, at the expense of the "old class" of moneyed business leaders. The growing importance of professionals and intellectuals in an increasingly knowledge-based world would supposedly increase the political influence of the new class.[74]

The tax protest movement that professionals helped to build in California seemed to be a living refutation of the theories that pointed to the supposedly leftist views of the "new class." Contrary to the arguments of Inglehart, professionals did not reject but rather championed materialist values. They opted not for militant protest but rather for electoral politics. Rather than expanding the scope of government programs, many professionals voted to slash them. Professionals searching for political power found it, not by challenging business leaders, but rather by allying with them at the local level.

The popularity of tax protests among professionals points to dangers of making sweeping conclusions about the political consciousness of professionals. A detailed social history of the tax revolt is useful because it highlights the political views of different types of professionals. The appeal of the tax revolt suggests that some types of professionals, who have been deemphasized by new-class theories, are actually more powerful than previously realized.

For example, the tax reduction movement attracted many lawyers in small partnerships practicing in fields such as real estate. These attorneys could themselves be considered small business owners, who dealt with other small business owners everyday. They were worlds apart from the more liberal but less numerous law school professors and attorneys specializing in public interest law, criminal law, and labor law. Furthermore, the tax reduction movement attracted many engineers and business service professionals, such as accountants and financial analysts. The movement attracted fewer artists, journalists, social scientists, and college professors, who generally hold more liberal views.[75]

In the politics of an upper-middle-class community, one would expect the more conservative business owners, managers, and business and technical professionals to prevail over the liberal professionals simply because the conservative occupations are more numerous. In the United States in 1979, as seen in a study divided by gender, there were 750,000 men in business or the conservative professions with earnings of $50,000 or more. These included business owners, corporate managers, sales supervisors and representatives, accountants, engineers, physical scientists, airline pilots, and navigators. In the same income bracket there were less than half as many men (320,000) in the liberal professions, including public-sector managers, architects, social workers, teachers, writers, artists, physicians, and health professionals. (Lawyers and judges were not tabulated.) Even in the $25,000 to $50,000 bracket, businessmen and men in conservative professions outnumbered those in liberal professions by three to one. Among women in the $50,000 and above bracket, there was a more even balance between those in business and conservative professions (28,000) and those in liberal professions (20,000). But this is overwhelmed by the startling fact that men outnumber women in the $50,000 and above bracket by eighteen to one.[76]

The history of the tax revolt also points to the political power of an older generation of professionals, as opposed to the 1960s generation that is supposedly rising in influence. The Woodstock generation of professionals, who did not fight in Vietnam, had at the time of Proposition 13 aged into their thirties and forties. They were the experts who, according to Inglehart, were serving in key congressional staff positions and other jobs that led to the top posts in government and business. But the tax reduction movement was the triumph of an older generation of professionals, who had fought in World War II or in Korea, and then had aged into their sixties. They had bought houses in California when land was cheap, mortgages were at 5 percent, and tax bills were two hundred dollars a year.

These fortunate people who arrived in California when dreams could still be golden became outraged at the property tax increases of the 1970s and mobilized for Proposition 13. They insisted that Prop. 13 contain a grandfather clause that distinguished between their generation and future generations of homeowners. Those who had already owned their home in 1978 would receive a bonus. Their property tax assessments were rolled back to the levels of 1975, just before home prices and assessments had gotten out of hand. But for younger Californians, the reality was not golden, only parched, dry brown. Younger homebuyers, who perhaps had delayed having children and had purchased after 1978, found that their assessments were equal to the market price they paid—a price outrageously inflated by the continuing California real estate boom.

In short, theories of the new class err when they portray younger or liberal professionals as powerful enough to lead or transform society through their expert knowledge. Such theories exaggerate when they portray professionals as a political force that can challenge the power of big business. But theories of the new class are useful because they highlight how the political consciousness of professionals was not monolithically conservative. The activists in the tax revolt who were liberal professionals, and even many who were business owners and managers, supported consumer and environmental regulations. Professionals wanted government amenities and limits to new construction and growth to protect the quality of their homes and their lives. Their stand on these issues has at least kept the politics of professionals from being a clone of big business conservatism.[77]

8

The Politics of Probusiness Tax Limitation

Oh Holy Father, please hear the concerns that are on people's minds as they try to hold their families together.[1]

There are moments when our prayers and the prayers of our friends and loved ones help to see us through and keep us on the right path.[2]

After the Proposition 13 uprising in California, the tax revolt was rampaging across the nation. Voters approved the Headlee Amendment in Michigan, limiting property taxes and state expenditures, and then Proposition 2½ in Massachusetts, drastically reducing property taxes. Howard Jarvis formed the American Tax Reduction Movement and barnstormed the nation, gathering two million signatures in support of the Kemp–Roth bill to lower federal income tax rates. The National Taxpayers Union and the National Tax Limitation Committee advocated a convention that would amend the U.S. Constitution to require a balanced federal budget each year. By 1989, with thirty-two state legislatures already in support, the approvals of just two more states would convene a convention instructed to write a highly controversial and inflexible economic policy directly into the U.S. Constitution.

How did the tax limitation movement spread throughout the nation? California seemed to offer a model for success. Howard Jarvis had brought together a diverse coalition—suburban businesses and realty boards together with homeowners and their neighborhood associations. The victory of Proposition 13 demonstrated that it was possible to unite probusiness and antistate constituencies.

Proposition 13 inspired measures such as Proposition 2½ in Massachusetts. But before that proposition passed, Massachusetts followed the example of the activists from the middle-income communities of Alhambra, San Gabriel, and Venice, California, who fought for a tax cut that would redistribute downward, away from big business and toward the blue-collar homeowner. Somewhere Karl Marx writes that history occurs, as it were, twice. He forgot to add that the first time is prophetic; the second, tragic.

The Working-Class Presence

In Dorchester, a working-class community south of downtown Boston, property tax assessments had climbed to the astounding rate of 119 percent of value, compared to 15 percent for downtown and around 22 percent for the better-off suburbs of West Roxbury, Allston, and Brighton. The Dorchester Community Action Committee (DCAC) organized neighborhood meetings where angry residents could file petitions to have their assessments reduced.

> We went to a meeting . . . and I found out this house should have been assessed for $7,500. . . . I said, gee, here I am $2,000 more a year than I should be paying. . . . I was getting the run-around here and I really got aggravated. . . . I'd just come out of the hospital, and I was so sick and weak, but I said, hey, I'm going to fight Kevin White [the mayor of Boston] if it's the last thing I do. . . .
>
> I wasn't working at the time because my kids were young. . . . It's only my husband's salary coming in, I said, how can we do this? I've worked so hard for eighteen years to have this home, I've made so many sacrifices, [and] I'll be damned [if] you're . . . going to take it away from me now, I said, I'll fight. . . .
>
> You've got to fight, you've got to stick together, you really do.[3]

And fight they did. They filed a huge stack of petitions to reduce assessments and met at City Hall to demand action. Neighbors called neighbors—twelve hundred had formed a telephone network—to tell about the next protest actions. During the 1975 city election campaign, they summoned Mayor White to a community meeting; White sent an assessing commissioner who was roundly criticized by a crowd of four hundred. Later, eight hundred people rode buses to protest near Kevin White's house.

At a time when Dorchester, with one-third of its population black, was fraught with racial tensions and outright riots over school busing, DCAC held some of the only community meetings where blacks, whites, and Hispanics could be seen together, and not fighting one another. A few days after a violent demonstration by an antibusing group, the South Boston Marshals, three hundred fifty persons crowded into a Catholic parish hall to discuss property tax abatements. Most of the whites in the audience opposed school busing; although one-quarter of the gathering was black, few had spoken up. As an elderly black man stood up, the entire hall became still:

> I want to talk about what we are doing here but I also want to talk about what happened this weekend. . . . Well, I don't care how you feel about certain issues but, all of us have common problems as we are paying way too much in taxes. And some people, we have heard tonight who they are, don't pay their fair share. And we pay more than our fair share. But I want to tell you there are people in this city, in high places and others, who would love to see us start fighting each other. But if we stick together and if we remember that we all need each other, we can win.

The man sat down. For a moment no one moved. Then, wild cheering broke out.[4]

Through meetings such as these, blacks and whites won lower property taxes that helped them to hold onto and improve their homes, contributing to the stability of a neighborhood that at one time seemed on its way to becoming a ghetto abandoned by the middle class. Over a four-year period, some 2,500 homeowners in Dorchester won assessment abatements.

In the white, lower-middle-class town of Somerville, it took years of organizing even to achieve more limited results. After four years of holding ward meetings on neighborhood problems, Somerville United Neighborhoods (SUN) charged that there was a surplus in the city treasury which the mayor was hiding so that he could lower the tax rate just before the next city election. SUN called officials before a meeting of three hundred fifty residents demanding an immediate tax cut. As aldermen equivocated, saying they needed more time to think about it, residents shouted, "How much time do you need?" The tax rate was cut, but only by 3 percent.[5]

The neighborhoods of Somerville bristled against not only politicians but also community business leaders, especially those involved in real-estate development.

> It's kind of hard for anybody, individuals or even a few people, to go up to city hall and get any action for the problems that they have. . . . [T]hey were in a [public housing] project or had struggled all their life to make a living and rented, and it was a struggle even paying the rent, when they saw somebody in their neighborhood buying two or three houses, and the

next thing you know it was torn down and apartment houses were going up. . . . Those are the people who really . . . wanted to fight building.

We were always in opposition to the chamber of commerce. That's a terrible organization in Somerville, eh!, absolutely disgusting. . . . I think most of the members are fine, as they are small businessmen and they are struggling as everybody else is, but the leadership, they're real estate interests in Somerville. . . . [One leader in the chamber] owned a great deal of property here in Somerville, he was a slumlord, and he had . . . done everything that we were basically against.

Consumers were concerned about their homes and neighborhoods; business owners, with profits. For one activist, this contrast was epitomized by a statement of the head of the chamber of commerce, who said that "he didn't think Somerville was a decent place to live. He was glad that he moved his family out of Somerville to Beverly."

He was right there at the right time to buy a lot of property at very reasonable prices and he took advantage of it, being in the real estate business. . . . These guys . . . got a hold of these houses a few years ago and then took advantage, somehow . . . of all these rehab[ilitation] programs and built the houses up, . . . and they still ended up having paid maybe $3,000 or $4,000 for a house and today they probably sell them for $100,000.[6]

SUN also protested that a shopping center developer had received a large abatement on his property taxes and that a developer of a 500-unit apartment project had his property taxes reduced to zero.

In their struggle to gain political influence, DCAC, SUN, and other groups in middle-income communities that composed Massachusetts Fair Share certainly did not have the support of large businesses or even the leading small businesses in the community. Fair share developed a characteristically militant posture; during one campaign for lower utility rates, Fair Share activists organized noisy picket lines at the electric and gas company headquarters and chased one unfortunate executive all the way home to his luxury high-rise building. But in contrast to California, the militancy in Massachusetts middle-income communities was harnessed to a different form of organization with different goals.

Fair Share groups had tens of thousands of dues-paying families. Fair Share operated with a budget of about $30,000 in Dorchester and $75,000 in Somerville; unlike its counterparts in California, it was able to hire several staff organizers, including activists from the federal program Volunteers in Service to America (VISTA). Organizers in a community formed sponsoring committees of clergy and other leaders and then went door to door, canvassing two thousand households and looking for perhaps two hundred persons willing to participate in a community meeting.[7]

Radical Statehouse

In California, middle-income communities had no self-empowering organizations and thus merely assisted in initiatives of other groups and followed Howard Jarvis as a media hero. Massachusetts Fair Share, however, developed an organization that enabled it to challenge big government somewhat more successfully. For example, the homeowners in Dorchester who filed for tax abatements received larger reductions compared to Californians who filed assessment appeals. And in 1978, when the Massachusetts budget surplus swelled to $200 million, Fair Share fought for and almost won a tax relief law—a circuit breaker, whereby the state would provide up to $500 for homeowners and renters who paid property taxes in excess of 8 percent of their household income.

At the hearings for the circuit-breaker bill, Mike Regan's testimony before state legislators was cut short. Then he warned, "Before we leave, we want you to know something. We want you to know . . . that we are just about ready to blow . . . our tops. . . . We are going to blow a fuse."[8] As the security guards gasped, he walked up to the committee chairperson, reached into his pocket, and placed two blown fuses on the table, followed by a procession of 150 other Fair Share activists who did likewise as the television lights glared.

During the last hectic days of the 1978 legislative session, Fair Share activists from Dorchester, Somerville, Chelsea, Lynn, and Springfield came in buses to occupy the capital. They stayed in shifts, so that for twenty-four hours, day after day, they were on the phone, calling; in the galleries, watching; and in the hallways, following, asking always: "How will you vote on the circuit-breaker bill?" When the bill was finally called up, Mike Regan came straight from his job at the candy factory to keep the vigil at the capital. At 6 A.M. he had to return to work, unable to afford losing a day's pay. As Mike Regan napped on a pallet in the candy warehouse, some of his compatriots fell exhausted and dozed on the benches in the statehouse. But most were on hand to see the Fair Share bill pass the Massachusetts house and then the senate.

Governor Michael Dukakis had criticized the circuit-breaker bill all along, preferring to use the state surplus to aid education and subsidize local courts. Dukakis had ten days to sign the bill, or the bill would lapse by pocket veto. On the ninth day, he had not signed. After discovering that Dukakis would appear that day in the town of Revere, Fair Share mobilized over one thousand protesters to pack the meeting hall. Inside, a few managed to ask questions of the governor; others were thrown out, pushed around, or arrested, as the overflow crowd outside grew more and more angry. The police kept a black government car in front as a decoy and used another car to take Dukakis out from a back exit and through the crowd. On the tenth day, Dukakis still did not sign, blocking the modest $50-million Fair Share plan for property tax relief.[9]

Big government in Massachusetts was forced to be a little more accommodating than in California but, in the end, was still unresponsive. City government did actively support one Fair Share campaign, but it was not to reduce property taxes, just to stop an impending quarter billion dollar tax increase for beleaguered homeowners. The increase stemmed from a 1974 Massachusetts Supreme Judicial Court decision, *Town of Sudbury* v. *the Commissioner of Corporations and Taxation,* in which the court ruled that localities had to assess all property—homes and businesses—at 100 percent of value. Since homes had been assessed at much lower rates compared to businesses, the Sudbury decision meant a huge increase in taxes for homeowners and an equally large reduction for business. In Boston, 100-percent valuation would increase tax bills for the average one-family home by $700, whereas the average commercial property would pay $1,700 less and an industrial plant $5,200 less.[10]

Fair Share proposed to split the tax roll and classify the property tax, assessing homes at 40 percent of value, commercial property at 50 percent, and industrial property at 55 percent, with a homeowner's exemption of $5,000 included for good measure. These tools of downward redistribution this time would be employed defensively, merely to stop the imminent shift of the tax burden from business to homeowners. Mayors threw their weight behind a program of restoring the status quo and preventing a tax increase on the homeowners, who would have thrown the mayors out of office. Kevin White poured a million dollars of city money into the 1978 campaign for the classification amendment, Question 1, while the Massachusetts Mayors Association worked statewide. Classification passed by a two-to-one margin.

Still, of all the states, Massachusetts had the highest effective tax rates on single-family homes and the highest property taxes as a percent of state personal income.[11] Even with classification, homeowners were just treading water. Many wanted to just pull the plug and drain the pool.

Fair Share devised a "tax-breaker" plan to reduce property taxes by 10 to 20 percent for owners of residential property, with landlords required to pass half their saving on to tenants. To compensate localities for lower revenues, the state would provide funds from new taxes to be levied on commercial banks and professional services offered by lawyers, real estate brokers, architects, and accountants. At one blow, Fair Share drove a wedge between the working class and the upper-middle class. For this Fair Share plan, the politicians, themselves lawyers, brokers, and accountants, were unresponsive.

In order to place the tax-breaker initiative on the 1980 ballot, Fair Share had to gather 60,000 signatures in just two months, October and November 1979. Now that the issue was reducing property taxes, the public employees who had worked for the classification amendment backed away. The teachers' association did not help the tax-breaker campaign because it would reduce revenues available for education. One public employees' union continually promised to collect 25,000 signatures but, with only one week to go, turned in only 2,000. With the weather growing colder day by day, all Fair Share staff took to the shopping malls, the town dumps, and even the early morning MTA trains, collecting signatures in a round-the-clock effort.[12] One could almost hear the trudge, trudge of the Scott Expedition pulling their own sleds in a desperate bid to reach the South Pole. Fair Share expired, 5,000 signatures short. Like the Scott Expedition, who had been beaten by a Scandinavian team, someone else had gotten there first.

Business-Populism in Suburban Massachusetts

Barbara Anderson led the expedition of the Citizens for Limited Taxation (CLT), which actually reduced property tax bills, not merely compensating for the unexpected tax increases brought on by the Sudbury decision. Their solution was Proposition 2½, which reduced property tax rates to 2½ percent of market value, resulting in a 1.5 billion dollar cut in tax collections statewide (and a 75-percent cut for Boston). As in Proposition 13, the cuts applied to both homeowners and businesses, with business getting the largest share of the relief.[13]

Politicians, fearing any significant reduction in government revenues, vigorously opposed proposals for a 2½-percent limit. Although Massachusetts representative Royall L. Switzler introduced a bill calling for a 2½-percent limit, a week after the passage of Proposition 13 in California, he received almost no support from legislators. The mayor of the town of Newton warned that a 2½-percent ceiling would lead to drastic cuts in services. "So people want to give up their library? Do they want their rubbish pickup once a month rather than once a week?" Only 5 Massachusetts house members out of 160 voted on May 1980 in support of a 2½-percent limit. Of 155 candidates for office surveyed before the November 1980 election, 76 percent opposed Proposition 2½ and 85 percent favored repealing it, amending it, or imposing new taxes to compensate for lost revenue.[14]

Frustrated by the inaction and the unresponsiveness of government, citizens formed a social movement that gathered the signatures to put Proposition 2½ on the ballot. This movement, headed by the group Citizens for Limited Taxation, then spearheaded the campaign that led a 59-percent majority of the voters to approve the proposition. Like the tax protest movement in California, the movement in Massachusetts brought together homeowners in upper-middle-class communities, the residents of middle-income communities attracted to a charismatic crusader, and the leading businesses in the suburbs (see table 8).

Edward F. King founded the Citizens for Limited Taxation in 1972

Table 8   *Massachusetts Tax Reduction Movements by Income Level in Communities*

Massachusetts Fair Share (Selected communities with active chapters):	*Median Household Income, 1979*
East Boston	$9,470
Chelsea	11,201
Dorchester	12,500
Somerville	14,401
Waltham	18,615

Citizens for Limited Taxation (Communities where taxpayers' groups endorsed Proposition 2½ by November 1977):	
Worcester	$14,116
Chicopee	15,452
Pittsfield	15,854
Quincy	17,376
Brookline	19,536
Marblehead	23,982
Holliston	25,822
Wellesley	32,547

Comparison areas:	
City of Boston	$12,530
Massachusetts	17,575
Boston Stnd. Metro. Statis. Area	18,694

by targeting his appeal to upper-middle-class professionals then making $50,000 and above. King was campaigning against a proposition that would have instituted a progressive tax on personal incomes in Massachusetts.

> It was a question . . . of getting a stockbroker, a good one, and saying, look, get all your compatriots. . . . Mortgage lenders in the banks, they all have an association. . . . It was relatively simple to get three or four key people that I knew from just regular business contacts. . . . Doctors, dentists, they were for me. . . . What you do to those people is just grab them by the throat and scare the daylights out of them.
>
> You say, look, the graduated income tax is going to be on the ballot. How much money do you make? . . . Let me show you what will happen to you if this passes. You do a few figures on paper [—For a taxable income of $50,000, the tax would have been $4,150—] and say, how would you like that? . . . This is what you'd pay and they all go [sucks in his breath to imitate the collective ah's of the audience]. . . . They go Holy Christ, what can I do about that? Well why don't you get a meeting of your friends. . . . If you've got a checkbook with you, you can give the money now. . . .
>
> We raised all kinds of money. That's how we built our grass-roots organization.[15]

Edward King could certainly give a straight pitch to the self-interest of the affluent. But like Howard Jarvis, King had a highly personal, emotional popularity among those who lived in South Boston and other middle-income communities.

> The working-class areas! . . . Any place where you found working people, those were my strongholds, yes indeed. . . . I was a working man's Republican. . . . I used to always talk about my background. My father was a meat cutter and my mother was a member of the International Union of Electrical Workers, and I used to always tell stories about unemployment and poverty. . . . I remember, I still do, I get dry mouth when I think about it. I remember my uncle. . . . I remember laying [sic] in bed at night waiting for my uncle's footsteps . . . because he brought the milk. We couldn't afford milk. . . . I'd hear the refrigerator door open and close, and my mother and father used to leave the room when he came up the stairs because they had too much pride to take the milk. . . . I used to talk about those things, those very real things that happened to me, and the image of the wealthy Republican . . . never stuck to me. . . .
>
> I used to march in the parades . . . in the working-class areas, in these heavily Democratic areas. It was like the Second Coming. . . . I just had a great rapport with those people and the feeling was mutual.

King's appeal was sentiment for the little guy and resentment for the big guy, which included not only big government but also big business.

> The bigger the business got, the less likely they were to like what we were doing. . . . The corporate barons never really liked us all that much. . . . There was an unholy alliance between what I call . . . the spenders and the lenders. . . . In Massachusetts . . . when the state government overspent its income it simply went to the First National Bank of Boston, the State Street Bank and Trust Company, the Bank of New England, and all the big banks, and borrowed millions and millions and millions of dollars and guaranteed to pay it back with seven, eight, nine, ten percent interest and guaranteed it at the expense of the taxpayers. . . . So we quickly found out that the banks were in bed with these [government] bastards. . . .
>   We had threats. I was called into one of the banks. . . . I have a witness. And I was told like a Mafia meeting, "Get off our turf." . . . [Question: Was it a personal threat to you physically?] If it would have been that I would have hit him. . . . It was very firm . . . not a physical threat: . . . You're not going to get funding any more, and you're going to make a lot of enemies . . . and I know you want to run for office someday, and you'll need friends. . . .
>   [Question: What about utilities?] They're regulated by the legislature and they were very careful, they didn't want to get too involved because they were afraid the legislature would wreak its vengeance on them. A lot of the big construction companies make their money building bridges and things for the state, so we found out . . . that our movement truly was a middle-class movement.

The Massachusetts Taxpayers Foundation, the voice of large banks, insurance companies, and utilities, opposed Proposition 2½ as too drastic. The foundation praised the more modest steps that the state legislature had already taken—lowering the capital-gains tax and the meals tax and limiting municipal spending.

But even if big business was no friend to the populist activities for Proposition 2½, small-scale businesses could still be part of We the people. According to the first executive director of CLT, small businesses provided much support. The owner of two sandwich shops, who later started a chain of over one hundred Papa Gino's pizza stores, contributed money and office space. CLT sent a mailing to the 13,000 members of the National Federation of Independent Business in the state. The Massachusetts State Automobile Dealers Association board of directors endorsed the proposition and contributed $20,000. (Prop. 2½ contained a provision reducing the excise tax on automobiles.) A few chambers of commerce (such as those of the South Shore, greater Lowell, and Framingham areas) provided help. Ed King spoke of the support from real estate businesses: "I have no quarrel with the real estate people in

Massachusetts. . . . They were very good. I went and spoke to different real estate groups around the state. They were receptive. They all put signs up in their windows; they gave us money."[16]

In California, the leaders of real estate and other suburban businesses were important, not only because they contributed directly to the tax revolt, but also because they helped to organize upper-middle-class homeowners in suburbs. The suburban businesses that played this key mediating role in Massachusetts were somewhat larger than in the California case. In Massachusetts they were the high-technology businesses along Route 128, which ringed the city of Boston.

Route 128, like the Pacific Coast Highway in southern California, is the road to the good job and the good life. The coast highway leads out to the beaches of Malibu and the marina at Newport Beach, and [literally] under the Los Angeles International Airport to the Hughes aircraft and space complex. Route 128 leads out to weekends on Cape Cod and in to the Lincoln Labs and the companies designing computers and communication and medical equipment. The quintessential intersection here is the interchange between Route 128 and the Concord Turnpike—the crossroads of American postwar modernism, born of the universities just to the east, hastened by the great Sputnik panic, and concretized in the architecture of shining functionality.

But as the miracle of Route 128 began to be mirrored by the lesser gods of Irvine, Sunnyvale, and Palo Alto, California—and of Austin, Texas; Chapel Hill, North Carolina; and even Phoenix, Arizona—a group of Route 128 firms formed the Massachusetts High Technology Council in 1977. In a few years the council grew to represent over one hundred corporations employing one hundred thousand persons. Massachusetts companies, competing nationally to attract more engineers and managers, found it difficult to recruit professionals to move to a state where the cost of living was high, the personal tax burden was 9 percent higher than in other states, and the property tax burden was the highest in the nation. Massachusetts high-tech firms complained about job offers that were turned down, vacancies that remained unfilled, and salary premiums of 20 to 30 percent that had to be offered.[17]

Concerns about their costs and the growth of their businesses led the High Tech Council to become involved in the problems of upper-middle-class consumers and homeowners. It became the business of the council to work for a lower cost of living and lower taxes for individuals. The council set out to reduce property taxes, not only on their own businesses but also for the homes of their professional employees.

Although the High Tech Council was a step up from suburban chambers of commerce and realty boards, the council's power nevertheless had its bounds and limits. The firms that composed the council were relatively new, especially when compared to those represented by the Massachusetts Taxpayers Foundation or the Associated Industries of Massachusetts (which spoke for manufacturing firms). The High Tech Council was not yet an established political interest group. The council, for example, proposed a fairly modest amendment to the Massachusetts constitution which would have limited overall state revenues to a percentage of state personal income. Even though the council, working with Citizens for Limited Taxation, gathered the required number of signatures, the Massachusetts legislature adjourned in July 1980 without even voting on the amendment.

Angered at the rebuff, the council decided to fund the campaign for Proposition 2½. The Citizens for Limited Taxation in September 1980 had only $19,000 to wage a campaign in the election that November. The council raised $246,000 for 2½, which helped to counteract the $547,000 from the Massachusetts Teachers Association in opposition to the proposition.[18] At the victory celebration for Proposition 2½, there was the spirit of Howard Jarvis, the ghost of Mass Fair Share, and, some say, the aroma of Papa Gino's pizzas.

The Rise of the National Taxpayers Union and the National Tax Limitation Committee

In localities throughout the United States taxpayers waged initiative campaigns like Propositions 13 and 2½, appealing to both businesses and citizens, and protesting against their tax burden and unresponsive government. The National Taxpayers Union encouraged these local efforts and tried to forge similar alliances in a nationwide political effort.

Founded in 1969, the National Taxpayers Union (NTU) grew slowly at first, attracting 1,800 members in its first year. In contrast to the Capitol-based interest groups who owned block-long office buildings and represented millions of constituents, the NTU rented a basement in the yet unfashionable southeast section of Washington and could claim only 6,000 members in 1973. Two years later, the NTU embarked on a membership drive. At the same time, it began a campaign to convince state legislatures to call a convention that would amend the U.S. Constitution to require a balanced budget.

The NTU did provide some assistance to the movement in California for Proposition 13. The NTU helped one taxpayers group in North Hollywood, the United Voters League, by providing ready-made articles for a local newsletter along with the names of potential volunteers from mailing list. The NTU helped to gather petition signatures, and it sent three organizers to California and provided $10,000 for advertisements during the campaign for Proposition 13. But despite this help, the Prop. 13 movement, with its thousands of volunteers and its small donations totaling millions of dollars, was essentially a home-grown product of California. The "new right," which later would initiate several of Ronald Reagan's policy departures, was at this time only a collection of political outsiders, almost extremists, still struggling for recognition.[19]

The new right did not create Proposition 13; rather, something of the reverse was true. The passage of Proposition 13 in California helped to inaugurate new alliances that helped to turn the new right into a national crusade. The executive vice-president of the National Taxpayers Union (NTU), joined the organization in the exciting days after Proposition 13 passed. He recounted, "It was an important moment in taxpayers' history because it gave everything a boost. Congress was scared; every politician in the country was scared. . . . You could sense the momentum—a lot of people got much more active. And since 1978, twenty states have passed tax- or spending-limitation laws."[20]

The success of Proposition 13 in California energized efforts throughout the nation. "The [balanced] budget amendment drive was given tremendous impetus in 1978 by the victory of Proposition 13 in California. . . . Proposition 13's astonishing success was a turning point for the taxpayers' movement and for the country itself." By 1979, the NTU had 130,000 members, was spending over two million dollars a year, and had convinced thirty states to support a constitutional convention to balance the budget.[21]

One reason for NTU's successes was that it managed to appeal to both businesses concerned about their tax bills and to grass-roots citizens concerned about taxes and government power. Between 1977 and 1984, NTU's principal publication, *Dollars and Sense,* contained many articles arguing that taxes harmed business and that taxes on businesses should be reduced. *Dollars and Sense* also frequently argued that politicians were unresponsive to citizens and the government wielded excessive power that jeopardized individual freedoms.[22]

Arguments against the power of government were also raised by the numerous state and local taxpayers organizations that cooperated with the NTU. In New York in 1978, 500 leaders of 80 local groups rallied to the cry of "More for the people, less for the state" and formed a coalition, the United Taxpayers of New York State, affiliated with the NTU. Another affiliate, the Connecticut State Taxpayers Association, was itself composed of 70 local groups. The United Taxpayers of New Jersey, an alliance of 200 groups, assisted in the NTU's balanced-budget campaign.[23]

In Oregon, Ray Phillips won his reputation as a fighter against taxes.

A former professional boxer turned boilermaker, Phillips founded the Oregon Taxpayers United, which eventually attracted some 35,000 supporters. Oregon Taxpayers United defeated a proposed state sales tax by a four-to-one margin during a 1985 referendum. Emphasizing citizen activism to exert power over government, Phillips urged, "As citizens we must study the issues, vote, and take control of our government."[24]

Activists also called for citizen power over government during a successful recall in 1983 of two Michigan state senators, David Serotkin and Philip Matsin, who had supported a 38-percent increase in the state income tax. Matsin was a Democrat representing a seemingly safe blue-collar district in Pontiac, where one out of four employees was a member of the United Auto Workers. Matsin was defeated even though he outspent the recall group by a ten-to-one margin. For Mick Steiner, chair of the recall group, the issue was taxation without representation and citizen power over government. "We proved that you can fight City Hall and win. We've held them [the politicians] accountable. . . . Now people realize that in spite of their political affiliation, if they aren't happy with their representation, those responsible can be taken out of office. It's called representative government."[25]

From its headquarters in Washington, the National Taxpayers Union espoused many of the same themes. On the eve of the 1980 elections, the NTU launched a "People Power Plan for the 1980s," an ambitious proposal for grass-roots organizing. A fund-raising letter proclaimed, "The truth is we've got a government of, by, and for [the] politicians and government employees." The goal of the plan was to "mobilize the massive power of the average American taxpayer. To mobilize *your* power. To make the government *responsive* to *you* once again."[26]

Beset with higher tax bills, many citizens felt that they were powerless and that the government was out of control. The Internal Revenue Service became a potent symbol of abusive government power. In a poll of the NTU membership, 91 percent replied that a priority should be working "to enact safeguards to protect taxpayers from IRS abuse." The NTU testified and lobbied for legislation strengthening the IRS Ombudsman, limiting IRS powers to seize property, allowing taxpayers to pay delinquent taxes in installments, and reimbursing legal costs for taxpayers who win court judgments against the IRS.[27]

In addition to its grass-roots support on issues about government power, the NTU succeeded in winning support from business. The NTU favored two changes in tax laws long sought by the business community—reducing the corporate income tax rate and ending the so-called double taxation of dividends. (Federal taxes are levied on both the corporation that declares a dividend and the individual who receives dividend income.) Furthermore, the NTU supported lowering the capital gains tax, arguing that this tax "reduces the amount of investment capital available to new emerging businesses."[28]

According to NTU chair James Davidson, small businesses are the prime supporters of his organization. Small businesses were concerned about fiscal policies and federal government deficits because these influence interest rates, which in turn affect consumer finance and the sales of small businesses, particularly real estate brokers and auto dealers. Small businesses depend on loans that are also vulnerable to high interest rates. In Michigan, for example, small businesses and trade associations such as the state association of realtors, the Michigan Chamber of Commerce, and the Michigan Association of Home Builders joined the NTU in lobbying the state legislature to call a constitutional convention to balance the budget.[29]

Small- and medium-size businesses had begun in the 1970s to exercise leadership in the suburbs of California, helping to give the homeowners a probusiness program. In Massachusetts, medium-sized, high-tech firms threw their support behind a property tax cut at a crucial moment. More businesses throughout the nation were actively working for probusiness tax limitation schemes, particularly the moderate initiatives like Michigan's Headlee Amendment, which limited the growth of government rather than slashing taxes. When it came time to pass the Reagan administration's major pieces of legislation—the Gramm–Latta budget resolution (1981), the Economic Recovery Tax Act of 1981, and the Gramm–Rudman–Hollings budget-balancing act, the nation's largest businesses, those companies on the *Fortune* magazine listings, were providing active support. Whereas large businesses had opposed Prop. 13, their increasing political activity now led them to join a tax limitation movement that was clearly espousing a probusiness program.

The Rise of Big Business Political Activism

Big business participation in the tax limitation movement was a product of a broader trend beginning in the mid-1970s—increased business activism in politics. The business community had been accustomed to using trade associations to lobby government administrators on behalf of a particular industry. By the late 1970s, however, the public affairs departments in large corporations were directing ambitious new efforts to appeal to the public, affect elections, and raise controversial policy issues. Two innovations in particular, advocacy advertising and the corporate political action committee, helped big business to increase its political clout.

Advocacy advertising differed from the promotion of a company's products and the traditional corporate-image advertising (the innocuous announcements on public television, for example, which keep the corporate name in the public mind associated with higher virtues). Advocacy advertising, on the contrary, directly addressed contentious political issues, emphasizing probusiness arguments and countering the claims of critics. The American Electric Power Company, for example, placed 5,690 print advertisements that attacked the U.S. Environmental Protection Agency's regulation of coal-burning power plants. W. R. Grace and Company bought ads to publicize its views on the federal income tax. Corporations spent $140 million on such advocacy advertisements in 1976; the Mobil Corporation alone spent $5 million. By the end of the decade roughly one in five major U.S. corporations were using advocacy ads.[30]

Another indication of business's increased political involvement was the political action committee. Political action committees (PACs) are organizations (with catchy acronyms like 6-PAC for a beer-industry group) that solicit campaign contributions from managers and workers in a firm or industry. By 1978, over 1,000 business PACs were contributing $17 million for federal races and another $20 million for other campaigns. (By contrast, labor contributions amounted to less than half these amounts.) In 1982, the Business Industry Political Action Committee (BIPAC) contributed $200,000 to 145 candidates and helped to direct the contributions of other business PACs to crucial elections.[31]

Business became more involved in politics, because government had become more involved with business. Government had enacted regulations on corporations, which the environmental, consumer, and public-interest movements had insisted upon. By 1975, over fifty thousand federal employees were administering regulations about occupational safety, consumer products, and clean air and water. In 1976 business spent over ten billion dollars to comply with such regulations. Whereas automobile production was almost completely unregulated by the federal government before 1966, in the decade that followed, the government specified detailed standards regarding fuel economy, exhaust emissions, and safety.[32]

In the late 1970s, executives of top corporations felt beleaguered by government regulations that encumbered managerial decisions about what to produce and how to produce it. Large businesses sought to counter their critics. One executive felt, "We need more political sophistication. We have to tell a state considering additional restrictions on business: 'The next plant doesn't go up here if that bill passes.' " Another urged, "We should cease to be patsies and start to raise hell."[33] Big business was mad at government and was not going to take it any more, either.

One way of getting back at the government was through the National Tax Limitation Committee (NTLC), founded by Lewis K. Uhler, who had been an advisor to Governor Ronald Reagan of California. NTLC's founders and officers included prominent conservatives such as Milton Friedman, M. Stanton Evans, and Clare Boothe Luce.

Business was a key constituency for the National Tax Limitation Committee. In Vermont for example, John Hunter, the president of the Vermont National Bank, was present at a meeting of local business leaders. "We were sitting around at the end of the meeting—it was about the [community] hospital, things like that—when we got on to the way the federal government keeps running up spending and debts. . . . Someone mentioned the movement to get a balanced-budget amendment to the Constitution." Hunter was soon heading the Vermont Tax Limitation Committee and was urging town meetings to pressure the state legislature to call for a constitutional convention to balance the budget. All in all, thirty thousand businesses, including forty listed in the *Fortune* directories of large corporations, contributed funds to the NTLC. Over one hundred business and trade associations are on record supporting the NTLC's balanced-budget amendment to the Constitution.[34]

Compared to the National Taxpayers Union, the National Tax Limitation Committee emphasizes the grass-roots less than business constituencies. The NTLC does not encourage local chapters. Rather, in order to reach its audience, the NTLC uses three major public relations firms and four regional directors to provide information to television, radio, and print outlets. In addition, the NTLC extensively utilizes computer-generated mailings. In the first years of its existence, the NTLC relied on mailing lists developed by Richard A. Viguerie, who also helped numerous "new right" and fundamentalist causes. In 1981 and 1982, the NTLC sent approximately 30 million pieces of mail to members and potential supporters.[35]

The increasing political activism of business in the late 1970s affected the course of the tax limitation movement. As homeowners, individual taxpayers, and citizens sought help in reducing their tax burden, they began to encounter a business community that, for its own reasons, was increasing its political activity. The success of Proposition 13 encouraged business to campaign for further tax reductions and limits. Businesses provided resources for the tax limitation movement but insisted on a program that would benefit businesses. The NTLC and the National Taxpayers Union are the latest examples of an alliance between business and grass-roots constituencies that has produced the revival of fiscal conservatism in the United States.

Conclusion:
Postcorporatist Protests
and the Reconstruction of
Inequality

The story of the consumers' tax revolt, and the probusiness tax limitation movement that followed, exemplifies how a protest can rebel against, and then reshape, major economic trends and political institutions in unforseen ways.

Political movements between 1800 and 1945 in the Western world battled over the key issues of economic production. In the United States, the Southern Farmers' Alliance and the populists defied the banks, merchants, and railroads; the Knights of Labor, the Wobblies, and other labor unions fought the business trusts, climaxing in the 1930s with the rise of the Congress of Industrial Organizations. Yet by the 1930s, labor unions, business, and the government were cooperating in a new pattern called corporatism.

The sparks of corporatism flickered in the National Recovery Administration, where the government organized groups of businesses to help determine production levels and prices. Corporatism became a steady glow as federal spending began to climb, and a hopeful ray when President Roosevelt built a political party in the blue-collar districts and established the National Labor Relations Board to recognize and regulate the trade union movement. Corporatism emerged into the spotlight during World War II, as the presidency coordinated the plans of the armed forces, gained the cooperation of big business, and enlisted the support of labor, now organized labor, by maintaining union membership in defense plants and by naming labor representatives to the War Labor Board. With labor, business, and war all united, this mighty corporatist machine emerged beaming and triumphant in a world that had been destroyed.

In Western Europe and Japan, former enemies and allies alike took up the corporatist model, outshining the victor as they reconstructed business cartels, expanded government administration, and remembered to include labor in the deal. But amid ambitious global arrangements, there were those whom the dominant institutions had forgotten, those whose stirrings created postcorporatist movements like the tax revolt.

These postcorporatist movements would begin with protests, though usually not about wages and production, but rather broad, sometimes ill-defined questions about the institutions that dominated economic and political life. The first anticorporatist grumblings in the United States took place around 1910 during the Progressive Era, even before the full implementation of corporatist trends. Business and government had already become national in scope, mega-bureaucratic in scale, and arrogant in their unresponsiveness. The new big businesses caused white-collar workers and professionals, uneasy about their status, to yearn for a society that would provide recognition and opportunities for the individual. In the cities, the power of political bosses led reformers on a crusade to weaken party organization and create a polity guided by individual informed citizens.

More recently, the maturing of corporatism has given rise to a generation of new postcorporatist movements—anti-institutional revolts that have challenged the policies and power of corporations, government agencies, labor unions, and universities. Anticorporatist movements have arisen on issues of race and gender, community, and peace and the environment, creating patterns of conflict different from the older class conflicts that had brought on corporatism and the welfare state earlier. New movements objected to their exclusion from corporatist institutions and raised issues about social life not encompassed by corporatist compromises.

The civil rights protests in the southern United States around 1960 first arose around issues of social life—the segregation of buses, schools, and public facilities. The black community went on to challenge discrimination in major corporatist institutions—government, trade unions, and employers. Although much of the black movement later made its accommodation with Democratic presidents, poverty programs, and black mayors, other protests quickly arose to further challenge corporatism. Inner-city communities protested against plans to demolish homes and build high-rise projects favored by the local corporatist coalition of downtown business, construction unions, and mayors and redevelopment agencies.

Socialist feminists shunned interest-group politics and argued for a comprehensive challenge to business, unions, and other patriarchal institutions that subjugated women. The antiwar movement sought to counterpoise itself against the military, defense contractors, and universities which supported the war in Vietnam. And the property tax revolt battled big government, which spent and spent to benefit its corporatist partners—economic development projects for business, and wages and pensions for public-sector unions.

The German sociologist Max Weber, writing around the beginning of the twentieth century, saw a society dominated by the narrow rationality of bureaucracies in government, business, the army, and the church, unresponsive to the populace and a threat to democracy itself. Even as anticorporatist protesters fought the iron cage of bureaucracy that Weber had so vividly described, they had to confront anew the economic divisions born of an earlier century, between those who owned businesses and those who worked for bosses. Postcorporatist movements became inextricably involved in the process whereby economic inequalities persisted, were compounded, and were recreated—the process first chronicled by Karl Marx. As movements fought corporatist bureaucracies, the movements articulated their programs for redistributing benefits and incomes, thereby clarifying the economic interests that they pursued, and the interests that were opposed.

Redistributive programs do not automatically arise just because the participants in a movement belong to a certain category of people that has an obvious group or class interest. Rather, programs evolve over time and are formed and reformulated through political processes. As protesting groups make affiliations with others and discover shared objectives and dispositions, so then do programs for reform develop.

In postcorporatist movements, a community is the place where a group creates the informal organizations that test friends and discover adversaries. The tax revolt was sustained by homeowners groups and other community organizations, which eventually banded together to gather petition signatures and campaign for Proposition 13. For the suburban homeowners groups, the major issues were not production but rather consumption, both by private households and in the public sector. Community life had been built on patterns of consumption, which were also patterns of inequality. As tax protest activists contested those structures of inequality, they took actions that nevertheless reconstructed further patterns of inequality.

Inequalities are perpetuated in many ways, sometimes out of bare necessity, sometimes by hidden, gradual trends. In blue-collar suburbs, as more dwellers crowd in seeking affordable housing, the cost of providing residents with government services increased, leading to higher tax rates compared to more affluent suburbs. Inequality some-times directly resulted from the policies of corporatist elites, such as urban renewal programs that provided subsidies for large developers while destroying homes for low-income people. Perhaps most interest-ing are the inequalities unwittingly reconstructed by movements that begin with the hope of reducing injustices and protesting the greater power of corporatist institutions.

Many tax protest activists during the years before Proposition 13 lived in working-class and lower-middle-class communities, where they soon sensed that big government and the corporatist institutions allied with government would be generally unresponsive to the problem of property tax bills too large for people to pay. Meanwhile, the leaders of small businesses in the suburbs sought to reduce their own tax bills and discov-ered that their power was bounded and did not extend to big city and big county government that controlled tax policy. Suburban business leaders sought to build popular pressures to counter the corporatist stranglehold on tax policy and gradually developed an affiliation with the homeown-ers in upper-middle-class communities.

Although these homeowners had the advantages of professional skills, high income, and education, they learned that their advantages were frustrated because they too were unable to influence the downtown corporatist institutions to reduce property taxes. Over time there was a noticeable change in how homeowners and businesses cooperated with each other and thought of each other. Tax protest leaders spoke less of downward redistribution programs.

The tax revolt became a movement of suburban businesses and profes-sionals who used their skills, resources, and influence in their communi-ties to organize a campaign directed against the higher levels of govern-ment and other corporatist institutions. The triumph of the tax revolt annihilated the corporatist complacency that the unrepresented could be taxed to pay off the interest groups. But the winning alliance also saw to it that the spoils of victory went to both homeowners and businesses, the latter, in fact, receiving most of the benefits. Here was an anticorporatist revolt, where the small property owner finally produced a program that further reconstructed inequality.

The little entrepreneurs, the managers with their demiurges, and the petty technicians who C. Wright Mills so aptly described four decades ago, did not vanish into apathy or fade into the political rearguard. Even as Mills was writing, in the small world of suburbia, neighbors met in living rooms, friends at the clubhouse, and Rotarians over breakfast to talk about their property tax bills. But out of these "micro" interactions, came the block clubs and homeowners associations, and finally the coali-tion of community groups that gave the property tax revolt its strength.

The community was the linkage between face-to-face interaction and "macro" processes involving inequalities and policies in the society at large.

But the consequences at the national level were not what the homeowners originally had in mind. Awakened by the success of Proposition 13, small business and eventually even the old corporatist enemy, large business, campaigned for the winning program of tax breaks for both business and middle-class individuals. The public-relations efforts for Proposition 2½ and the Kemp–Roth bill gave wide publicity to supply-side and probusiness arguments. As Milton Friedman toured the country and the Laffer Curve became a household phrase, probusiness ideologies emerged ascendant in the mind of the middle class. Born of changing affiliations in communities and matured by historical processes, small property owners gained a class consciousness of sorts, but quite the opposite of what Marx had favored.

Not all postcorporatist movements, of course, end up promulgating probusiness beliefs and programs that redistribute income from the poor upward to the affluent. Postcorporatist movements turned left as well as right. The consumerist movements inspired by Ralph Nader have challenged major corporations; one consumers' group in 1988 used a California ballot initiative to drastically limit the rates charged by auto insurance companies. Environmental movements have demanded that businesses disclose the hazards of workplace chemicals and compensate employees for injuries caused by asbestos and coal dust.

But typically, postcorporatist movements take more contradictory, ambiguous, or untold positions about business and economic inequality. The antiwar movement confronted defense industries, but college students' opposition to being drafted meant that low-income and minority youth were disporportionally killed in Vietnam. Although the feminist movement has created opportunities for professional and business women, it has had fewer successes improving the lot of secretaries and clerks.

The story of the tax revolt is relevant to other postcorporatist movements. This is so not because history must repeat itself, nor because business necessarily wins the old battle of employer versus worker. The case of the tax revolt exemplifies the processes that other postcorporatist movements must go through, the pressures that they face, and the issues that they necessarily confront.

By raising social issues that corporatist planners have not considered and by organizing groups excluded from corporatist compromises, postcorporatist movements usually face the indifference or the outright opposition of powerful corporatist institutions. Localized protests must be unified into a movement that can effectively challenge the larger political institutions of region, state, and nation where corporatist interests have established their hold. Even when the movement's leadership makes a challenge, the problem remains of keeping that leadership responsive to the members, and authentic to the movement's original mission. Too often postcorporatist movements are not built with a clear program but are unified around the charismatic style of populist leaders who can turn conservative, like Jerry Rubin or Eldridge Cleaver.

Studying the social origins of a movement through in-depth interviews, one can understand how movement activists developed a folk wisdom about their position in society and what ought to be done about it. The historian's craft can uncover the story of how activists built a movement that resonated with folk wisdom. Studying how a movement's actions actually affected the structures of inequality can help individuals to better grapple with the powers and the trends that constrain their choices and their lives.

APPENDIX
Research Methods for Studying Social Movement History

Not being a participant in the tax revolt, I gathered information about it by using several interrelated research methods: historical, quantitative, and qualitative.

Archival Research

The first task, suitable for a historian, was to document the rather obscure events during the early years of the tax protest movement in California. I focused the investigation on the times and places that generated most of the property tax protests—Los Angeles, Orange, and Riverside Counties—culminating with the passage of Proposition 13 in 1978 and stretching back thirty years before. Beginning with the index and the newspaper clipping ("morgue") files to the *Los Angeles Times,* I then expanded my search of morgue files to include twelve other newspapers in southern California, including the daily community newspapers with the largest circulations in the three major suburbs of Los Angeles— the Van Nuys *Valley News* (San Fernando Valley), the Torrance *Daily Breeze* (southcoast beach communities), and the *San Gabriel Valley Tribune.* The *Los Angeles Times* was comprehensively indexed, but it often ignored protests that arose in outlying suburban communities, focusing instead on downtown politicians. Community newspapers provided better coverage of tax protests but filed old clippings unsystematically.

Tax protest activity reached peaks in three years (1957, 1964, and 1976). Within each year, I chose the thirty-day period of maximum participation and then scanned every issue of the *Valley News, Daily Breeze,* and the *Tribune* for that period, looking for articles about additional events. Morgue file research, like other archival work, requires one to persist in requesting creative categories of files, inside which then trivial, and now critical, information might be stored. Aiding my search was a growing list of persons, neighborhoods, and names of organizations involved in tax issues. For the communities that repeatedly erupted in tax protests, I sought to gain a sense of the context of the protests by investigating the history of other community controversies around issues such as urban redevelopment and growth.

The file of newspaper clippings provided information about the key protests, campaigns, and persons in the three-decade movement to reduce property taxes. This documentation, interesting in its own right, served to open up new avenues of research. Newspaper articles suggested lines of questioning in the interviews (see below) and were shown to informants to stimulate recollection and comment.

Coding of Events

I then sought to uncover any broad patterns in the protest events which might be related to other regularities or social structures in society at large. This required me to systematically compare protests that arose in different times in different communities by gathering the same information about each of the protests.[1] I coded the newspaper accounts of all tax *protest events,* that is, public meetings and demonstrations where the major issue was high property taxes. For each protest event, I determined the location (census tract and name of community), the date, and the number of participants. In the press accounts of tax protests, there was probably less error in estimates of the number of participants, compared to, for example, descriptions in the nineteenth century of large and dispersed crowd actions. This is so because the great majority of the tax protest events involved participants seated in an auditorium or another public facility for a long period of time, so reporters were likely to have made fairly accurate estimates. Actions involving persons in a large outdoor area (e.g., scattered along streets) tended to involve few persons. Approximately 100 protest events were coded and were then grouped into **protest sequences,** that is, the events within one community during a fiscal year. There were 36 protest sequences, each of which drew a total attendance at events of 100 or more (table 2, 77–78).

For each protest sequence, I also examined press accounts for the reactions of business and government leaders, including the elected and top appointed officials of the City of Los Angeles and County of Los

Angeles. Government leaders could issue critical or supportive statements, or might consult with protesters, form study committees, or make changes in government spending or taxation.[2] I also determined the stance of government leaders in suburban towns, in those cases where communities had constituted themselves as independent political jurisdictions. (Towns and communities in California suburbs generally had populations of around 50,000, ranging from 10,000 to 150,000.)

I also examined how community business leaders reacted to tax protests. These community business leaders, who usually owned or managed small businesses employing fewer than fifty persons, were active in the community's chamber of commerce or realty board. In such organizations, a major role was usually played by small businesses with interests in land who favored growth of the community. Community business leaders could offer verbal and financial support to tax protests, and might even lead them.

It was soon apparent that the response of business and government leaders depended upon whether the protests originated in affluent or in middle-income communties. I devised a measure of community socioeconomic status (SES) using U.S. Census reports. One measure of community SES was median family income. Family income was measured, instead of the income of families and unrelated individuals, in order to better portray the conditions of homeowners, who comprised a major constituency of the tax revolt. The median family income of a community was then divided by the figure for the Los Angeles–Long Beach Standard Metropolitan Statistical Area (L.A. SMSA) for the same year. (To obtain yearly figures from decennial data, I used linear interpolation.)[3] The resulting family income ratio was not drastically affected by increases in dollar values caused by inflation. The family income ratio, in short, was designed to measure relative consumer welfare.

Another measure of community SES was the percentage of professional, technical, and managerial workers. Included in this group are small business owners; excluded are sales and clerical workers without administrative responsibilities. The percentage of professionals in each community was divided by the figure for the L.A. SMSA in the same year. This occupations ratio was averaged with the income ratio described above to form a relative affluence index.

Areas with a relative affluence index greater than or equal to 1.30 were termed upper-middle class. Middle-income communities were those where the relative affluence index was at least 0.60 but less than 1.30.[4] These limits are comparable to the ones used by social scientists debating about the size of the middle class in the United States. Some define middle-class families as those earning incomes between 75 percent and 125 percent of the median; others use a higher upper limit of

1.42 times the median, or $43,800 in 1987.[5] Using the relative affluence index, I was able to systematically compare the responses of business and government leaders to protests that arose in communities of different socioeconomic status.

Extended Interviews

Interviews provided insights into the central process that this book explores—how movement activists interpret the unresponsiveness of big government and other institutions and then formulate courses of action, thereby defining the goals and interests that the movement pursues. The important actors here were the heads of the protest committees and the taxpayers and homeowners groups that provided the organizational basis of the tax revolt. The redistributive agenda of the tax revolt was set by the ideas and decisions of these activists and not by the beliefs of the general public or the decisions of the voters.

In other words, the relevant "universe" to be studied was not millions of California voters but rather a small group of movement activists. These were the activists, numbering in the hundreds, who in the early stages of the tax revolt organized signature-gathering campaigns. These activists were not the one million who signed the last petition that put Proposition 13 on the ballot. The methodological task, then, was *not* to survey a large sample of voters whose views were representative of all voters in California. It was to conduct as many interviews as possible with the key activists in tax protests before Proposition 13.

I developed an expanding list of activists' names from newspaper articles discovered through morgue files, indexes, and scans of back issues. Also helpful was a list of forty names published in 1976 in the first issues of the *Taxpayer's Watchdog* newsletter. I utilized the mailing lists and contacts supplied personally by Howard Jarvis, Paul Gann, the Citizens for Property Tax Relief (Palos Verdes peninsula), and the Taxpayer's Watchdog organization. (This San Fernando Valley group provided a list of sixty names in Los Angeles County.) Informants were asked to provide names and phone numbers of other activists, which produced a snowball effect of many additional names in the early stages of the research project, tapering off at the end as the suggested names had already been interviewed. Interviews were also conducted with real estate professionals and business executives who had been politically active in local government issues, and with officials in the county assessor's office in Los Angeles, along with protest activists and business leaders in Massachusetts.

The major obstacle to obtaining interviews was not securing permission but merely locating and contacting the activists, particularly those involved in protests in 1957 and 1964. Some detective work was called for; I traced individual residences through old phone books and neighborhood acquaintances. A total of 120 interviews, most of them lasting around three hours, were conducted between 1981 and 1988.

The tax protest activists selected for interviews had detailed and valuable knowledge about local events which written primary sources had largely ignored. To use a fixed-response, public opinion questionnaire with the activists would be as inappropriate as administering such a questionnaire to a retired presidential cabinet member. The first part of the interviews with the tax protest activists resembled the oral history interviews that historians conduct with high government officials.[6]

During the interviews, informants were asked to confirm and elaborate on the data that had already been gathered from newspaper articles, documents, and previous interviews. The informants were continually asked to be specific, in order to reconstruct as detailed an account as possible of political processes and movement programs. Interviewers asked for clarification when informants lapsed into providing generalized, stereotyped, idealized, or blatantly self-serving accounts. The informants were also asked to provide accounts of previous protests in the community on issues such as housing, environment, government services, redevelopment, and growth.

What was important was not only an accurate account of events but also information about how the protesters had interpreted the events back then and had acted accordingly. Thus, the second portion of the in-depth interview was focused on the past beliefs that the protesters held when they had been most active in the movement. What was needed was information about how the activists interpreted the response (or lack of response) of government and business leaders. How did those interpretations affect the strategies or alliances the activists devised to deal with their lack of political influence?

For each interview, I composed a list of questions covering topics such as the informant's views about how government had responded to tax protests, about relations with protest groups that had arisen in other communities, about leaders and organizations that had attempted to unify the tax protest movement, and about the tactics, programs, and political doctrines commonly advocated during tax protests.

The questions were not asked in the same order for each interview. Each interview was a unique performance. As informants gave their detailed accounts, they usually volunteered answers to many questions without having been asked directly. Once an informant's flow of conversation began to move to a new topic, the interviewer would take the opportunity to pose the detailed questions that had been prepared in advance about that topic. Interviewers avoided interrupting informants with a question that would abruptly change topics. Only toward the end of the session would the interviewer proceed through the list and ask questions that remained unanswered.

In order to maintain the focus on the informant's views in the past, the interviewer's questions continually used the past tense and cue phrases such as "thinking back," "back then," and "in 1957." When informants lapsed into giving their present views on current topics, they were steered back into discussions about past events and opinions.[7]

In short, the methodological task was not to garner the opinions of the voting public but rather to study the interpretations made by a small group of activists about a specific political situation in the past. This was best accomplished not by using a fixed-response survey of a sample, but rather through utilizing a combination of oral-history interviewing and in-depth interviewing. To elaborate the processes of interaction and interpretation, one needs to systematically code primary data to establish the flow of events and their patterns, and then to conduct interviews that explore how activists formulated and then reformulated their political views.

Notes

Acknowledgments

1. Bill Haber (activist in Californians for Proposition 13 and Tarzana Property Owners Association), interview with the author's research project, Sociology Department, UCLA (Tarzana, Calif.: April 23, 1987).

Introduction

1. Alvin Rabushka and Pauline Ryan, *The Tax Revolt* (Stanford, Calif.: Hoover Institution, 1982), 37. A CBS-*New York Times* Poll revealed 51- to 24-percent support for a measure like Proposition 13; the Harris Poll also revealed two-to-one support among those with an opinion.

The provisions of Proposition 13 were summarized on initiative petitions as follows: "Limits ad valorem taxes on real property to 1% of value except to pay indebtedness previously approved by voters. Establishes 1975–76 assessed valuation as base value of property for tax purposes. Limits annual increases in value. Provides for reassessment after sale, transfer, or construction. Requires ⅔ vote of Legislature to enact any change in state taxes designed to increase revenues. Prohibits imposition by state of new ad valorem, sales, or transaction taxes on real property. Authorizes specified local entities to impose special taxes except ad valorem, sales and transaction taxes on real property."

2. Alvin Rabushka, "Tax and Spending Limits," in *The United States in the 1980s,* ed. Peter Duignan and Alvin Rabushka (Stanford, Calif.: Hoover Institution, 1980), 85–108. Austin Ranney, "The Year of the Referendum," *Public Opinion* 1 (December 1978), 26–27. Rabushka and Ryan, *Tax Revolt,* 189–194. *New York Times,* "Nationwide Tax Revolt Is Showing No Signs of Abating, Survey Finds," August 5, 1979.

By mid-1980, a total of seventeen states had adopted an overall limit on taxes and/or expenditures. Eight of these limits were the result of initiatives or referenda. See Winnifred M. Austermann and Daniel Pilcher, "The Tax Revolt Transformed," *State Legislatures* 6 (July/August 1980), 25–33. Austin Ranney, "The Year of the Referendum," *Public Opinion* 5 (December 1982–January 1983), 12–13.

3. According to Robert Kuttner in *The Revolt of the Haves: Tax Rebellions and Hard Times* (New York: Simon and Schuster, 1980): "The corporate tax lobby was distinctly uncomfortable with the crude, unreined populism of a Howard Jarvis and his remarkably similar counterparts in other states: Jim Wittenburg, the leader of Oregon's tax revolt, a convicted bad-check artist; Idaho's Don Chance, a retired insurance salesman; Bob Tisch, a rural Michigan drains commissioner."

4. Ibid., 293, 151.

5. *Chicago Sun-Times,* "Taxpayers United Plans Tax Strike in Lake County," April 26, 1978. *Chicago Tribune,* "James Tobin's War on Taxes," October 22, 1978. *Dollars and Sense,* "NTU Backs Illinois Taxpayers' Revolt," August 1978.

6. Barbara Anderson (executive director, Citizens for Limited Taxation), interview with the author's research project, Sociology Department, UCLA (Boston: December 17, 1984).

7. Ibid.

8. P. M. Williams and S. J. Reilly, "The 1980 U.S. Election and After," *Political Studies* 30 (1982), 371–392. See also Jerome L. Himmelstein and James A. McRae, Jr., "Social Conservatism, New Republicans, and the 1980 Election," *Public Opinion Quarterly* 48 (Fall 1984), 592–605. Richard B. Wirthlin, "The Republican Strategy and Its Electoral Consequences," in *Party Coalitions in the 1980s,* ed. Seymour Martin Lipset (San Francisco: Institute for Contemporary Studies, 1981), 235–266.

9. "What's Fair," *Time,* April 16, 1984. See also U.S. Congress, Joint Economic Committee, "Fairness and the Reagan Tax Cuts" (Washington, D.C.: Government Printing Office, 1984). In *The New Class War: Reagan's Attack on the Welfare State and Its Consequences* (New York: Pantheon, 1982), Frances Fox Piven and Richard A. Cloward estimate that 85 percent of the reductions in personal income and estate taxes went to taxpayers with incomes greater than $50,000 per year.

1. Whose Interests? Whose Programs?
Redistributing the Property Tax Burden

1. For a family with four exemptions.

2. Although an individual has an interest in obtaining the group advantage, the individual may or may not have an interest in contributing to the collective effort to achieve the group interest. See Mancur Olson, Jr., *The Logic of Collective Action: Public Goods and the Theory of Groups* (Cambridge: Harvard University Press, 1965).

3. Adam Prezworski, *Capitalism and Social Democracy* (Cambridge: Cambridge University Press, 1985).

4. "Writer Explores Reasons for Screaming County Tax Hike," *San Pedro News Pilot*, December 2, 1957.

5. Ibid. See the annual publication *Tax Payers' Guide*, published by the County of Los Angeles, Office of the Auditor. "Irate Property Owners Complain about Tax Hike," *San Gabriel Valley Tribune*, November 7, 1957. "Thousands Irate as Big Tax Bills Are Received in Mails," *Van Nuys Daily News*, c. November 7, 1957.

6. Law firm partner involved in Watson's campaign and in lawsuits of businesses to gain lower assessments (name withheld), interview with the author's research project, Sociology Department, UCLA (Los Angeles: August 20, 1984). "Many Changes, Thanks to Watson," *Torrance Daily Breeze*, July 23, 1965. "Committee Formed to Back Watson," *Torrance Daily Breeze*, May 27, 1962.

7. Felix J. Weil, "Assessor Watson's New County-Wide Reappraisal System" (Statewide Homeowners Association, Los Angeles, 1964, document in the author's collection). Philip E. Watson, "A Stranger at the Door," *Glendale News Press*, April 20, 1965. Los Angeles County, Department of the Assessor, "Biennial Report 1961–1963" and "Biennial Report 1965–1967." "Assessed Valuation Hits $14.4 Billion," *Valley News* (Van Nuys, Calif.), July 12, 1966. Los Angeles County, Office of the Assessor, press release, July 11, 1966, document in the author's collection. Beginning in 1974, the sale prices of properties anywhere near California's cities were increasing significantly year after year.

8. Diane Paul, *The Politics of the Property Tax* (Lexington, Mass.: D. C. Heath, 1975), 93; see also pp. 91–112. Kuttner, *Revolt,* 34–36.

9. Kuttner, *Revolt.* Around the same time, the California State Board of Equalization was reducing the property tax assessments on large public utility corporations from 50 to 25 percent. Such property accounted for 12.1 percent of all assessments in fiscal 1965 but only 6.7 percent in 1978. See William H. Oakland, "Proposition 13—Genesis and Consequences," *National Tax Journal,* Supplement, 32 (June 1979), 387–409.

10. Large increases also occurred in selected neighborhoods in Chatsworth Lake (a newer, upper-middle-class area, up 92 percent) and in gentrifying beach communities like Venice and Westchester (up about 70 percent). Meanwhile, the assessments on commercial property in downtown Los Angeles actually decreased 12.7 percent. California State Board of Equalization, Property Tax Department, Assessment Standards Division, "Assessment Practices Survey, Los Angeles County, 1972–73." Tax Increase Eased by Valuation Rise," *Los Angeles Times,* July 15, 1975; "Assessment Protest Filings Quadruple," July 29, 1975. Lydia G. Kinzer and Shirley W. Moltz, "A Longitudinal View of Sales Data for a Computer-assisted Appraisal Program," *Assessor's Journal* 10 (October 1975), 41–56.

11. California State Board of Equalization, Department of Property Taxes, Assessment Standards Division, "Assessment Practices Survey, Los Angeles

County, 1978–79." "Assessments Skyrocket 14%, Hit Top Level in County History," *Valley News,* July 13, 1976. "Property Taxes: Increases Cut Deep Into Budgets," *Los Angeles Times,* August 1, 1976, sec. II.

12. Ironically, Watson's defense in 1967 was that he was not offering a special favor to the Newberry Company, because other businesses had also received the same benefit, a reduction in the assessment rate from 45 percent to 25 percent when he took office. "Watson Faces Trial," *Torrance Daily Breeze,* February 7, 1967. "Watson Intervened in Two Tax Cases, Report Says," *Los Angeles Times,* March 16, 1977, sec. I; "Bellino Rigged Report—Watson," March 25, 1977, sec. I; "Less Rise Seen in Commercial Property Values," May 21, 1978, sec. I.

13. Frank Levy, "On Understanding Proposition 13," *The Public Interest* 56 (Summer 1979). Oakland, "Proposition 13," and California State Board of Equalization, "Annual Report 1978–79" (Sacramento, Calif., 1979), taken together indicate that between fiscal 1974 and 1978, net assessed value of all single-family residences increased 110 percent, whereas nonresidential property increased 36.6 percent.

14. Net assessed values include the exemptions for homeowners. The fiscal 1979 estimate was made prior to the passage of Proposition 13. California, Legislative Analyst, "An Analysis of Proposition 13" (Sacramento, Calif., May 1978), 25; California, Legislative Analyst, "Budget Analysis," 1977–1978 (Sacramento, Calif., 1977), A-32. Oakland, "Proposition 13." California's director of finance calculated that single-family residences accounted for 35.5 percent of assessments in fiscal 1973, increasing to 40.5 percent in fiscal 1977. "Outside Forces Siphon Funds—Tax Bills Grow," *Los Angeles Times,* October 21, 1977, sec. II. Levy, "Proposition 13."

15. Robert Kuttner and David Kelston, *The Shifting Property Tax Burden* (Washington, D.C.: Conference on Alternative State and Local Policies, 1979).

16. Jack Citrin, "Do People Want Something for Nothing: Public Opinion on Taxes and Government Spending," *National Tax Journal,* Supplement, 32 (June 1979), 114. Kuttner, *Revolt,* 147; Oakland, "Proposition 13," 391. Helen F. Ladd and Julie Boatright Wilson, "Who Supports Tax Limitations: Evidence from Massachusetts' Proposition 2½," *Journal of Policy Analysis and Management* 2 (1983), 261. For those requiring proof that people voted for Proposition 13 because they thought that their taxes were too high, Sears and Citrin constructed a model to see which demographic variables, symbolic predispositions, attitudes, and self-interests could best explain voting for tax limitation initiatives. In this model (which accounted for 27.5 percent of the variance) the variable with the largest direct impact (standardized coefficient) on voting in favor of the initiatives was the voter's perception that taxes were too high. David O. Sears and Jack Citrin, *Tax Revolt: Something for Nothing in California* (Cambridge: Harvard University Press, 1982), 121, 210.

17. Richard Close (president, Sherman Oaks Homeowners Association), interview with the author's research project, Sociology Department, UCLA (Century City, Calif.: March 9, 1982).

18. Kuttner, *Revolt,* 138, 154–155. Kuttner and Kelston, *Shifting Tax.*

19. One national survey indicated that 68 percent approved of a "higher tax

rate for wealthier people." Of those who agreed, 44 percent strongly agreed. "*Los Angeles Times* Poll," no. 81 (May 3, 1984), question 64.

20. Elliott Sclar, Ted Behr, Raymond Torto, and Maralyn Edid, "Taxes, Taxpayers and Social Change: The Political Economy of the State Sector," *Review of Radical Political Economics* 6 (1974), 147. Kuttner, *Revolt,* 319. Janice Perlman, "Grassrooting the System," *Social Policy* 7 (September–October 1976), 4–20. Robert K. Brandon, Jonathan Rowe, and Thomas H. Stanton, *Tax Politics: How They Make You Pay and What You Can Do about It* (New York: Pantheon, 1976), 268. Rabushka, "Tax Limits," 97.

21. Dean C. Tipps, "California's Great Property Tax Revolt: The Origins and Impact of Proposition 13," unpublished manuscript.

22. Sears and Citrin, *Tax Revolt,* 118. "Big Winners for California's Tax Cuts," *Los Angeles Times,* June 5, 1983. "Rich Got Richer Throughout State," in "Prop 13: A Year Later," reprinted from a series published in the *Long Beach Independent Press–Telegram,* June 10–17, 1979, 35. Oakland, "Proposition 13." California, Assembly Committee on Revenue and Taxation and Assembly Committee on Local Government, "The Property Tax Four Years after Proposition 13: Assessment Issues, Allocation Issues, Litigation: A Briefing Book" (Sacramento, Calif., 1982).

23. Evelle Younger, who won the Republican primary for governor in 1978, made a carefully qualified statement. Although he declined to advocate Proposition 13, Younger said he would personally vote for the measure. "Politicians Got Down-To-Earth Lessons on Taxes and Spending," *Los Angeles Times,* June 19, 1983. Howard Jarvis with Robert Pack, *I'm Mad as Hell: The Exclusive Story of the Tax Revolt and Its Leader* (New York: Times Books, 1979), 88, 102, 117, 127.

24. In 1977, for example, the officers of Cal-Tax were vice-presidents, comptrollers, or general managers for taxes of Southern Pacific, Union Oil, Pacific Gas and Electric, J. G. Boswell, and Southern California Edison Company. "Oliver Thomas Will Head Cal-Tax in 1977," *Cal-Tax News* 18 (March 1, 1977), 1.

25. "Opinion," *Cal-Tax News* 17 (February 15, 1976), 2; "Opinion," *Cal-Tax News* 16 (August 1976), 2; "An Alternative to Jarvis, Behr," *Cal-Tax News* 10 (February 15, 1978), 1. Jerry Vorpahl and Robert Berson, "Special Report: Business Grades the Legislature," *Pacific Business* 61 (November–December 1971), 26. The California Real Estate Association supported lower property taxes in general but did not specifically endorse Proposition 13 or its rival on the ballot, Proposition 8.

26. California Taxpayers' Association, "Cal-Tax Position Paper on Proposition 13, The Jarvis/Gann Property Tax Limitation Initiative" (Sacramento, Calif.: February 28, 1978). Kirk West (executive vice-president, California Taxpayers' Association), memo to the Board of Directors, "Jarvis/Gann Initiative—*Preliminary* Analysis of Impact on California Business," January 30, 1978. Both at the Institute of Governmental Studies Library, University of California at Berkeley.

27. "Soul Searching at B of A," *Los Angeles Times,* June 4, 1978, sec. I.

Bank of America, "Position Paper on the State Property Tax Relief Measures, Propositions 8 and 13 on the June 6 Primary Ballot" (San Francisco: April 13, 1978). Document at the Institute of Governmental Studies Library, University of California at Berkeley.

28. Howard P. Allen (president, Southern California Edison; chair, No on 13 campaign), interview with the author's research project, Sociology Department, UCLA (Rosemead, Calif.: August 10, 1981).

2. Theories of Inequality and an Interactive Approach to Power

1. Thus always to tyrants (the state motto of Virginia).

2. Sears and Citrin, *Tax Revolt,* analyzes the vote in California for Proposition 13 and succeeding tax-cutting initiatives. Paul N. Courant, Edward M. Gramlich, and Daniel L. Rubinfeld, "Why Voters Support Tax Limitation Amendments: The Michigan Case," *National Tax Journal* 33 (March 1980), 1–20.

3. E. E. Schattschneider, *The Semi-Sovereign People: A Realist's View of Democracy in America* (New York: Holt, Rinehart, and Winston, 1960). Peter Bachrach and Morton S. Baratz, "The Two Faces of Power," *American Political Science Review* 56 (1962), 947–952. Steven Lukes, *Power: A Radical View* (New York: Macmillan, 1974). For a critique of the theory of nondecisions, see Nelson W. Polsby, *Community Power and Political Theory* (New Haven: Yale University Press, 1963).

4. Matthew Crenson, for example, in *The Un-Politics of Air Pollution* (Baltimore: Johns Hopkins University Press, 1971), examines the decision of officials in Gary, Ind., not to reduce air pollution. Crenson's analysis of this nondecision yields interesting results because the neighboring city of East Chicago, Ill., did abate pollution. Crenson documents how attempts to reduce pollution in Gary were frustrated by the major corporation in that town, U.S. Steel.

5. Robert Dahl, *Who Governs? Democracy and Power in an American City* (New Haven: Yale University Press, 1961).

6. Manuel Castells, *The City and the Grassroots: A Cross-Cultural Theory of Urban Social Movements* (Berkeley, Los Angeles, London: University of California Press, 1983).

7. For different definitions of class interest, see Ira Katznelson, *City Trenches: Urban Politics and the Patterning of Class in the United States* (Chicago: University of Chicago Press, 1981), 201 ff.

8. Richard Hofstadter, *The Age of Reform: From Bryan to FDR* (New York: Vintage, 1955). Richard Hofstadter, "The Pseudo-Conservative Revolt," in *The Radical Right,* ed. Daniel Bell (New York: Doubleday, 1964), 85; Seymour Martin Lipset, "The Sources of the 'Radical Right,'" in *The Radical Right,* 308, 338. Joseph Gusfield, *Symbolic Crusade: Status Politics and the American Temperance Movement* (Urbana, Ill.: University of Illinois Press, 1963).

9. Seymour Martin Lipset and Earl Raab, *The Politics of Unreason: Right-Wing Extremism in America, 1790–1977* (Chicago: University of Chicago Press, 1978).

10. Lipset and Raab, *Unreason,* use the term "Quondam Complex" to refer to the backward-looking character of right-wing movements. See pp. 223, 460, 487, 489, 504. For the lack of group attachments, what Lipset and Raab call "anomic status preservatism," see pp. 156, 460.

11. For critiques of theories arguing that social breakdown causes movements, see the following: Ralph Turner, "Needed Research in Collective Behavior," *Sociology and Social Research* 42 (1958), 463. Michael Rogin, *The Intellectuals and McCarthy: The Radical Specter* (Cambridge: MIT Press, 1967). Charles Tilly, *From Mobilization to Revolution* (Reading, Mass.: Addison-Wesley, 1978), 18. Bert Useem, "Solidarity Model, Breakdown Model, and the Boston Anti-Busing Movement," *American Sociological Review* 45 (1980), 357–369.

12. This spatial dimension is absent in conflicts over the federal income tax which tend to pit economic interest groups against one another. Debates over maintaining deductions for business entertainment and home mortgages, for example, place the restaurant industry at odds with the construction industry.

13. James Q. Wilson, *The Amateur Democrat: Club Politics in Three Cities* (Chicago: University of Chicago Press, 1962), 96–109. Edward C. Banfield and James Q. Wilson, *City Politics* (Cambridge: Harvard University Press, 1965).

14. For a summary and analysis of the literature on "practical incorporation," see J. A. Agnew, "Homeownership and the Capitalist Social Order," in *Urbanization and Urban Planning in Capitalist Society,* ed. Michael Dear and Allen J. Scott (London: Methuen, 1981), 457–480.

15. For a description and critique of "conversion theory," which emphasizes how suburbs convert their residents to political conservatism, see Robert C. Wood, *Suburbia: Its People and Their Politics* (Boston: Houghton Mifflin, 1958).

16. Louis Hartz, *The Liberal Tradition in America* (New York: Harcourt Brace Jovanovich, 1955). For a more critical treatment of how the liberal consensus is the self-interest of property owners, see C. B. Macpherson, *The Political Theory of Possessive Individualism: Hobbes to Locke* (London: Oxford University Press). Cf. Norbert Wiley, "America's Unique Class Politics: The Interplay of the Labor, Credit, and Commodity Markets," *American Sociological Review* 32 (August 1967), 529–541.

17. Barry Schwartz (ed.), *The Changing Face of the Suburbs* (Chicago: University of Chicago Press, 1976). Bennett M. Berger, *Working Class Suburb: A Study of Auto Workers in Suburbia* (Berkeley and Los Angeles: University of California Press, 1960). According to some studies, the racial, economic, and other differences *between* suburbs can explain voting patterns better than suburban versus urban differences. See for example, Frederick M. Wirt, Benjamin Walter, Francine F. Rabinovitz, and Deborah R. Hensler, *On the City's Rim: Politics and Policy in Suburbia* (Lexington, Mass.: D. C. Heath, 1972).

18. John R. Logan, "Growth, Politics, and the Stratification of Places," *American Journal of Sociology* 84 (1978), 404. Harvey Molotch, "The City as a Growth Machine: Toward a Political Economy of Place," *American Journal of Sociology* 82 (1976), 309–332. John R. Logan and Harvey Molotch, *Urban For-*

tunes: The Political Economy of Place (Berkeley, Los Angeles, London: University of California Press, 1987).

19. As Adam Przeworski put it, "Economic struggles . . . always appear historically in their concrete articulation within the totality of struggles, always in a form molded by political and ideological relations. . . . Hence the organization of economic struggles is not determined uniquely by the structure of the system of production. . . . [I]n each concrete conjuncture struggles to organize, disorganize, or reorganize classes are not limited to struggles between or among classes." "Proletariat into a Class: The Process of Class Formation from Karl Kautsky's *The Class Struggle* to Recent Controversies," *Politics and Society* 7 (1977), 372, 386.

20. "*[T]he organizational structures of states indirectly influence the meanings and methods of politics for all groups in society*. . . . Definitions of what is feasible or desirable in politics depend in part on the capacities and the qualities that various groups attribute to state organizations and to the officials and politicians who operate them." Ann Shola Orloff and Theda Skocpol, "Why Not Equal Protection? Explaining the Politics of Public Social Spending in Britain, 1900–1911, and the United States, 1880s–1920," *American Sociological Review* 49 (December 1984), 726–750, emphasis in original.

21. Whereas the upper-middle class in the 1970s opposed taxes because of the effective administrative capacity of the tax collection organizations, the upper-middle class around 1900, according to Orloff and Skocpol (ibid.) opposed social programs because the state bureaucracy was as yet ineffective, encrusted with the patronage and corruption of political machines.

22. The voting majority of three supervisors is referred to as "the three kings."

Other studies also reveal that community groups have some power over issues within their own community but very little over issues affecting large constituencies. For example, a study of sixteen community-based groups in Atlanta, Boston, and Los Angeles concluded that although the groups had some impact on neighborhood issues, the groups lacked the power to influence the citywide school system. The groups "generally avoid and are virtually powerless in, all aspects of policy-making in the major policy areas of budget, personnel, and curriculum." Smaller units of organization, such as block clubs, have even less influence. Douglas Yates, *Neighborhood Democracy* (Lexington, Mass.: D. C. Heath, 1973), 35. Marilyn Gittell, *Limits to Citizen Participation: The Decline of Community Organizations* (Beverly Hills, Calif.: Sage, 1980), 37, 156.

23. In a survey of thirty-nine major works about community power, John Walton concluded that the major issue in the research was whether the leaders in a community formed one cohesive group, two factions, a shifting coalition of interests, or formed no consistent pattern whatever. John Walton, "A Systematic Survey of Community Power Research," in *The Structure of Community Power,* ed. Michael Aiken and Paul Mott (New York: Random House, 1970), 443–464.

24. Dahl, *Who Governs?,* 86, 163, 320. Big city governments are not particularly responsive to community groups or to the general citizenry. Local politics

often lacks elaborate formal procedures (such as open hearings, second and third readings, and compromises between two-chambered legislatures), all of which place decisions more in the public view. The media devotes less effort to reporting local politics, compared to national politics. Paul E. Peterson, *City Limits* (Chicago: University of Chicago Press, 1981), 122.

25. Ralph H. Turner and Lewis M. Killian, *Collective Behavior,* 2d ed. (Englewood Cliffs, N.J.: Prentice-Hall, 1972), use the term "power orientations." See also Tilly, *Mobilization.*

26. Doug McAdam, "Tactical Innovation and the Pace of Insurgency," *American Sociological Review* 48 (1983), 735–754. Steven E. Barkan, "Legal Control of the Southern Civil Rights Movement," *American Sociological Review* 49 (1984), 552–565. See Craig Jenkins, *The Politics of Insurgency* (New York: Columbia University Press, 1984) for the stance of the growers against the farmworkers movement.

27. As Karl Mannheim wrote, "The re-interpretation of . . . continuous and coherent change in meaning becomes the main concern of our modern historical sciences." *Ideology and Utopia: An Introduction to the Sociology of Knowledge,* trans. Louis Wirth and Edward Shils (New York: Harcourt, Brace, and World, 1936), 69.

Some contemporary exponents of the interpretive tradition are: Herbert Blumer, *Symbolic Interactionism: Perspective and Method* (Englewood Cliffs, N.J.: Prentice-Hall, 1969), 5, 10. Anthony Giddens, *New Rules of Sociological Method: A Positive Critique of Interpretative Sociologies* (New York: Basic, 1976), 105, 124. Clifford Geertz, *The Interpretation of Cultures* (New York: Basic Books, 1973), 5, 99, 140. Like the religious rituals that Geertz describes, the political events in this book have changed the beliefs of the participants. However, my approach places greater emphasis, as it must in the contemporary era, on the creation of new beliefs rather than the prepetuation of traditions. My approach also differs from the extreme individualistic and biological approach that J. David Lewis and Richard L. Smith—*American Sociology and Pragmatism: Mead, Chicago Sociology, and Symbolic Interaction* (Chicago: University of Chicago Press, 1980)—attribute to John Dewey and to Blumer.

The interpretive tradition may be contrasted to social-psychological theories such as value-expectancy theory and attribution theory, which have recently been used to analyze belief systems in social movements. See Bert Klandermans, "Mobilization and Participation: Social-Psychological Expansions of Resource Mobilization Theory," *American Sociological Review* 49 (1984), 583–600. Myra Marx Ferree and Frederick D. Miller, "Mobilization and Meaning: Toward an Integration of Social Movements," *Sociological Inquiry* 55 (1985), 38–51.

28. For the importance of the changing beliefs in social movements, see Turner and Killian, *Collective Behavior.* Gusfield, *Symbolic Crusade.* The collective-behavior perspective has emphasized that movement participants and the public constantly interpret their situations and their actions, leading to changing definitions of the goals of social movements.

29. Alain Touraine, *The Voice and the Eye: An Analysis of Social Movements* (Cambridge: Cambridge University Press, 1981), 66, and others who write about

the "new social movements" discuss how movements can affect the basic cultural orientations of a society.

30. In this point about preservationist movements, I disagree with the otherwise excellent arguments of Ferree and Miller, "Mobilization and Meaning," 45. They emphasize how "reactive" social movements couch their discourse in terms of the dominant ideology and, hence, do not need to formulate a new ideology. According to Ferree and Miller, the task of forming new beliefs is reserved for movements that withdraw from society or raise new demands not in accord with existing arrangements.

31. In this book, I highlight the fluidities of cultural change, rather than conceptualizing culture as relatively fixed, basic assumptions about reality.

The fundamentals of political culture in the United States contain ambiguities and possibilities that have animated two centuries of contention. Take the example of American individualism. One interpretation, made by the political left, has emphasized egalitarianism and anti-elitism and has attacked the privileges of special interests, upholding measures to help individuals advance. American individualism has also been interpreted as antistatism, however, which has fueled movements of the radical right. The tax protesters were all Americans, and all individualists, and again they had to choose between left and right. The culture of individualism provides no clear-cut legacy to social movements. Culture bequeaths only a set of complex issues that each generation of activists must creatively try to resolve.

32. Antigrowth movements have been more successful in upper-middle-class suburbs compared to working-class areas. See Molotch, "Growth Machine." John R. Logan, "Industrialization and the Stratification of Cities in Suburban Regions," *American Journal of Sociology* 82 (1976), 333–352. Jeffrey R. Henig, *Neighborhood Mobilization: Redevelopment and Response* (New Brunswick, N.J.: Rutgers University Press, 1982).

33. This coalition condemned government bureaucracy, in contrast to the Progressive Era confluence at the turn of the century, when a coalition of upper-middle-class reformers and local business leaders *increased* the authority of rationalized city agencies and city managers. See Martin Schiesl, *The Politics of Efficiency: Municipal Administration and Reform in America, 1880–1920* (Berkeley, Los Angeles, London: University of California Press, 1977). James Weinstein, *The Corporate Ideal in the Liberal State, 1900–1918* (Boston, Beacon Press, 1968). Samuel P. Hays, "The Politics of Reform in Municipal Government in the Progressive Era," *Pacific Northwest Quarterly* 55 (October 1964), 157–169.

34. See Geertz's discussion (*Interpretation,* 95) of the effects of religious symbols and rituals. George Herbert Mead uses the term "I" to refer to the subject who makes an individual creative response to the interpretations of others. Dealing with a different subject, E. P. Thompson, *The Making of the English Working Class* (New York: Vintage, 1963), 12–13, writes: "There is the . . . orthodoxy, in which the great majority of working people are seen as passive victims. . . . My quarrel with [this is] . . . that it tends to obscure the agency of working people, the degree to which they contributed by conscious

efforts, to the making of history." See also Samuel Bowles and Herbert Gintis, *Democracy and Capitalism: Property, Community, and the Contradictions of Modern Social Thought* (New York: Basic, 1987), for an extended discussion of structures of power, political learning, and political action.

35. For works that utilize the interpretive tradition of symbolic interactionism to analyze political actions and conflicts, see George Francis Cronk, "Symbolic Interactionism: A 'Left-Meadian' Interpretation," *Social Theory and Practice* 2 (Spring, 1973). Peter M. Hall, "A Symbolic Interactionist Analysis of Power," in *Perspectives in Political Sociology,* ed. A. Effrat (Indianapolis, Ind.: Bobbs-Merrill, 1972), 35–75.

36. Research in the field of social movements is just beginning to tackle the question of how redistributional programs and interests are constructed. For example, Ronald Aminzade, "Capitalist Industrialization and Patterns of Industrial Protest: A Comparative Urban Study of Nineteenth-Century France," *American Sociological Review* 49 (1984), 437–453, in a study of nineteenth-century French workers, argues that different paths of industrial development in three communities led workers to pursue a variety of interests—maintaining the traditional work day, raising wage rates, and challenging work practices and discipline.

37. McAdam, "Tactical Innovation"; and Doug McAdam, *Political Process and the Development of Black Insurgency* (Chicago: University of Chicago Press, 1982). The change in power relations was that the blacks had moved out from the control of the cotton plantation system and had developed indigenous institutions in Southern cities. In the North, the black vote had become an important constituency in national elections.

For changes in the orientation of student activists, see Doug McAdam, *Freedom Summer* (New York: Oxford University Press, 1988).

38. Other rational-actor models have focused on explaining why individuals contribute to a movement. Rational-actor models have been used to explain decisions such as an individual's joining an organization, taking a leadership role in the organization, or expressing a willingness to engage in action. Rational-actor models have had little to say about how movements formulate goals and programs and clarify and redefine their interests.

39. Tilly, *Mobilization,* 98–142. The goals that a group articulates for itself provide a good indication of group interests in the short run. Tilly believes that an analysis of class relations (along with the process of statemaking) can predict what interests people pursue "on the average and in the long run." Tilly, *Mobilization,* 61, 118. However, I contend that the interests a movement chooses to advance through its program cannot be easily deduced.

In some of his historical analyses, Tilly does suggest that the contention for political power can affect which interests a movement pursues. For example, as commoners challenged the increasingly centralized power of the French state in the seventeenth century, protesters began to express more class antagonism against merchants and prominent local landowners. Protesters ceased to ally with local notables against the crown, as they did during the Fronde. Charles Tilly, *The Contentious French* (Cambridge: Harvard University Press, 1986),

152, 161. Tilly's historical work (*Mobilization*, 241) provides fascinating details of how, in the rural province of Burgundy in the nineteenth century, tax protests still arose. In 1830 a crowd of winegrowers and workers in Beaune shouted "Down with excise taxes" and occupied the town square. In Meursault, winegrowers drove out the tax men. Small property owners and their subordinates had developed a common program opposing centralized state power.

40. For some movements, achieving power can become such a concern that the movement will abandon its previous program. The archetypical case is a communist movement that, despite its promises, establishes an authoritarian state. Movements that begin by upholding certain interests soon discover that, in order to wield power, actions must be taken promoting a very different set of interests. The hopes of many a great revolution, to borrow a phrase from Leon Trotsky, have been betrayed.

41. Michael Schwartz, *Radical Protest and Social Structure: The Southern Farmers Alliance and Cotton Tenancy, 1880–1890* (New York: Academic Press, 1976), especially p. 188, which chronicles the changing interests pursued by an important social movement.

42. Roberto Michels, *Political Parties* (Glencoe, Ill.: Free Press, 1949). For a critique, see Mayer Zald and Roberta Ash, "Social Movement Organizations, Growth, Decay and Change," *Social Forces* 44 (1966), 327–341. Other literature on changing goals in movements focuses on successful or defeated movements and, thus, is less applicable to the formative phase of a movement, which we are examining in the case of the tax revolt. See Sheldon L. Messinger, "Organizational Transformation: A Case Study of a Declining Social Movement," *American Sociological Review* 20 (1955), 3–10. Mayer N. Zald and Patricia Denton, "From Evangelism to General Service: On the Transformation of the YMCA," *Administrative Science Quarterly* 8 (June 1963), 214–234.

43. John D. McCarthy and Mayer N. Zald, "Resource Mobilization and Social Movements: A Partial Theory," *American Journal of Sociology* 82 (1977), 1112–1141. For an organizational approach to changing goals that is closer to our own, see Philip Selznick, *TVA and the Grass Roots* (New York: Harper and Row, 1965). Selznick, however, stresses how the goals of grass-roots democracy were abandoned because of pressure from larger property owners (farmers) and established interest groups, in contrast to our analysis of how goals changed because of democratic pressures from smaller property owners.

44. During the electoral campaign for Proposition 13 in 1978, Howard Jarvis did secure the services of campaign consultants to develop media advertising.

45. As Przeworski argues, "By recognizing the objective nature of ideological and political relations, this formulation permits us to analyze the effects of these relations upon the process in the course of which classes are continually organized, disorganized, and reorganized." "Proletariat," 385.

46. This is the lesson of Karl Polanyi's masterful interpretation of world history, *The Great Transformation* (Boston: Beacon Press, 1944). For discussions of communal solidarity in movements, see Bruce Fireman and William A. Gamson, "Utilitarian Logic in the Resource Mobilization Perspective," in *The Dynamics of Social Movements*, ed. Mayer N. Zald and John D. McCarthy

(Cambridge, Mass.: Winthrop, 1979), 3–44. Ferree and Miller, "Mobilization and Meaning," 41, 46. Anthony Oberschall, *Social Conflict and Social Movements* (Englewood Cliffs, N.J.: Prentice-Hall, 1973). Close-knit networks, sometimes found in isolated communities, can generate intense feelings of solidarity and can sustain unique world views that justify rebellion.

47. Thompson, *Working Class,* 9–10.

3. Probusiness Leaders and Consumers' Movements in Communities

1. Dr. Paul Peppard (honorary co-chair, Citizens for Property Tax Relief; town council member for Palos Verdes Estates), interview with author's research project, Sociology Department, UCLA (Palos Verdes Estates, Calif.: July 17, 1987).

2. Marge Flynn (office manager, Citizens for Property Tax Relief), interview with author's research project, Sociology Department, UCLA (Redondo Beach, Calif.: July 23, 1987).

3. Bill Haber, interview.

4. Probusiness economists Milton Friedman and Arthur Laffer supported Prop. 13 in 1978 but were not involved in tax protests before then.

The conceptually clearest and the most elaborate sources for the revival of probusiness conservatism are books published after 1978. But before this time, the same ideas were publicized widely through magazines, newspapers, and broadcast journalism. These latter sources exposed tax protest activists of the 1970s to probusiness creeds.

5. Heritage Foundation, *An Agenda for Progress* (Washington, D.C.: The Foundation, 1981). William Simon, *A Time for Truth* (New York: Reader's Digest Press, 1978). David A. Stockman, *The Triumph of Politics: How the Reagan Revolution Failed* (New York: Harper and Row, 1986). Paul Craig Roberts, *The Supply Side Revolution: An Insider's Account of Policymaking in Washington* (Cambridge, Mass.: Harvard University Press, 1984). Sidney Blumenthal, *The Rise of the Counter-Establishment: From Conservative Ideology to Political Power* (New York: Times Books, 1986).

6. George Gilder, *Wealth and Poverty* (New York: Basic, 1981).

7. The monetarist emphasis on stringency sometimes provoked the ire of more expansionist supply siders. See Kevin Phillips, *Post-Conservative America* (New York: Random House, 1982), 138.

8. Milton and Rose Friedman, *Free to Choose: A Personal Statement* (New York: Harcourt Brace Jovanovich, 1980). The Friedmans differ somewhat from the supply siders discussed above because the Friedmans' defense of capitalism rests on the argument that capitalism maximizes consumer sovereignty—that consumers can get it if they really want by purchasing on free markets.

9. Conflicts over consumption, what Weber called the "means of sustenance" (in contrast to the means of production) can become the most important form of conflict in a society. For example, Weber argues that through the Middle Ages, groups frequently contended over the price of bread. "This fight spread until it

involved all those commodities essential to the way of life." See Max Weber, *From Max Weber: Essays in Sociology,* trans. Hans Gerth and C. Wright Mills (New York: Oxford University Press, 1958), 88, 93, 186. For an analysis of consumption in advanced industrial societies, see C. Wright Mills, *White Collar: The American Middle Classes* (New York: Oxford, 1951).

10. Robert Kuttner, "The Declining Middle," *Atlantic Monthly* (July 1983), 60–72. Cf. Robert J. Samuelson, "Economic Report: Middle-Class Media Myth," *National Journal* 15 (December 1983). Bruce Steinberg, "The Mass Market Is Splitting Apart," *Fortune* (November 28, 1983), 76–81. "Population Puzzle: Is the U.S. Middle Class Shrinking Alarmingly?" *Wall Street Journal,* June 20, 1984.

11. Robert Holsworth, *Public Interest Liberalism and the Crisis of Affluence: Reflections on Nader, Environmentalism, and the Politics of a Sustainable Society* (Cambridge, Mass.: Schenkman, 1980). Hans Gorey, *Nader and the Power of Everyman* (New York: Grosset and Dunlap, 1975).

12. Paul Blumberg, *Inequality in an Age of Decline* (New York: Oxford University Press, 1980), 183, 202.

13. For a critique of individualistic theories and practices in American society, see Robert N. Bellah, Richard Madsen, Anne Swidler, William M. Sullivan, and Steven M. Tipton, *Habits of the Heart: Individualism and Commitment in American Life* (Berkeley, Los Angeles, London: University of California Press, 1985).

14. Anthony Giddens, *Class Structure of the Advanced Societies* (New York: Harper and Row, 1973), 109, has suggested that a major feature of the "structuration" of classes are "distributive groupings," which share similar patterns of consumption of goods. A prime example of such a distributive group is a segregated residential neighborhood. John Rex and Robert Moore, *Race, Community, and Conflict* (London, Oxford University Press, 1967), highlights the processes that formed three distinctive groupings of housing in England. The white middle class owns its own homes; the white working class occupies government-provided housing, whereas ethnic groups rent slum housing.

15. Morris Janowitz, *The Community Press in an Urban Setting* (Glencoe, Ill.: Free Press, 1951). Community attachments are undercut when households move, but the extent of residential mobility in the United States should not be overestimated. Sixteen percent of the U.S. population (including children) changed dwellings between March 1982 and March 1983. Individuals aged twenty to twenty-nine did much of the moving; the middle-aged and the elderly, less. Of those between forty-five and fifty-four years of age, 8.1 percent moved in 1982–1983; between fifty-five and sixty-four, 5.9 percent, and sixty-five and older, 4.9 percent.

16. These processes are characterized by Gerald Suttles's phrase, "the defended neighborhood." Gerald Suttles, *The Social Construction of Communities* (Chicago: University of Chicago Press, 1972), 40, 240. Jane Jacobs, *The Death and Life of Great American Cities* (New York: Random House, 1961). Jessie Bernard, *The Sociology of Community* (Glenview, Ill.: Scott Foresman), 188.

17. James O'Connor, *The Fiscal Crisis of the State* (New York: St. Martin's,

1973). Peter Saunders, *Social Theory and the Urban Question* (London: Hutchinson, 1981), 261.

18. "Directory of Taxpayer Groups," *Taxpayer's Watchdog,* (November 1976), 2. After Proposition 13 passed, the *Los Angeles Times* published a list of seventeen homeowners associations in the San Fernando Valley which held regular meetings.

In other parts of the United States, homeowners were also particularly active in property tax reduction campaigns. Of the 29,000 persons in Milwaukee who signed an initiative in 1978 to limit property taxes to 1 percent, 74 percent were homeowners (56 percent in the adult population were homeowners). See Robert M. Stein, Keith E. Hamm, and Patricia K. Freeman, "An Analysis of Support for Tax Limitation Referenda," *Public Choice* 40 (1983), 187–194.

19. Similarly, Oliver P. Williams's study of suburbia concludes that the residents wanted government to lower taxes, provide amenities, and preserve the social character of their communities. See Oliver P. Williams, Harold Herman, Charles Liebman, and Thomas Dye, *Suburban Differences and Metropolitan Policies* (Philadelphia: University of Pennsylvania Press, 1965), 216.

20. Marilyn Noorda (chair, taxation committee, Sherman Oaks Homeowners Association), interview with author's research project, Sociology Department, UCLA (Camarillo, Calif.: February 14, 1982). Frank Lalli, "The New Middle-Class Dream: I Just Want to Hang on to What I've Got," *New West* (October 25, 1976), 20–28. "Property Taxes: Increases Cut Deep into Budgets," *Los Angeles Times* (August 1, 1976), sec. II.

21. Harry Cimring, letter to the editor, *Los Angeles Times* (September 25, 1976), sec. II. Jean F. Noss, letter to the editor, *Los Angeles Times* (September 25, 1976), sec. II.

22. William B. Scott, *In the Pursuit of Happiness: American Conceptions of Property from the Seventeenth to the Twentieth Century* (Bloomington, Ind.: Indiana University Press).

23. "Property Taxes: Increases Cut Deep into Budgets," *Los Angeles Times,* August 6, 1976, sec. II.

24. Lalli, "Middle-Class Dream," 25. As James Scott argues in *The Moral Economy of the Peasant* (New Haven, Conn.: Yale University Press, 1976), taxes that are *inflexible* and ignore the peasants' *ability to pay* are likely to be viewed as unjust, thereby inciting rebellion. Chapter 1 of this book has traced how the property tax became inflexible because of "reform" measures; higher sale prices automatically produced higher tax bills with little leeway for adjustment or appeal. The property tax was determined not by the ability to pay and current income but by the current value of property.

25. Thompson, *Working Class,* 486. See Craig Calhoun, *The Question of Class Struggle* (Chicago: University of Chicago Press, 1982) for a lengthy discussion of "reactionary radicals" in nineteenth-century England.

26. M. Stephen Weatherford, "Popular Participation and Representation in the Urban Environment: The School Desegregation Issue in Los Angeles," *ERIC Reports* ED166267 (1978). Noorda, interview. United Organizations of Taxpayers, board member (name withheld), interview with author's research

project, Sociology Department, UCLA (Los Angeles, February 16, 1982). The daily newspaper *Valley News* (Van Nuys, Calif.) provided the best coverage of the antibusing movement in the Valley.

27. Sears and Citrin, *Tax Revolt,* 168. The two-question measure of racism was significantly correlated with support for the tax revolt (a total effect of 0.21, and a direct effect of 0.11 measured by the standardized coefficients in a multiple-regression model). Useem, "Anti-Busing."

28. Sears finds strong correlations between such racially prejudiced attitudes and the opposition to busing. David O. Sears, Carl P. Hensler, and Leslie K. Speer, "Whites' Opposition to 'Busing': Self-Interest or Symbolic Politics?" *American Political Science Review* 73 (1979), 369–384. Miller argues that specific concerns about educational programs were not strong predictors of opposition to busing, compared to other predictors, racism and general program concerns (such as commitment to integration). Steven D. Miller, "Contemporary Racial Conflict: The Nature of White Opposition to Mandatory Busing," Ph.D. dissertation, Political Science Department, UCLA, 1981. One attempt to explain the opposition to a local school-busing plan concluded that the most important factors were a rejection of the goals of integration and a denial that the government should take action on such issues. Douglas S. Gatlin, Michael W. Giles, and Everett F. Catalo, "Policy Support within a Target Group: The Case of School Desegregation," *American Political Science Review* 72 (1978), 985–995.

However, some opinion polls indicate that whites who oppose school busing do not particularly espouse racial prejudice. Johnathan Kelly, "The Politics of School Busing," *Public Opinion Quarterly* 38 (1974), 23–39. Arthur L. Stinchcombe and D. Garth Taylor, *On Democracy and School Integration* (Plenum, 1980), 177–179.

29. Gary Orfield, *Must We Bus? Segregated Schools and National Policy* (Washington, D.C.: Brookings Institution, 1978), 109. Useem, "Anti-Busing." Seymour Martin Lipset and William Schneider, *The Confidence Gap: Business, Labor, and Government in the Public Mind* (New York: Free Press, 1983), 39. The distinction made here between prejudice (discussed in the previous paragraph) versus other claims of ethnic advantage is similar to the distinction J. B. McConahay and J. C. Hough, Jr., make between "redneck racism" and "symbolic racism." "Symbolic Racism," *Journal of Social Issues* 32 (1976), 23–45. See also David Wellman's distinction in *Portraits of White Racism* (Cambridge: Cambridge University Press, 1977) between "prejudice" and "white racism"; and Herbert Blumer, "Race Prejudice as a Sense of Group Position," *Pacific Sociological Review* 1 (Spring, 1958), 3–7.

30. Thorstein Veblen, *The Theory of the Leisure Class: An Economic Study of Institutions* (New York: A. M. Kelley, 1899; Boston: Houghton Mifflin, 1973). Weber, *From Max,* 189, emphasis added in the quotation. Weber extensively discussed ethnic status groups, which, because of custom and ritual, cannot easily intermingle or intermarry with members of dominant groups.

Chicago, Washington, D.C., San Francisco, Los Angeles, Houston, and other cities have long histories of neighborhood associations that have sought to exclude minority residents. Such associations have exerted social pressure on white homeowners, have intimidated minority homebuyers, and have attempted to enforce covenants (restrictions included in deeds to real estate) forbidding sales to minorities. Neighborhood associations have also campaigned against government plans to locate low-income public housing in white communities.

31. Julia Wrigley's field research on the antibusing movement in Boston reveals that businesses larger than neighborhood retail outlets did not support the movement. Untitled manuscript, Sociology Department, UCLA, 1987.

32. Robert Ryan (president, Abalone Cove Homeowners Association; secretary, Peninsula Advisory Council, a coalition of homeowners groups), interview with the author's research project, Sociology Department, UCLA (Rancho Palos Verdes, Calif.: July 22, 1987).

33. Peppard, interview. Save Our Coastline, "The History of the 4th City Campaign, Palos Verdes Peninsula," 1972, document in the author's collection. 4th City Campaign Committee, letter to peninsula residents, April 1972, document in the author's collection.

34. Don Hill (homeowners association liaison and steering committee member, Citizens for Property Tax Relief), interview with the author's research project, Sociology Department, UCLA (Rancho Palos Verdes, Calif.: May 19, 1987). Marineland was later purchased by Harcourt Brace Jovanovich who, in a surprise shift, decided to support the incorporation of a new town. After the growth limiters won, Marineland suffered a fall in business and was closed down in 1987 as part of a corporate reorganization. One final petition drive sought to save the animals at Marineland. Flipper, his cousins, and related assets were not liquidated for use as glue in textbook bindings.

35. "Developers, Residents Clash at Open Space Hearing," *Palos Verdes Peninsula News,* September 27, 1972. President, Palos Verdes Peninsula Advisory Council, to Local Agency Formation Commission, "Application to Initiate Proceedings for Incorporations of Cities," c. 1972, document in the author's collection. "Dream of Fourth City on Peninsula Comes True," *Los Angeles Times,* August 30, 1973, Centinela South Bay Edition, Sec. VII.

36. ". . . Battling 'Bigness,' " *Torrance Daily Breeze,* c. 1972, document in the author's collection.

37. Robert Ryan, interview. Bryan Hardwick Associates, news release for Committee for Incorporation of the 4th City, August 17, 1973, document in the author's collection.

38. Don Hill, interview.

39. Tarzana Property Owners Association, Inc., *TOPA Newsletter,* November 1975, document in the author's collection.

40. Frank Popper, *The Politics of Land Use Reform* (Madison, Wis.: University of Wisconsin Press, 1981).

41. Dan Shapiro (president, Studio City Residents Association), "L.A.: Its Luster Has Tarnished," *Daily News,* April 13, 1986.

42. Sears and Citrin, *Tax Revolt,* 48, 57, 80, 86.

43. James A. Davis, "Conservative Weather in a Liberalizing Climate: Change in Selected NORC General Social Survey Items, 1972–78," *Social Forces* 58 (1980), 1129–1156. Everett Carll Ladd, Jr., "What the Voters Really

Want," *Fortune* 98 (December 18, 1978), 40–48. Everett Carll Ladd, Jr., with Marilyn Potter, Linda Basilick, Sally Daniels, and Dana Suszkiw, "The Polls: Taxing and Spending," *Public Opinion Quarterly* 43 (Spring, 1979), 126–135.

Two years after the passage of Proposition 13, pluralities still favored increases in spending on twelve services (but not welfare). In one study conducted immediately before the 1980 election, a plurality of the public favored no cuts in federal health and education services. During the Reagan administration, even when respondents were asked in general terms about government social spending, respondents expressed favorable attitudes. For example, majorities of 52 to 59 percent favored a "great deal more" or "somewhat more" spending for federal domestic programs in three polls taken between December 1983 and May 1984. Fifty-seven percent in January 1985 opposed Reagan's proposals to reduce spending on social services. Markus, Gregory B., "Political Attitudes during Election Year: A Report on the 1980 NES Panel Study," *American Political Science Review* 76 (1982), 538–560. *Los Angeles Times, The Los Angeles Times Poll*, no. 93 (January 24, 1985), question 29; no. 74 (December 15, 1983), question 38; no. 75 (February 9, 1984), question 18; no. 81 (May 3, 1984), question 30.

44. Jarvis, *I'm Mad*, 118–123.

45. Zane L. Miller, *Suburb: Neighborhood and Community in Forest Park, Ohio, 1935–1976* (Knoxville, Tenn.: University of Tennessee Press, 1981). Miller argues that in the 1970s there was a heightened emphasis on self-fulfillment through career and consumption at the expense of traditional civic virtues.

46. Terry N. Clark and Lorna Ferguson, *City Money: Political Processes, Fiscal Strain, and Retrenchment* (New York: Columbia University Press, 1983), also see the "new fiscal populism" as a mixture of liberal and conservative views, but a somewhat different mixture. Clark argues that the new fiscal populists avoided expressing antiminority views. In this he differs from the argument in this chapter and the findings of Sears and Citrin, *Tax Revolt*, 210, who linked the tax revolt to symbolic racism.

47. Sears and Citrin claim that conservative voters were somewhat more likely to give retrospective support to a package of Proposition 13 and later tax initiatives. The direct effect, measured by the standardized coefficient, was 0.10 in a multivariate model. *Tax Revolt*, 210.

48. Phillips, *Post-Conservative*, 126.

49. Tribune Media Services, Inc., Orlando, Fla., *The Harris Survey*, no. 17 (February 28, 1985). Using an eight-point conservative-to-liberal scale, the Gallup Poll in 1978 found that 33 percent identified themselves as either "far right," "substantially right of center," or "moderately right of center." Those "just slightly right of center" were tabulated with the 43 percent who were moderates. "Opinion Roundup," *Public Opinion* 1 (September–October 1978), 33. The National Opinion Research Center found that 33.5 percent in 1978 identified themselves as extremely conservative, conservative, or slightly conservative. See Davis, "Conservative Survey," 1138.

50. "Opinion Roundup," *Public Opinion* 1 (September–October 1978), 38. Davis, "Conservative Survey," 1138. Lipset and Schneider, *Confidence Gap*,

320. In addition, 69 percent of conservatives agree that the government should set safety standards in factories. See CBS News/*New York Times* Poll, January 12, 1978.

51. Karl A. Lamb, *As Orange Goes* (New York: W. W. Norton, 1974), 221. Lloyd Free and Harvey Cantril, *The Political Beliefs of Americans: A Study of Public Opinion* (New Brunswick, N.J.: Rutgers University Press, 1967), characterized the American public as ideological conservatives and operational liberals. Americans seemed to articulate generalized conservative views but, at the same time, defended many specific liberal positions.

52. Philip Converse, "The Nature of Belief Systems in Mass Publics," in *Ideology and Discontent,* ed. David Apter (New York: Free Press, 1964). Converse went on to argue that large sections of the mass public possessed no meaningful belief systems about political matters. This assertion has been the source of much controversy. Norman R. Luttbeg, "The Structure of Beliefs among Leaders and the Public," *Public Opinion Quarterly* 32 (1968), 398–409, for example, argues that the mass public, like elites, does indeed articulate structured beliefs about local government policy. Luttbeg explains 65 percent of the variance in public opinions on issues (compared to 74 percent for a sample of elites) by using five factors pertaining to child rearing, taxation, inner-city areas, recreation, and growth. One need not accept the more extreme formulation of Converse's claims to argue that the political views of the mass public, like those of grass-roots activists, are not organized as coherent ideologies and are worlds apart from the programs of probusiness conservative leaders.

53. Clinton Rossiter, *Conservatism in America* (New York: Knopf, 1955), 8, uses the term "the conservatism of possession" to describe this phenomenon.

54. Converse, "Belief Systems." More recently, when a CBS News/*New York Times* poll (April 1981, pt. 2) asked people to define the difference between a conservative and a liberal, 52 percent chose no opinion. George Horace Gallup, *The Gallup Poll: Public Opinion 1935–1971* (New York: Random House, 1972), 2244. Pamela Johnston Conover and Stanley Feldman, "The Origins and Meaning of Liberal/Conservative Self-Identifications," *American Journal of Political Science* 25 (1981), 617–645; "How People Organize the Political World: A Schematic Model," *American Journal of Political Science* 28 (1984), 95–123.

55. Willard Mullins, "On the Concept of Ideology in Political Science," *American Political Science Review* 66 (June 1972), 498–510. Mullins contrasts this emphasis on purposive action with other approaches to ideology that stress the emotional response to symbols.

56. My focus is on how beliefs are shaped when groups interact with political structures, rather than on how individuals process their beliefs through a preexisting mental structure. My approach thus contrasts to that of Conover and Feldman, "Schematic Model," who draw on recent social-psychological literature and use the term "schema" to refer to a cognitive structure that processes information. My concept of group interpretations places more emphasis on the macro-sociological level. Sears and Citrin, *Tax Revolt,* 76, also discusses schemata, which they define as a consistent set of political attitudes that are mildly intercorrelated and, when analyzed by factor analysis, load on the same factor.

My concept of political interpretation also differs from their term "symbolic predisposition," which refers to the individual's attitudes toward an object or a narrow set of objects, for example, blacks and other ethnic minorities. Cf. Dennis Chong, Herbert McClosky, and John Zaller, "Patterns of Support for Democratic and Capitalist Values in the United States," *British Journal of Political Science* 13 (1982), 434, who discuss the apparently consistent attitudes that arise from the projection of psychological dispositions such as authoritarianism.

4. Middle Americans and Generalized Unresponsiveness

1. Property and Homeowners of the San Gabriel Valley, secretary (name withheld), interview with the author's research project, Sociology Department UCLA (Alhambra, Calif.: July 14, 1982).

2. "Mike Rubino to Run for City Council," *Alhambra Post Advocate,* March 24, 1965.

3. Jarvis, *I'm Mad,* 97.

4. "2,000 Protest Hike in Taxes," *Alhambra Post Advocate,* November 11, 1964.

5. "Taxpayers Storm into Civic Center," *Los Angeles Times,* November 20, 1964.

6. Mike Rubino (founder, Alhambra Property Tax Protest Committee), interview with the author's research project, Sociology Department, UCLA (Alhambra, Calif.: August 14, 1981, and January 21, 1982).

7. David Morgan (director of Hollywood Better Government Association), interview with the author's research project, Sociology Department, UCLA (Hollywood, Calif.: May 4, 1987).

8. Richard Carman (president of San Gabriel Valley Taxpayers Association and Better Government Association, California), interview with the author's research project, Sociology Department, UCLA (San Gabriel, Calif.: February 26, 1988).

9. "Supervisors' Gadfly Enjoys Role," *San Gabriel Valley Tribune,* December 13, 1977. Carman, interview.

10. "Rubino, Assessor Agree They 'Agree,' " *Alhambra Post Advocate,* n.d., c. 1964.

11. United Organizations of Taxpayers, board member (name withheld), interview with the author's research project, Sociology Department, UCLA (Van Nuys, Calif.: April 27, 1987).

12. Recall that big city, county, and metropolitan government are distinguished from the governments of towns and communities, which have populations of around fifty thousand.

13. San Gabriel Taxpayers Association, "Agenda for Meeting on Friday, June 13, 1969," leaflet. See also Howard Jarvis, letter (April 1969), document in the author's collection. The anger aroused by this issue was evident in an eariler letter that spoke of the "senseless inflationary irresponsibility of some of our administrators. Between the spiraling property taxes and the gradual suppres-

sion of free speech most people have decided enough is enough and they are ready to call a spade a spade and fight back hard." Richard M. Carman, letter to Hon. John L. E. Collier, June 18, 1965, document in the author's collection.

14. Bill R. Hutton, interview with the author's research project, Sociology Department, UCLA (North Hollywood, Calif.: January 22, 1987). Coalition of Homeowners and Renters of Los Angeles County, co-founder (name withheld), interview with the author's research project, Sociology Department, UCLA (Venice, Calif.: February 26, 1987).

15. Property and Homeowners of the San Gabriel Valley, secretary, interview.

16. North Hollywood Homeowners Association, vice-president (name withheld), interview with the author's research project, Sociology Department, UCLA (Los Angeles: January 21, 1987).

17. Herbert Gans, *The Levittowners: Ways of Life and Politics in a New Suburban Community* (New York: Pantheon, 1967). Ann Lennarson Greer, *The Mayor's Mandate: Municipal Statecraft and Political Trust* (Cambridge, Mass.: Schenkman, 1974).

18. Better Government Association, "Accomplishments & Goals," leaflet, c. 1975, document in the author's collection. Howard Jarvis, *I'm Mad*, 284.

19. "Taxpayers Storm into Civic Center," *Los Angeles Times,* November 20, 1964; Rubino, interview.

20. Fiscal years (column A) rather than calendar years provide a more convenient interval for grouping the events. This is true because in Los Angeles County, property taxation and, hence, tax protest are geared to a fiscal-year cycle. Protests typically begin when assessments are mailed out at the beginning of the fiscal year in July. Communities protest again when tax bills are sent out in November and may continue to protest in the next calendar year.

21. As explained in the appendix, the relative affluence index (column E) for Lomita, for example, is the average of two ratios—first, the median family income of Lomita divided by the figure for the metropolitan area and, second, the percentage of professional workers divided by the metropolitan figure.

22. A total of four protests gained the support of community political leaders. Three of these protests took place in communities with relative-affluence indexes near the top of the range (San Marino, 1976, and Palos Verdes peninsula, 1977) or an attendance figure at the top of the range (West Covina, 1958).

These results built upon previous models of social movements. Anthony Oberschall, "Loosely Structured Collective Conflict: A Theory and an Application," in *Research in Social Movements, Conflict and Change,* vol. 3, ed. Louis Kriesberg (Greenwich, Conn.: JAI Press, 1980), 45–68. Tilly, *Mobilization,* 106–115. Tilly's discussion of the authorities' reaction to social movements needs to be modified to analyze the response of community leaders. According to Tilly, authorities will facilitate a social movement when the protesting group itself is acceptable and when the group uses acceptable tactics. Tilly operationalizes group acceptability as the power of the group. I have found, however, that the affluence of the protesting community is a major factor determining whether community leaders approve of a group.

Tilly argues that authorities find small-scale actions more acceptable than large ones. Although this may be the case for collective violence, the opposite holds true in a democracy when a social movement uses peaceful and constitutional means. Ralph H. Turner, "The Public Perception of Protest," *American Sociological Review* 34 (December 1969), 815–831, suggests that small protests that pose little threat may lead the authorities to dismiss the protests as deviance and take an unfavorable stand. This argument is substantiated by the finding that it is the large-scale protest that is likely to gain the support of community leaders.

23. *San Gabriel Valley Tribune,* August 6, 1976; September 25, 1976.

24. Coalition of Homeowners and Renters of Los Angeles County, cofounder, interview.

25. San Gabriel Valley Taxpayers Association, news release, "Subject: Initiative Petition," October 10, 1971, document in the author's collection. Emphasis in original. "People Power Displays Real Muscle: Volunteers Work Round the Clock for Jarvis Amendment," *Alhambra Post-Advocate,* November 11, 1971.

26. The percentage was 8 in 1980 and 15 in 1984. Although most of the questions in opinion polls refer to the federal government, citizens were also concerned about representation at the local level.

27. Lipset and Schneider, *Confidence Gap,* 17. Gallup, *The Gallup Poll,* 127. These questions are evidence of what has been termed low *external* efficacy. External efficacy refers to the respondent's judgments of institutions and systems outside the individual. It can be distinguished from *internal* efficacy, which focuses on the individual and his or her perceived ability to influence surroundings. Low internal efficacy would be indicated by a yes response to the statement, "Sometimes politics and government seem so complicated that a person like me can't really understand what's going on." Several studies have indicated that low external efficacy, combined with high internal efficacy, are connected with protest activities. See Jeffrey M. Paige, "Political Orientation and Riot Participation," *American Sociological Review* 36 (October 1971): 810–820.

28. Donald I. Warren, *The Radical Center: Middle Americans and the Politics of Alienation* (Notre Dame, Ind.: University of Notre Dame Press, 1976). See also James D. Wright, *The Dissent of the Governed: Alienation and Democracy in America* (New York: Academic Press, 1976), 135–143.

29. Sears and Citrin, *Tax Revolt,* 29, argues that distrust of government was particularly important in the California tax revolt because it led to a rapid increase in support for Proposition 13 immediately before the June 1978 election. In May 1978, the assessor of Los Angeles County was faced with the task of sending out tax bills that showed dramatic increases from the previous year. Political elites first sought to postpone mailing the bills until after the election. Later, bowing to public pressure, officials let worried taxpayers travel to City Hall to see their bills. Some politicians then tried to halt the assessment increases and instead sought to raise the tax rate for all taxpayers. This, however, merely angered those who had been spared an assessment increase. Thus, politicians activated popular perceptions that government was seeking to placate, manipulate, and fool the public.

30. Courant et al., "Tax Limitation." David Lowery and Lee Sigelman, "Un-

derstanding the Tax Revolt: Eight Explanations," *American Political Science Review* 75 (December 1981), 963–974. Daniel Yankelovich and Larry Kaagan, "One Year Later: What It Is and What It Isn't," *Social Policy* (May/June 1979), 19–23. Sears and Citrin's survey in *Tax Revolt* included one question about respondents' views about government power. Unfortunately, in their data analysis, one variable combined and contaminated the responses to that question with responses to another question about trust of government, an analytically separate concept.

31. Morgan, interview.

32. Coalition of Homeowners and Renters of Los Angeles County, cofounder, interview.

33. Morgan, interview.

34. Lipset and Schneider, *Confidence Gap*, 29, 168. "Opinion Roundup: The Balance Sheet on Business," *Public Opinion* 5 (October–November 1982), 24. For similar findings using qualitative methods, see David Halle, *America's Working Man: Work, Home, and Politics Among Blue-Collar Property Owners* (Chicago: University of Chicago Press, 1984), chaps. 9, 12.

35. Lipset and Schneider, *Confidence Gap*, 36, 89, 165. Similarly, a series of Harris Polls revealed that the percentage of the public having a "great deal of confidence" in "major companies" fell from 55 percent in 1966, to 22 percent in 1978 (the year that Proposition 13 passed), to 19 percent in 1984. *Harris Survey,* no. 112 (December 17, 1984). Gallup's percentages are higher because Gallup respondents could choose among two positive responses compared to one in the Harris Poll. Gallup, *The Gallup Poll,* 176.

The overall negative view of business coexists with some positive attitudes. Although the public expresses displeasure with big business, the public praises the free enterprise system and the technological accomplishments of business in creating new products. "Opinion Roundup: The Balance Sheet on Business," *Public Opinion* 5 (October–November 1982), 21.

36. Morgan, interview.

37. Coalition of Homeowners and Renters of Los Angeles County, cofounder, interview.

38. Rubino, interview.

39. Carman, interview.

40. Ibid.

41. Frank Wittenberg (board member, United Organizations of Taxpayers), interview with the author's research project, Sociology Department, UCLA (West Hollywood, Calif.: April 30, 1987).

42. United Organizations of Taxpayers, volunteer signature solicitor in Orange County, Calif. (name withheld), interview with the author's research project, Sociology Department, UCLA (Leisure World, near Rossmoor, Calif.: May 7, 1977).

43. Rubino, interview.

44. Morgan, interview. This contrasts to the pattern in upper-middle-class communities, where differences between homeowners and chambers of commerce were reconciled (see chap. 7). Citizens Against the Formation of a Rede-

velopment Agency in the City of San Gabriel, "Won't You Help," leaflet, n.d., document in the author's collection; original sentences used all capital letters.

45. *Alhambra Post-Advocate*, November 11, 1971. Richard Carman, letter to supporters, March 1975, document in the author's collection.

46. Irving Gilman (president, Monterey Park Taxpayers Association), interview with the author's research project, Sociology Department, UCLA (Monterey Park, Calif.: August 2, 1982). *Taxpayer's Watchdog*, March 1977, 3. The Tax Justice Act is California Senate Bill 154, introduced on January 18, 1977, by Senators Petris, Alquist, Dunlap, et al. This leftist reform bill was drastically amended and then languished for a year and a half. Ironically, after Proposition 13 passed, it was quickly rewritten and served as the bailout bill giving state aid to tax-starved localities.

47. Joyce Blaine (president and cofounder of the Van Nuys Homeowners Association), interview with the author's research project, Sociology Department, UCLA (Van Nuys, Calif.: August 6, 1982).

48. North Hollywood Homeowners Association, vice-president, interview. The median family income there in 1976 was $15,302, or 1.12 that for Los Angeles County. Another activist in a middle-income community in the San Fernando Valley also felt that the local chamber of commerce had not been supportive of any citizens' causes. See Van Nuys Homeowners Association, former president (name withheld), interview with the author's research project, Sociology Department, UCLA (Van Nuys, Calif.: February 10, 1987).

49. El Segundo Taxpayers Association, cofounder and newsletter editor (name withheld), interview with the author's research project, Sociology Department, UCLA (El Segundo, Calif.: July 29, 1980).

50. Unified Homeowners and Renters Groups of Los Angeles County, "An Open Letter to The Los Angeles County Taxpayers . . . ," c. 1977; Citizens' Tax Advisory Committee, Group 13, "Proposals for Tax Reform," n.d.; Coalition of Homeowners and Renters of Los Angeles County, "News Release: Public's Tax Reform Proposal," n.d. Documents in the author's collection.

51. Samuel Huntington, *American Politics: The Promise of Disharmony* (Cambridge: Harvard University Press, 1981), 33, 86.

5. Middle-Income Communities in Search of Power

1. Fred Kimball (publisher of magazine for apartment owners, field deputy for Philip Watson, consultant on paid signature solicitation), interview with the author's research project, Sociology Department, UCLA (Agoura, Calif.: August 6, 1984).

2. Property and Homeowners of the San Gabriel Valley, secretary, interview. Property and Homeowners of the San Gabriel Valley, director (name withheld), interview with the author's research project, Sociology Department, UCLA (San Gabriel, Calif.: July 21, 1982).

3. Houston Myers (president, Property and Homeowners of the San Gabriel

Valley), interview with the author's research project, Sociology Department, UCLA (Alhambra, Calif.: February 6, 1982).

4. Myers interview. California, Fair Political Practices Commission, "Campaign Contribution and Spending Report, November 2, 1976, General Election" (Sacramento, Calif.: Office of State Printing, 1977). California, Secretary of State, "Statement of Vote, General Election, November 2, 1976" (Sacramento, Calif.: Office of State Printing). American Independent Party, "California State Platform," adopted in convention, Sacramento, Calif., 1980, mimeo, document in the author's collection.

5. Property and Homeowners of the San Gabriel Valley, director, interview.

6. Howard Farmer (founder and president, United Voters League; state vice-chairperson, Citizens Asserting Supremacy over Taxation), interviews with the author's research project, Sociology Department, UCLA (North Hollywood, Calif.: March 27, 1982, and May 22, 1982). Rutenberg and Rutenberg, interview.

7. Pablo Campos (activist, Citizens Asserting Supremacy over Taxation), interview with the author's research project, Sociology Department, UCLA (Los Angeles: August 4, 1984).

8. Gilman, interview.

9. Coalition of Homeowners and Renters of Los Angeles County, cofounder, interview. Tax Coalition, "Participants, Tax Coalition Meeting: Summary of Discussion," December 5, 1976, document in the author's collection.

10. Coalition of Homeowners and Renters of Los Angeles County, cofounder, interview.

11. United Organizations of Taxpayers, volunteer signature solicitor in Orange County, interview.

12. Howard Farmer, interview.

13. Los Angeles County Property Owners Association (forerunner to the United Organizations of Taxpayers), president (name withheld), interview with the author's research project, Sociology Department, UCLA (Los Angeles: 1984), date withheld.

14. Farmer, interview. United Organizations of Taxpayers, volunteer signature solicitor in Orange County, Calif., interview.

15. Coalition of Homeowners and Renters of Los Angeles County, cofounder, interview.

16. Bill Hutton, letter to the editor published in the *Valley News,* n.d., c. 1980, document in the author's collection.

17. Curtis H. Stevens (president, Coordinating Council, San Fernando Valley Area Association), interview with the author's research project, Sociology Department, UCLA (Northridge, Calif.: January 31, 1987).

18. *Alhambra Post-Advocate,* November 11, 1971; June 17, 1972.

19. Better Government Association of California, "Release #2" (South Whittier, Calif., 1978), document in the author's collection.

20. North Hollywood Homeowners Association, president (name withheld), interview with the author's research project, Sociology Department, UCLA (North Hollywood, Calif.: August 11, 1982). Sun Valley Homeowners Associa-

tion, president (name withheld), interview with the author's research project, Sociology Department, UCLA (Sun Valley, Calif.: September 8, 1982).

21. Property and Homeowners of the San Gabriel Valley, secretary, interview.

22. Farmer, interview.

23. Gilman, interview. Blaine, interview.

24. "Culver City Tax Protest Draws 700," *Santa Monica Evening Outlook,* September 13, 1966. "Glendale Leads in Tax Strike," *Glendale News Press,* December 8, 1966. The median family income in Culver City was 1.11 times the figure for the Los Angeles metropolitan area.

25. Howard Jarvis, *I'm Mad,* 13, 118; and "American Liberty Is Based Upon Individual Property Rights," 1976, leaflet in the author's collection.

26. Property and Homeowners of the San Gabriel Valley, secretary, interview. El Segundo Taxpayers Association, cofounder, interview. Sun Valley Homeowners Association, president, interview. North Hollywood Homeowners Association, president, interview.

27. Ed Salzman, "Dear Landlord: You Have a Friend in Howard Jarvis," *New West* (February 27, 1978), 68.

28. Field Institute, *The California Poll,* Release #975, June 2, 1978. Middle-income voters supported Proposition 13. Voters with an opinion and with family incomes between $10,000 and $14,999 were 57 percent in favor of Proposition 13; those with incomes between $15,000 and $19,999 were 60 percent in favor. (In the City of Los Angeles, the median family income in 1976 was $14,030. In this poll, the state was 63 percent in favor and voted the next week 65 percent in favor.)

Coalition of Homeowners and Renters of Los Angeles County, "Which Is It To Be?—The Legislature's SB-1 (Prop. 8) or the People's Prop. 13" (Venice, Calif., 1978), document in the author's collection; coalition, cofounder, interview.

29. Rubino, interview.

30. The weighted average was equal to (Sigma $[A_c][N_c]$) / N_t; N_c is the attendance at events in a community in a fiscal year, A_c is the relative affluence index of the community that year, and N_t is the attendance for all events in the decade.

6. Community Business Leaders: Bounded Power and Movement Alliances

1. Jarvis, *I'm Mad,* 239.

2. Peter Searles (public relations consultant for Proposition 14 in 1972), interview with the author's research project, Sociology Department, UCLA (North Hollywood, Calif.: August 7, 1984).

3. "New Buildings Will Raise Skyline for Sherman Oaks," *The News,* November 10, 1966.

4. Mills, *White Collar,* 59.

5. In the 1980s, Parker was one of the largest land developers in Santa Barbara County.

6. The ratio of a community's median family income divided by the metro-

politan figure, averaged with a similar ratio for the percentage of professional workers, yields the affluence index. See appendix.

7. "Citizens Flood Covina 'Tax Watchdog' Protest Meeting," *San Gabriel Valley Tribune,* November 10, 1957.

8. Art Jett (activist in West Covina Citizens Committee for Fair Taxation), interview with the author's research project, Sociology Department, UCLA (West Covina, Calif.: August 15, 1983).

9. Cf. Molotch, "Growth Machine," who uses the term "growth machine" to refer to both these community small-business leaders and economic elites at the metropolitan level.

10. The differing reactions also stemmed from the smaller size of the Alhambra protest. In Alhambra during 1964–1965, five meetings attracted 3,190 persons, less than one-third the total attendance in the Covina Valley.

11. "City Council Girds for Tax War," *Los Angeles Mirror News,* November 20, 1957. However, the resulting adverse publicity from Legg's statement led him to attend the very next tax protest meeting and distribute leaflets advertising how he had reduced county spending on two occasions. "Valley-wide Tax Protest Meeting to Determine Recall Action Plans," *San Gabriel Valley Tribune,* November 24, 1957, sec. C; John Hiatt (activist in West Covina Citizens Committee for Fair Taxation), interview with the author's research project, Sociology Department, UCLA (West Covina, Calif.: August 25, 1983). Jett, interview.

12. This pattern of response—increasing participation without granting tangible advantages—can be termed formal cooptation. Philip Selznick, "Foundations of the Theory of Organization," *American Sociological Review* 13 (1948), 25–35.

13. "Real Estate Boards Move for Fair Tax," *San Gabriel Valley Tribune,* December 18, 1957. Jett, interview.

14. Harold Johnson (activist in West Covina Citizens Committee for Fair Taxation), interview with the author's research project, Sociology Department, UCLA (West Covina, Calif.: August 24, 1983). Arthur J. Vidich and Joseph Bensman, *Small Town in Mass Society: Class, Power, and Religion in a Rural Community* (Garden City, N.Y.: Doubleday, 1960).

15. Jett, interview.

16. The power of community business leaders is also limited by the much greater power of metropolitan, national, and international business elites. For example, local businesses in Santa Barbara, even when they joined forces with environmental groups and some upper-class residents of the community, failed to control pollution from offshore oil drilling. Even though this pollution threatened the community's economic base of tourism, retirement, and educational work, community business leaders were no match for the major oil corporations. In recent years, large enterprises, such as real estate chains, publishing empires, and land developers who operate at the metropolitan and national level, have been overshadowing the community-based real estate office, newspaper, and contractor. Harvey Molotch, "Capital and Neighborhood in the United States," *Urban Affairs Quarterly* 14 (1979), 289–312. Harvey Molotch and John Logan,

"Tensions in the Growth Machine: Overcoming Resistance to Value-Free Development," *Social Problems* 31 (1984), 483–499.

17. See Everett Cherrington Hughes, *The Growth of an Institution: The Chicago Real Estate Board* (1931; reprint New York: Arno Press, 1979), for a study of a real estate board with a long history of political involvement on issues such as zoning, rent control, banking, taxation, and the structure of local government. See also Janowitz, *Community Press*. C. Wright Mills and Melville J. Ulmer, "Small Business and Civic Welfare," in *The Structure of Community Power*, ed. Michael Aiken and Paul E. Mott (New York: Random House, 1970), 124–154.

18. Searles, interview.

19. The issue of open housing was a critical one for California and the nation. Because of white opposition and the practices of local governments, banks, and the federal government, less than 5 percent of the suburban population in 1970 was black. Many of these "suburbanized" blacks were concentrated in distinctive areas not far from the central city. See Brian Berry, *The Open Housing Question: Race and Housing in Chicago, 1966–1976* (Cambridge, Mass.: Ballinger, 1979), 375. Charles Abrams, *Forbidden Neighbors* (New York: Harper, 1955), 181. Michael Danielson, *The Politics of Exclusion* (New York: Columbia University Press, 1976).

There is some disagreement about the degree to which segregated housing can be blamed on the attitudes and actions of white homeowners. Harvey Molotch, *Managed Integration: Dilemmas of Doing Good in the City* (Berkeley, Los Angeles, London: University of California Press, 1972), argues that de facto housing segregation in Chicago's South Shore stemmed from the structure of the real estate market, which led large numbers of blacks to purchase homes in the few areas that were open to them.

20. Thomas Casstevens, "Berkeley," in *The Politics of Fair Housing Legislation*, ed. Lynn Eley and Thomas Casstevens (San Francisco: Chandler, 1968), 215–236.

21. "Housing Initiative Titled: Petitions Gathering Signatures for Public Vote," *California Real Estate Magazine* 44 (December 1963), 5; "Petition Signers Set New Record, Qualify Initiative for Public Vote," *California Real Estate Magazine* 44 (March 1964). Thomas Casstevens, *Politics, Housing, and Race Relations: California's Rumford Act and Proposition 14* (Berkeley: University of California, Institute of Governmental Studies, 1967), 61. It should be noted, however, that several realty boards in the San Francisco Bay Area opposed the proposition. See Raymond Wolfinger and Fred I. Greenstein, "The Repeal of Fair Housing in California: An Analysis of Referendum Voting," *American Political Science Review* 52 (September 1968), 753–769.

In his first campaign for governor of California, Ronald Reagan called for the repeal of the Rumford Act. Assembly member Rumford was defeated in the ensuing Reagan landslide. See John H. Denton, *Apartheid American Style* (Berkeley, Calif.: Diablo Press, 1967), 34.

22. Denton, *Apartheid*, 19. "N.A.A.C.P. Joins Attack on Detroit Housing Law," *New York Times*, December 22, 1964, 21. Howard D. Hamilton, "Direct

Legislation: Some Implications of Open Housing Referenda," *American Political Science Review* 54 (March 1970), 124–137.

23. Law firm partner involved in Watson's campaign and in lawsuits of businesses to gain lower assessments (name withheld), interview with the author's research project, Sociology Department, UCLA (Los Angeles: August 20, 1984).

24. Ibid.

25. John Patrick Kearney (field deputy to Philip Watson), interview with the author's research project, Sociology Department, UCLA (Los Angeles: August 14, 1984).

26. Law firm partner (name withheld), interview.

27. "Watson Accused of Fraud, Sued for $2 Million," *Los Angeles Times,* October 5, 1968. The names of campaign donors and the amounts given were obtained from the records of the secretary of state, California State Archives, Sacramento, Calif. Macco Realty was developing one thousand acres statewide and contributed $25,000, with William Baker listed at the Macco address contributing another $12,500. (Baker was president of the company.) "Foes of Prop 9 Receive Largest Financial Help," *Los Angeles Times,* October 31, 1968.

28. Whitaker and Baxter (Public Relations and Campaign Management), "A Report, General Election, November 5, 1968" (San Francisco, 1968); "Supervisors Assail Watson Spending in Prop. 9 Campaign," *Los Angeles Times,* October 9, 1968. Kenneth Hahn, a liberal county supervisor, was the source of the direct quotation.

29. Dugald Gillies, "Major Tax Reform Proposals Expected for 1970," *California Real Estate Magazine* (January 1970), 5; "Action Plan Formed for 'Yes' Vote on Proposition 14," *California Real Estate Magazine* (September 1972), 8. "Voters Facing Dilemma Over Property Tax Limit Proposal," *Los Angeles Times,* September 17, 1972; "State Employees Association Spends $1.6 Million Backing Prop. 15," *Los Angeles Times,* November 1, 1972, 3.

30. Searles, interview.

31. Ibid.

32. Ibid.

33. "Meet Toby Roth: Realtor and Politician," *Real Estate Today* (November 1979), 39. Lucian Davis (director, Los Angeles County Board of Realtors and California Association of Realtors), interview with the author's research project, Sociology Department, UCLA (Los Angeles: August 14, 1984).

34. Jean Poulson (president, Los Angeles County Board of Realtors; director, California Association of Realtors and National Association of Realtors), interview with the author's research project, Sociology Department, UCLA (La Canada/Flintridge, Calif.: August 9, 1984). Poulson adds that what motivated real estate professionals to become politically active was "a different type of leadership, a more concerned leadership nationally, statewide, that could pass this on down to the *grassroots,* and made the individual agent in the field more aware of the political consequences for not being involved" (emphasis added).

See also Donald H. Bouma, "Analysis of the Social Power Position of a Real

Estate Board," in *The Structure of Community Power*, ed. Michael Aiken and Paul E. Mott (New York: Random House, 1970), 367–377, for a case study of a realty board which revealed that once the board took a stand on a ballot initiative, all realtors had to publicly support the position and had to gather a quota of signatures for the initiative.

35. "First, and Still the Best," *The Apartment Owner* (August 1984), 22. "The New Mood of Local Government," *California Real Estate Magazine* (March 1977), 5. California Association of Realtors, "The Tax Limitation Plan," (Los Angeles: The Association, 1977).

36. Of the ten persons who signed the articles that incorporated the United Organizations, two (Grace and Elmer Bieck) lived in a census tract where the median family income was $18,711 in 1969 or about 1.71 times the figure for Los Angeles County. One other person lived in a census tract with a median family income of 1.33 times the county figure. The other seven directors, including Jarvis, James Christo, and an early president of the UO, lived in middle-income neighborhoods.

37. This and other quotations in this section are from Harry Crown, interview with the author's research project, Sociology Department, UCLA (Sepulveda, Calif.: September 1984). Crown lived in a census tract where the median family income in 1967 was $11,270 or 1.15 times that of the Los Angeles metropolitan area. (The relative affluence index in Crown's tract was 1.06.)

38. *The Apartment Owner*, August 1984, 22.

39. This and other quotations in this section are from Milton Rubin, interview with the author's research project, Sociology Department, UCLA (Los Angeles: September 11, 1984).

40. *San Gabriel Valley Tribune*, December 7, 1966. *Glendale News Press*, December 7, 1966.

41. In 1960 the median family income in Bellflower was $7,015, almost exactly equal to the figure for the Los Angeles–Long Beach metropolitan area.

42. *The Register*, July 8, 1971.

43. *The Register*, April 6, 1971, 13.

44. "Jarvis Amendment's OC Leaders Named," *The Register*, November 1971, undated clipping in morgue file, folder 300, Amendment. James Earle Christo, interview with the author's research project, Sociology Department, UCLA (Bellflower, Calif.: August 11, 1981; August 17, 1984).

45. This and other quotations in this section are from Christo, interview.

46. *The Register*, August 13, 1971.

47. *The Register*, July 8, 1971; July 14, 1971; October 28, 1971. Jarvis, *I'm Mad*, 29. *Long Beach Independent Press Telegram*, September 17, 1970.

48. Jarvis, *I'm Mad*, 247–248.

49. Ibid., 254–255.

50. *The Register*, August 14, 1971; September 19, 1971; March 20, 1972. Jarvis, *I'm Mad*, 67–68, 89. *Glendale News Press*, July 16, 1976; July 17, 1976; August 24, 1977. However, Jarvis (*I'm Mad*, 69) in his autobiography claims that he "never discussed the present amendment [Proposition 13] with anybody in the apartment industry."

51. Jarvis, *I'm Mad,* 72, 116, 118.

52. *Glendale News Press,* November 18, 1976. Howard Jarvis, "American Liberty Is Based Upon Individual Property Rights," 1976, document in the author's collection.

53. Communities with high attendance at tax protest events also had high increases in assessments. Since fiscal 1949, in the thirteen communities where 500 or more persons reportedly attended tax protest events during a year, the median increase of assessed valuations during the year of protest was 27.0 percent. Among the sixteen communities where yearly reported attendance was from 100 to 500, the median assessment increase was 14.8 percent. This compares to a 6.8 percent median annual increase for Los Angeles County between 1949 to 1978.

54. Recall that the dividing line between middle-income communities and upper-middle-class ones was defined as a relative affluence index of 1.3. One can be certain that the communities in the *clearly* upper-middle-class group (affluence indexes greater than 1.4) actually fell above the 1.3 cutoff, with only a 5-percent chance that the high index resulted from census sampling error.

The calculations for these conclusions are as follows. Assuming a town has 10,000 workers and one-sixth were asked to state their profession: 32.5 percent say they were professionals. According to U.S. Census data, the adjusted standard error is 1.21 percent. Using a 95-percent confidence interval, the finding can be expressed as 32.5 percent plus or minus 2.42 percent. Assuming that the metropolitan area had 25-percent professionals, the professional ratio for the town would be 1.30 plus or minus 0.097, or 1.2 to 1.4. Only four communities had a sampled universe of less than 10,000 and hence were subject to a larger sampling error.

7. Frustrated Advantage in Upper-Middle-Class Communities

1. Flynn, interview.

2. *Taxpayer's Watchdog,* editor (name withheld), interview with the author's research project, Sociology Department, UCLA (Sherman Oaks, Calif.: July 22, 1982).

3. Joe Amorelli (treasurer, Californians for Proposition 13), interview with the author's research project, Sociology Department, UCLA (Tarzana, Calif.: September 10, 1982).

4. *Taxpayer's Watchdog,* editor (name withheld), interview.

5. "Thousands Back Tax Protest Organization," *Valley News,* July 22, 1976.

6. "Homeowner Groups Set Meeting on Tax Relief," *Valley News,* September 5, 1976.

7. "Legislature Fails to Agree on Property Tax Relief Bill," *Valley News,* September 15, 1977.

8. William Robert James McQueen, *Community Groups in the Eastern Santa Monica Mountains: With Special Reference to the Beverly Glen Residents Associa-*

tion, M.A. thesis, Dept. of Geography, University of California at Los Angeles, 1979.

9. Irma Dobbyn (president, Tarzana Property Owners Association), interview with the author's research project, Sociology Department, UCLA (Tarzana, Calif.: February 4, 1987).

10. Ralph Orr (activist with the Sand Area Residents Association, Manhattan Beach), interview with the author's research project, Sociology Department, UCLA (Manhattan Beach, Calif.: February 14, 1987).

11. Regis Kennedy (president, Tarzana Property Owners Association), interview with author's research project, Sociology Department, UCLA (Tarzana, Calif.: August 12, 1982).

12. Seth Larsen (activist, Highland Property Owners Group), interview with the author's research project, Sociology Department, UCLA (Los Angeles: August 13, 1984).

13. Orr, interview.

14. Hill, interview. For a discussion of the homeowners' opposition to growth on the peninsula which led to the incorporation of the city of Rancho Palos Verdes, see chap. 3.

15. "County Tax Vote Stirs Criticism of Hayes," *Torrance Daily Breeze,* July 7, 1976; "Hayes Forms Tax Panels," *Torrance Daily Breeze,* July 20, 1976.

16. Jeannette Mucha (public-relations and press officer for Citizens for Property Tax Relief), interview with the author's research project, Sociology Department, UCLA (Redondo Beach, Calif.: July 6, 1987).

17. Gunther Buerk (board member, homeowners association on Rocking Horse Road; president, Palos Verdes Peninsula Advisory Council; founding city council member, city of Rancho Palos Verdes), interview with the author's research project, Sociology Department, UCLA (Rancho Palos Verdes, Calif.: July 2, 1987).

18. Brentwood Homeowners Association, executive secretary and director (name withheld), interview with the author's research project, Sociology Department, UCLA (Brentwood, Calif.: July 27, 1982).

19. Jim Hatch (steering committee, Citizens for Property Tax Relief), interview with the author's research project, Sociology Department, UCLA (Rancho Palos Verdes, Calif.: May 15, 1987). Ernest Dynda (director of the Agoura–Los Virgenes Chamber of Commerce; president of the United Organizations of Taxpayers), interview with the author's research project, Sociology Department, UCLA (Agoura Hills, Calif.: July 27, 1987).

20. Jane Nerpel (founder, Californians for Proposition 13; administrator, Taxpayers Watchdog), interview with the author's research project, Sociology Department, UCLA (Van Nuys, Calif.: February 4, 1982).

21. Recall that the relative affluence index is the ratio of the median family income over the figure for the L.A. area, averaged with the ratio of the percentage of professional employees over the L.A. figure.

The vast majority of blue-collar workers do not make an upper-middle-class income. For example, when Proposition 13 passed in 1978, unionized and middle-aged steelworkers and printers made less than 1.3 times the median family income, but graduates of law school usually started work at salaries greater than 1.3 times the median. See Blumberg, *Inequality*, 76. Assuming a one-income family, associate and full professors in large state universities generally earned upper-middle-class incomes, whereas assistant professors did not. A few high administrators earned upper-class incomes, in excess of $120,000.

22. Mucha, interview.

23. Haber, interview.

24. Ibid.

25. Also, 130 labor and public employee organizations contributed $1.8 million, and the top officers and lobbyists (not the rank and file) could be considered to be politically influential.

26. The emphasis here on the discrepancy between political power and socioeconomic inequality differs from the existing literature on status inconsistency. That literature examines the different dimensions of socioeconomic inequality itself, such as education, income, and occupation, and attempts to link political behavior to status discrepancies (such as having a high education but low income).

27. James K. Lee (chairman, Citizens for Property Tax Relief), interview with the author's research project, Sociology Department, UCLA (Los Angeles: July 30, 1982).

28. Noorda, interview. Close, interview. Darrow Miller (director, Cheviot Hills Homeowners Association), interview with the author's research project, Sociology Department, UCLA (Cheviot Hills, Calif.: August 9, 1982).

29. Brentwood Homeowners Association, executive secretary and director, interview.

30. Kennedy, interview.

31. Brentwood Homeowners Association, executive secretary and director, interview.

32. Lee, interview.

33. Ibid.

34. Maurice Hart, letter to the editor, *Valley News*, August 4, 1976.

35. Emphasis added. Brentwood Homeowners Association, executive secretary and director, interview.

36. Peppard, interview.

37. Brentwood Homeowners Association, executive secretary and director, interview. Miller, interview.

38. One would expect to find more harmonious relations between upper-middle-class homeowners and local business leaders in those locales where the issues of growth were not as salient. Specifically, although controversies over urban growth did exist in Sherman Oaks, Brentwood, and other Valley and hillside communities in 1976, the controversies were far less intense compared to the ones in West Covina in 1957. Relations between the upper-middle class and community business leaders were likely to be more cooperative if the area's growth rate had leveled off. During the 1950s, the number of housing units in West Covina increased by 891 percent; upper-middle-class homeowners frequently fought with community business leaders on growth issues. In the 1970s the housing units on the Palos Verdes peninsula increased by 89 percent; in Sherman Oaks,

13 percent; and Brentwood, 2 percent. This made possible more harmonious relations between community businesses and the upper-middle class.

39. Amorelli, interview.

40. *Taxpayer's Watchdog,* editor, interview.

41. Ibid.

42. Buerk, interview.

43. Mucha, interview.

44. Buerk, interview.

45. Peppard, interview.

46. Ibid.

47. Ibid.

48. This tax rate was applied in fiscal 1976 to an assessed value that was one-quarter of market value.

49. Steve Frank (president, CIVICC; vice-president, BUSTOP), interview with the author's research project, Sociology Department, UCLA (Sepulveda, Calif.: August 30, 1982).

50. Ibid.

51. Dan Hon (founding chair of the Canyon County Formation Committee, Santa Clarita Valley), interview with the author's research project, Sociology Department, UCLA (Newhall, Calif.: September 14, 1982).

52. "County Secession Move On," *Torrance Daily Breeze,* August 31, 1975. The resentment against paying for the inner-city welfare roles was heightened because the inner city was largely black and Hispanic. One study done for the secession movement revealed that the proportion of the population on welfare in the South Bay was the same as the rest of Los Angeles County. But many believed that the welfare payments in the South Bay were legitimate because the recipients were white. "All these little blonde girls you saw riding around with two little kids in the back of the Volkswagen were on welfare, and they're all living in Palos Verdes. . . . What we didn't have was an excessive population of black people. . . . You could almost count it—lily white." South Bay secession movement, activist (name withheld), interview with the author's research project, Sociology Department, UCLA (place and date withheld).

53. Dynda, interview.

54. Ibid. Dan Shapiro (president, Studio City Residents Association), interview with the author's research project, Sociology Department, UCLA (Studio City, Calif.: January 27, 1986).

55. Jim Walker (leader, South Bay secession movement), interview with the author's research project, Sociology Department, UCLA (Catalina Island, Calif.: August 11, 1987).

56. Hon, interview.

57. Bill New (organizer, People's Advocate) interviews with the author's research project, Sociology Department, UCLA (West Los Angeles, Calif.: May 29, 1982, and June 18, 1982).

58. Kathy Bergstrom (steering committee, Citizens for Property Tax Relief), interview with the author's research project, Sociology Department, UCLA (Hermosa Beach, Calif.: September 4, 1982).

59. Close, interview. Noorda, interview.

60. Warren Stearns (president, North Santa Monica Homeowners Association), interview with the author's research project, Sociology Department, UCLA (Westwood, Calif.: August 5, 1982).

61. Eunice McTyre (secretary, Taxpayers Watchdog), interview with the author's research project, Sociology Department, UCLA (Chatsworth, Calif.: July 15, 1982). *Taxpayer's Watchdog,* editor, interview.

62. Farmer, interview.

63. Virgil Elkins (board member, United Organizations of Taxpayers; Orange County chairman, Taxpayers, Inc.; president, Orange County Taxpayers Association), interview with the author's research project, Sociology Department, UCLA (Santa Ana, Calif.: March 18, 1982).

64. Lyle Cook (activist in campaign for Proposition 13; candidate for state assembly, American Independent Party), interview with the author's research project, Sociology Department, UCLA (Fresno, Calif.: September 18, 1987). Paul Gann (founder, People's Advocate), interview with the author's research project, Sociology Department, UCLA (Carmichael, Calif.: August 28, 1987). One tax reduction petition that Paul Gann unsuccessfully circulated contained several progressive provisions—an increase in the homeowner's exemption and a provision mandating that renters be given tax relief as well as homeowners. When Jarvis and Gann decided to join forces and were negotiating the specific provisions of what became Proposition 13, Gann insisted that assessments should be limited as well as the tax rate; this provision would benefit homeowners, whose assessments were rising faster than business's. Proposition 13 did contain a provision limiting the annual increase in assessments to 2 percent (regardless of the inflation of market prices, which was much higher). Gann and Jarvis agreed, however, that the reduction in tax rates to 1 percent would apply to both business and homeowners.

Gann argued against higher taxes on businesses because they would then merely raise prices the consumers would have to pay: "I've been in and worked with the free enterprise system and I know that business doesn't pay taxes. Business collects the money but they collect it from the people who they do business with. So we, the people, pay the taxes whether big business collects it and turns it over to the government or we send it in direct." Gann, interview.

65. *Glendale News Press,* June 6, 1978; May 27, 31, 1978.

66. Lee, interview.

67. Haber, interview. Frank, interview. Charles Betz (board member, United Organizations of Taxpayers), interview with the author's research project, Sociology Department, UCLA (West Los Angeles, Calif.: February 16, 1982).

68. *Valley News,* April 9, 1978. In addition, the Hillsborough Homeowners Association of San Mateo County, which represented a wealthy residential community in northern California, contributed $9,000.

69. Elkins, interview. *Taxpayer's Watchdog,* editor, interview.

70. Frank, interview.

71. Poulson, interview. Lee, interview.

72. In the 40th, 39th, 38th, and 37th Assembly Districts, respectively. The inner-city 47th District voted 35 percent in favor of Proposition 13.

High-income individuals supported Proposition 13 strongly. The higher the income, the stronger the support. 68 percent of those earning above $30,000 (1.6 times the L.A.–SMSA median in 1978) favored the proposition immediately before the election. Field Institute, *The California Poll,* Release #975, June 2, 1978.

High-income earners were also likely to be homeowners; this group strongly favored Proposition 13. In a multicausal model, the direct effect (controlling for proximate variables) of homeownership on support for the tax revolt, as indicated by the standardized coefficient, was +0.12. Income had a total effect of +0.16 but a direct effect of zero. Sears and Citrin, *Tax Revolt,* 96–100, 207–212.

73. Poll data indicates that professionals and business elites oppose policies to redistribute wealth from the affluent to the poor. Steven Brint, "The Political Attitudes of Professionals," *Annual Review of Sociology* 11 (Palo Alto, Calif.: Annual Reviews, Inc., 1985), 389–414.

74. Ronald Inglehart, "Post-Materialism in an Environment of Insecurity," *American Political Science Review* 75 (December 1981), 880–900. Alvin W. Gouldner, *The Future of Intellectuals and the Rise of the New Class* (New York: Seabury Press, 1979). Gouldner argued that professionals would lean to the left not because of their newly found power but rather because of their deprivation; many highly educated persons faced dismal employment prospects. Everett Carll Ladd, Jr., "The New Lines Are Drawn: Class and Ideology in America," *Public Opinion* 1 (July/August 1978), 48–53.

75. Fifty-four percent of college grads voted for Prop. 13, a smaller percentage than the electorate. Exit poll, *Los Angeles Times,* June 7, 1978. Nathan Glazer, "Lawyers and the New Class," in Robert L. Bartley, et al., *The New Class?* ed. B. Bruce Biggs (New Brunswick, N.J.: Transaction, 1979). Brint, "Professionals."

76. For example, across the entire United States in 1979, there were only 23 female mechanical engineers and 53 female airline pilots and navigators making $50,000 or above, compared to 3,896 and 20,976 men in the same job categories and income level. U.S. Bureau of the Census, *1980 Census of the Population, Detailed Population Characteristics, United States Summary,* sect. A, vol. 1, pt. 1 (Washington, D.C.: Government Printing Office, 1982).

77. Brint, "Professionals." The professionals' support of environmental issues is probably not an indication of their postmaterialism. The desire for a home in an aesthetic environment, for example, by necessity is also a desire for a more expensive home. Environmentalism is the icing on the materialistic cake. Lipset and Schneider, *Confidence Gap,* 245.

8. The Politics of Probusiness Tax Limitation

1. Typical invocation for a Fair Share community meeting. Michael Ansara (cofounder, Massachusetts Fair Share, Harvard Strike, 1969), interview with the

author's research project, Sociology Department, UCLA (Boston: December 1984).

2. Ronald Reagan, *Ronald Reagan's Weekly Radio Addresses,* vol. 1, *The First Term* (Wilmington, Del.: Scholarly [*sic*] Resources, Inc., 1987).

3. Jean Tomaszycki (activist, Dorchester Community Action Committee), interview with the author's research project, Sociology Department, UCLA (Dorchester, Mass.: December 1984). Joanne Corbett, Neal Michaels, Dale Mitchell, and Diane Muellner, "Property Tax Classification in Massachusetts: An Alternative to 100% Revaluation," report prepared for Massachusetts Fair Share, mimeo, c. 1978.

4. Ansara (recalling the speaker's words), interview.

5. Lou Finfer (staff organizer for Dorchester Community Action Committee and Somerville United Neighborhoods), interview with the author's research project, Sociology Department, UCLA (Boston: December 1984).

6. Warren Banbury (cochair, taxation committee, Somerville United Neighborhoods), interview with the author's research project, Sociology Department, UCLA (Medford, Mass.: December 1984).

7. Finfer, interview. Ansara, interview. Ansara claims that at its peak, Fair Share had 140,000 dues-paying families statewide with 60 community organizers and another 140 staff fund solicitors.

8. Mike Regan (activist in Chelsea Fair Share), interview with the author's research project, Sociology Department, UCLA (Boston: December 1984). *Boston Globe,* April 12, 1978; *Boston Herald-American,* April 12, 1978.

9. Regan, interview. Mark Dyen (president of Massachusetts Fair Share, Harvard Strike, 1969), and Carolyn Lucas (chair, Fair Share tax committee), interview with the author's research project, Sociology Department, UCLA (Boston: December 1984). *Daily Evening Item* (Lynn, Mass.), June 27, 1978. Ansara, interview. *Boston Herald-American,* July 11, 1978.

10. John Avault, Alex Ganz, and Daniel M. Holland, "Tax Relief and Reform in Massachusetts," *National Tax Journal* 32 (1979): 289–304.

11. Kuttner, *Revolt,* 313–315. Avault, et al., "Tax Relief." Classification did not take effect in a locality until the State Revenue Department certified that properties had been reassessed at 100 percent of value, a task that many localities were unwilling to undertake.

12. Dyen and Lucas, interview.

13. The proposition also limited property tax collections to the previous year's total plus 2.5 percent, reduced the auto excise tax to 2.5 percent, and eliminated many practices associated with higher local government spending (such as programs mandated by state government but not funded by the state, binding arbitration for police and firefighters' salary issues, and the power of school boards to spend money without local government approval).

14. *Boston Globe,* June 11, 1978; June 15, 1978; May 6, 1980; October 30, 1980.

15. Edward F. King (founding executive director, Citizens for Limited Taxation, not to be confused with Edward J. King, former governor of Mass.), interview with the author's research project, Sociology Department, UCLA

(Boston: December 1984). For a listing of community organizations supporting Proposition 2½, see "Endorsers of Tax Limitation," *Taxachusetts* 1 (November 1977), 4.

16. King, interview. Don Feder, interview with the author's research project, Sociology Department, UCLA (Boston: December 1984). Committee for Limited Taxation, "Memo #2—Preparing for the Petition Drive," document in the author's collection. Anderson, interview. The literature of the National Federation of Independent Business emphasizes the problems of small business and sometimes criticizes large business. See Richard Hamilton, *Restraining Myths: Critical Studies of U.S. Social Structure and Politics* (Beverly Hills, Calif.: Sage, 1975), 247. Pauline Zywaski (treasurer, Citizens for Limited Taxation), interview with the author's research project, Sociology Department, UCLA (Holliston, Mass.: December 1984).

17. Massachusetts High Technology Council, "A New Social Contract for Massachusetts," mimeo, c. 1978; "Why a High Technology Council?" pamphlet, c. 1983.

Of the 29 companies that had representatives on the High Technology Council's Board of Directors, 19 did not have sufficient sales to be ranked among the top 1,000 U.S. industrial corporations. See *Fortune Double 500 Directory* (New York: Time, Inc., 1980). Those 10 firms listed in the directory had sales ranging from $112 million to $2.4 billion. Four ranked in the top 500 and 6 ranked 501 to 1,000.

18. Dekkers L. Davidson, "The Massachusetts High Technology Council," Harvard Business School case studies 0-383-026 and 0-383-027 (Boston: HBS Case Services, 1982).

19. Another new-right group, the Conservative Caucus, gained the affiliations of a tax protest group in Redondo Beach and one in Glendale. Several tax activists had been recruited to the caucus when its national chair, Howard Phillips, made a series of local appearances. Ray Maloney (activist in Revolt Against Government Excesses; district director, Conservative Caucus), interview with the author's research project, Sociology Department, UCLA (Long Beach, Calif.: August 16, 1982).

20. *Dollars and Sense,* November 1984, 2. This is a publication of the National Taxpayers Union and should not be confused with a periodical with the same title published by the Union for Radical Political Economics.

21. *Dollars and Sense,* November 1979, 8; November 1984, 2.

22. A content analysis of *Dollars and Sense* revealed that 20 percent of its arguments about taxes were in favor of business interests and 30 percent against the power of government and the IRS. Both of these figures are above the medians (14 and 13 percent, respectively) for the antitax publications found in the Right-Wing Collection of the University of Iowa Library and four other libraries. Clarence Y. H. Lo, "The Pro-Business and Anti-Government Sides of the Tax Revolt," Sociology Department, UCLA, 1986, photocopy.

23. *Dollars and Sense,* February 1979, 4; April–May 1979, 5; September 1978, 1.

24. *Dollars and Sense,* November 1985, 2.

25. *Dollars and Sense,* January–February 1984, 6.

26. *Dollars and Sense,* September 1980, 5; April 1984, 2.

27. *Dollars and Sense,* May–June 1984, 9; April 1984, 3.

28. *Dollars and Sense,* October 1978, 8; September 1978, 1.

29. *Kansas City* (Mo.) *Times,* May 29, 1982, 1. David Keating (executive vice-president, National Taxpayers' Union), interview with the author's research project, Sociology Department, UCLA (Washington, D.C.: February 5, 1986). *Dollars and Sense,* December 1985–January 1986, 4.

30. Parkash S. Sethi, *Advocacy Advertising and the Large Corporation* (Lexington, Mass.: Lexington Books, 1977), 8, 115–178. David Vogel, "The Power of Business in America: A Re-appraisal," *British Journal of Political Science* 13 (1982), 19–43. Michael Useem, *The Inner Circle: Large Corporations and the Rise of Business Political Activity in the U.S. and the U.K.* (New York: Oxford, 1984), 129.

31. Michael Maliban (ed.), *Parties, Interest Groups and Campaign Finance Laws* (Washington, D.C.: American Enterprise Institute, 1980). Elizabeth Drew, *Politics and Money* (New York: Macmillan, 1983). Vogel, "Business." Useem, *Inner Circle,* 134.

32. Vogel, "Business."

33. Leonard Silk and David Vogel, *Ethics and Profits: The Crisis of Confidence in American Business* (New York: Simon and Schuster, 1976), 46, 51–53, 66–67, 71.

34. "Rebellion Against Deficits," *Nation's Business,* March 1984, 22–24. National Tax Limitation Committee, "About the National Tax Limitation Committee," leaflet, n.d.

35. This direct mail program was awarded the Gold Echo Award presented by the Direct Mail Marketing Association. National Tax Limitation Committee, "Biennial Report, 1981–82," pamphlet. "Moving to Limit U.S. Spending," *Washington* [D.C.] *Star,* June 8, 1978, 1. "Reagan's Speech Elates Lobbyists," *New York Times,* May 1, 1982. "The Grass-Roots Revolt Against Federal Deficits," *Fortune,* November 28, 1983, 51. "Drive for Balanced Budget Amendment Turns to States," *Washington Times,* February 1, 1984, 3c.

Appendix: Research Methods for Studying Social Movement History

1. Tilly, *Mobilization.*

2. For a typology of the authorities' responses to social movements, see William A. Gamson, *The Strategy of Social Protest* (Homewood, Ill.: Dorsey, 1975).

3. For data on 1976 see City of Los Angeles, Department of City Planning, Data Support Unit, "Estimated Median Family Income by Planning District within Geographic Area, 1969–1976," mimeo, March 1979.

4. Communities with an affluence index of less than 0.60 can be termed deprived. For example, 1.45 million residents lived in the central Los Angeles area (including Watts, East Los Angeles, and Hollywood), which had a relative

affluence index of 0.55. The federally defined poverty line in 1987 was 0.38 times the median family income, or $11,611 for a family of four.

5. See chap. 3, n. 10, for the debate on the size of the middle class.

6. Paul Thompson, *The Voice of the Past: Oral History* (New York: Oxford, 1978). Lewis A. Dexter, *Elite and Specialized Interviewing* (Evanston, Ill.: Northwestern University Press, 1970).

7. Robert K. Merton, Marjorie Fiske, and Patricia L. Kendall, *The Focused Interview: A Manual of Problems and Procedures* (Glencoe, Ill.: Free Press, 1956).

Bibliography

Abrams, Charles. *Forbidden Neighbors*. New York: Harper, 1955.

Agnew, J. A. "Homeownership and the Capitalist Social Order." In *Urbanization and Urban Planning in Capitalist Society*, ed. Michael Dear and Allen J. Scott. London: Methuen, 1981.

Aminzade, Ronald. "Capitalist Industrialization and Patterns of Industrial Protest: A Comparative Urban Study of Nineteenth-Century France." *American Sociological Review* 49 (1984), 437–453.

Avault, John, Alex Ganz, and Daniel M. Holland, "Tax Relief and Reform in Massachusetts." *National Tax Journal* 32 (1979), 289–304.

Bachrach, Peter, and Morton S. Baratz. "The Two Faces of Power." *American Political Science Review* 56 (1962), 947–952.

Banfield, Edward C., and James Q. Wilson. *City Politics*. Cambridge: Harvard University Press, 1965.

Barkan, Steven E. "Legal Control of the Southern Civil Rights Movement." *American Sociological Review* 49 (1984), 552–565.

Bellah, Robert N., Richard Madsen, Anne Swidler, William M. Sullivan, and Steven M. Tipton. *Habits of the Heart: Individualism and Commitment in American Life*. Berkeley, Los Angeles, London: University of California Press, 1985.

Berger, Bennett M. *Working Class Suburb: A Study of Auto Workers in Suburbia*. Berkeley and Los Angeles: University of California Press, 1960.

Bernard, Jessie. *The Sociology of Community*. Glenview, Ill.: Scott Foresman, 1973.

Berry, Brian. *The Open Housing Question: Race and Housing in Chicago, 1966–1976*. Cambridge, Mass.: Ballinger, 1979.

Blumberg, Paul. *Inequality in an Age of Decline.* New York: Oxford University Press, 1980.

Blumenthal, Sidney. *The Rise of the Counter-Establishment: From Conservative Ideology to Political Power.* New York: Times Books, 1986.

Blumer, Herbert, "Race Prejudice as a Sense of Group Position." *Pacific Sociological Review* 1 (1958), 3–7.

———. *Symbolic Interactionism: Perspective and Method.* Englewood Cliffs, N.J.: Prentice-Hall, 1969.

Bouma, Donald H. "Analysis of the Social Power Position of a Real Estate Board." In *The Structure of Community Power,* ed. Michael Aiken and Paul E. Mott. New York: Random House, 1970.

Bowles, Samuel, and Herbert Gintis. *Democracy and Capitalism: Property, Community, and the Contradictions of Modern Social Thought.* New York: Basic, 1987.

Brandon, Robert K., Jonathan Rowe, and Thomas H. Stanton. *Tax Politics: How They Make You Pay and What You Can Do About It.* New York: Pantheon, 1976.

Brint, Steven. "The Political Attitudes of Professionals." *Annual Review of Sociology* 11 (Palo Alto, Calif.: Annual Reviews, Inc., 1985).

Calhoun, Craig. *The Question of Class Struggle.* Chicago: University of Chicago Press, 1982.

California, Assembly Committee on Revenue and Taxation and Assembly Committee on Local Government, "The Property Tax Four Years After Proposition 13: Assessment Issues, Allocation Issues, Litigation: A Briefing Book." Sacramento, Calif., 1982.

California, Fair Political Practices Commission. "Campaign Contribution and Spending Report, November 2, 1976, General Election." Sacramento, Calif., 1977.

California, Legislative Analyst. "Budget Analysis, 1977–1978." Sacramento, Calif., 1977.

———. "An Analysis of Proposition 13." Sacramento, Calif., May 1978.

California, Secretary of State. "Statement of Vote, General Election, November 2, 1976." Sacramento, Calif., 1976.

California State Board of Equalization. "Annual Report 1978–79." Sacramento, Calif., 1979.

California State Board of Equalization, Property Tax Department, Assessment Standards Division. "Assessment Practices Survey, Los Angeles County, 1972–73." Sacramento, Calif., 1973.

California State Board of Equalization, Department of Property Taxes, Assessment Standards Division. "Assessment Practices Survey, Los Angeles County, 1978–79." Sacramento, Calif., 1979.

Casstevens, Thomas. *Politics, Housing, and Race Relations: California's Rumford Act and Proposition 14.* Berkeley, Calif.: University of California, Institute of Governmental Studies, 1967.

———. "Berkeley." In *The Politics of Fair Housing Legislation,* ed. Lynn Eley and Thomas Casstevens. San Francisco: Chandler, 1968.

Castells, Manuel. *The City and the Grassroots: A Cross-Cultural Theory of Urban Social Movements.* Berkeley, Los Angeles, London: University of California Press, 1983.

Chong, Dennis, Herbert McClosky, and John Zaller. "Patterns of Support for Democratic and Capitalist Values in the United States." *British Journal of Political Science* 13 (1982), 401–440.

Citrin, Jack. "Do People Want Something for Nothing: Public Opinion on Taxes and Government Spending." *National Tax Journal,* Supplement, 32 (1979), 113–129.

Clark, Terry N., and Lorna Ferguson. *City Money: Political Processes, Fiscal Strain, and Retrenchment.* New York: Columbia University Press, 1983.

Conover, Pamela Johnston, and Stanley Feldman. "The Origins and Meaning of Liberal/Conservative Self-Identifications." *American Journal of Political Science* 25 (1981), 617–645.

————. "How People Organize the Political World: A Schematic Model." *American Journal of Political Science* 28 (1984), 95–123.

Converse, Philip. "The Nature of Belief Systems in Mass Publics." In *Ideology and Discontent,* ed. David Apter. New York: Free Press, 1964.

Courant, Paul N., Edward M. Gramlich, and Daniel L. Rubinfeld. "Why Voters Support Tax Limitation Amendments: The Michigan Case." *National Tax Journal* 33 (1980), 1–20.

Crenson, Matthew. *The Un-Politics of Air Pollution.* Baltimore: Johns Hopkins University Press, 1971.

Cronk, George Francis. "Symbolic Interactionism: A 'Left-Meadian' Interpretation." *Social Theory and Practice* 2 (1973), 313–333.

Dahl, Robert. *Who Governs? Democracy and Power in an American City.* New Haven: Yale University Press, 1961.

Danielson, Michael. *The Politics of Exclusion.* New York: Columbia University Press, 1976.

Davidson, Dekkers L. "The Massachusetts High Technology Council." Harvard Business School case studies 0-383-026 and 0-383-027. Boston: HBS Case Services, 1982.

Davis, James A. "Conservative Weather in a Liberalizing Climate: Change in Selected NORC General Social Survey Items, 1972–78." *Social Forces* 58 (1980), 1129–1156.

Denton, John H. *Apartheid American Style.* Berkeley, Calif.: Diablo Press, 1967.

Dexter, Lewis A. *Elite and Specialized Interviewing.* Evanston, Ill.: Northwestern University Press, 1970.

Drew, Elizabeth. *Politics and Money.* New York: Macmillan, 1983.

Ferree, Myra Marx, and Frederick D. Miller. "Mobilization and Meaning: Toward an Integration of Social Movements." *Sociological Inquiry* 55 (1985), 38–51.

Fireman, Bruce, and William A. Gamson. "Utilitarian Logic in the Resource Mobilization Perspective." In *The Dynamics of Social Movements,* ed. Mayer N. Zald and John D. McCarthy. Cambridge, Mass.: Winthrop, 1979.

Fortune Magazine. *The Fortune Double 500 Directory.* New York: Time, Inc., 1980.

Free, Lloyd, and Harvey Cantril. *The Political Beliefs of Americans: A Study of Public Opinion.* Reprint, New Brunswick, N.J.: Rutgers University Press, 1967.

Friedman, Milton, and Rose Friedman. *Free to Choose: A Personal Statement.* New York: Harcourt Brace Jovanovich, 1980.

Gallup, George Horace. *The Gallup Poll: Public Opinion, 1935–1971.* New York: Random House, 1972.

Gamson, William A. *The Strategy of Social Protest.* Homewood, Ill.: Dorsey, 1975.

Gans, Herbert J. *The Levittowners: Ways of Life and Politics in a New Suburban Community.* New York: Pantheon, 1967.

Gatlin, Douglas S., Michael W. Giles and Everett F. Catalo. "Policy Support within a Target Group: The Case of School Desegregation." *American Political Science Review* 72 (1978), 985–995.

Geertz, Clifford. *The Interpretation of Cultures.* New York: Basic, 1973.

Giddens, Anthony. *Class Structure of the Advanced Societies.* New York: Harper and Row, 1973.

———. *New Rules of Sociological Method: A Positive Critique of Interpretive Sociologies.* New York: Basic, 1976.

Gilder, George. *Wealth and Poverty.* New York: Basic, 1981.

Gittel, Marilyn. *Limits to Citizen Participation: The Decline of Community Organization.* Beverly Hills, Calif.: Sage, 1980.

Glazer, Nathan. "Lawyers and the New Class." In Robert L. Bartley et al., *The New Class?* ed. B. Bruce Biggs. New Brunswick, N.J.: Transaction, 1979.

Gorey, Hans. *Nader and the Power of Everyman.* New York: Grosset and Dunlap, 1975.

Greer, Ann Lennarson. *The Mayor's Mandate: Municipal Statecraft and Political Trust.* Cambridge, Mass.: Schenkman, 1974.

Gouldner, Alvin W. *The Future of Intellectuals and the Rise of the New Class.* New York: Seabury Press, 1979.

Gusfield, Joseph. *Symbolic Crusade: Status Politics and the American Temperance Movement.* Urbana, Ill.: University of Illinois Press, 1963.

Hall, Peter M. "A Symbolic Interactionist Analysis of Power." In *Perspectives in Political Sociology,* ed. A. Effrat. Indianapolis, Ind.: Bobbs-Merrill, 1972.

Halle, David. *America's Working Man: Work, Home, and Politics among Blue-Collar Property Owners.* Chicago: University of Chicago Press, 1984.

Hamilton, Howard D. "Direct Legislation: Some Implications of Open Housing Referenda." *American Political Science Review* 54 (1970), 124–137.

Hamilton, Richard. *Restraining Myths: Critical Studies of U.S. Social Structure and Politics.* Beverly Hills, Calif.: Sage, 1975.

Hartz, Louis. *The Liberal Tradition in America.* New York: Harcourt Brace Jovanovich, 1955.

Hays, Samuel P. "The Politics of Reform in Municipal Government in the Progressive Era." *Pacific Northwest Quarterly* 55 (1964), 157–169.

Henig, Jeffrey R. *Neighborhood Mobilization: Redevelopment and Response.* New Brunswick, N.J.: Rutgers University Press, 1982.

Heritage Foundation. *An Agenda for Progress.* Washington, D.C.: The Foundation, 1981.

Himmelstein, Jerome L., and James A. McRae, Jr. "Social Conservatism, New Republicans, and the 1980 Election." *Public Opinion Quarterly* 48 (1984), 592–605.

Hofstadter, Richard. *The Age of Reform: From Bryan to FDR.* New York: Vintage, 1955.

———. "The Pseudo-Conservative Revolt." In *The Radical Right,* ed. Daniel Bell. New York: Doubleday, 1964.

Holsworth, Robert. *Public Interest Liberalism and the Crisis of Affluence: Reflections on Nader, Environmentalism, and the Politics of a Sustainable Society.* Cambridge, Mass.: Schenkman, 1980.

Hughes, Everett Cherrington. *The Growth of an Institution: The Chicago Real Estate Board.* 1931. Reprint, New York: Arno Press, 1979.

Ingelhart, Ronald. "Post-Materialism in an Environment of Insecurity." *American Political Science Review* 75 (1981), 880–900.

Jacobs, Jane. *The Death and Life of Great American Cities.* New York: Random House, 1961.

Janowitz, Morris. *The Community Press in an Urban Setting.* Glencoe, Ill.: Free Press, 1951.

Jarvis, Howard, with Robert Pack. *I'm Mad as Hell: The Exclusive Story of the Tax Revolt and Its Leader.* New York: Times Books, 1979.

Jenkins, J. Craig. "Resource Mobilization Theory and the Study of Social Movements." *Annual Review of Sociology* 9 (Palo Alto, Calif.: Annual Reviews, Inc., 1983).

———. *The Politics of Insurgency.* New York: Columbia University Press, 1984.

Katznelson, Ira. *City Trenches: Urban Politics and the Patterning of Class in the United States.* Chicago: University of Chicago Press, 1981.

Kelly, Johnathan. "The Politics of School Busing." *Public Opinion Quarterly* 38 (1974), 23–39.

Kinzer, Lydia G., and Shirley W. Moltz. "A Longitudinal View of Sales Data for a Computer-Assisted Appraisal Program." *Assessor's Journal* 10 (1975), 41–56.

Klandermans, Bert. "Mobilization and Participation: Social-Psychological Expansions of Resource Mobilization Theory." *American Sociological Review* 49 (1984), 583–600.

Kuttner, Robert. *The Revolt of the Haves: Tax Rebellions and Hard Times.* New York: Simon and Schuster, 1980.

———. "The Declining Middle." *Atlantic Monthly* (July 1983), 60–72.

Kuttner, Robert, and David Kelston. *The Shifting Property Tax Burden.* Washington, D.C.: Conference on Alternative State and Local Policies, 1979.

Ladd, Everett Carll Jr. "The New Lines are Drawn: Class and Ideology in America." *Public Opinion* 1 (1978), 48–53.

———. "What the Voters Really Want." *Fortune* (1978), 40–48.

Ladd, Everett Carll Jr., with Marilyn Potter, Linda Basilick, Sally Daniels, and Dana Suszkiw. "The Polls: Taxing and Spending." *Public Opinion Quarterly* 43 (1979), 126–135.

Ladd, Helen F., and Julie Boatright Wilson. "Who Supports Tax Limitations: Evidence from Massachusetts' Proposition 2½." *Journal of Policy Analysis and Management* 2 (1983), 256–279.

Lalli, Frank. "The New Middle-Class Dream: I Just Want to Hang on to What I've Got." *New West* (October 25, 1976), 20–28.

Lamb, Karl A. *As Orange Goes.* New York: W. W. Norton, 1974.

Levy, Frank. "On Understanding Proposition 13." *The Public Interest* 56 (1979), 66–89.

Lewis, J. David, and Richard L. Smith. *American Sociology and Pragmatism: Mead, Chicago Sociology, and Symbolic Interaction.* Chicago: University of Chicago Press, 1980.

Lipset, Seymour Martin. "The Sources of the 'Radical Right.' " In *The Radical Right,* ed. Daniel Bell. New York: Doubleday, 1964.

Lipset, Seymour Martin, and Earl Raab. *The Politics of Unreason: Right-Wing Extremism in America, 1790–1977.* Chicago: University of Chicago Press, 1978.

Lipset, Seymour Martin, and William Schneider. *The Confidence Gap: Business, Labor, and Government in the Public Mind.* New York: Free Press, 1983.

Lo, Clarence Y. H. "Mobilizing the Tax Revolt: The Emergent Alliance between Homeowners and Local Elites." In *Research in Social Movements, Conflict and Change,* vol. 6 (Greenwich, Conn.: JAI Press, 1984), 293–328.

———. "The Pro-Business and Anti-Government Sides of the Tax Revolt." Sociology Department, University of California at Los Angeles, 1986, photocopy.

Logan, John R. "Industrialization and the Stratification of Cities in Suburban Regions." *American Journal of Sociology* 82 (1976), 333–352.

Logan, John R. "Growth, Politics, and the Stratification of Places." *American Journal of Sociology* 84 (1978), 404–416.

Logan, John R., and Harvey Molotch. *Urban Fortunes: The Political Economy of Place.* Berkeley, Los Angeles, London: University of California Press, 1987.

Los Angeles City, Department of City Planning, Data Support Unit. "Estimated Median Family Income by Planning District within Geographic Area, 1969–1976." Los Angeles, March 1979.

Los Angeles County, Department of the Assessor. "Biennial Report." Los Angeles, various years.

Los Angeles County, Office of the Auditor. *Tax Payers' Guide.* Los Angeles, various years.

Lowrey, David, and Lee Sigelman. "Understanding the Tax Revolt: Eight Explanations." *American Political Science Review* 75 (1981), 963–974.

Lukes, Steven. *Power: A Radical View.* New York: Macmillan, 1974.

Luttbeg, Norman R. "The Structure of Beliefs among Leaders and the Public." *Public Opinion Quarterly* 32 (1968), 398–409.

McAdam, Doug. *Political Process and the Development of Black Insurgency.* Chicago: University of Chicago Press, 1982.

———. "Tactical Innovation and the Pace of Insurgency." *American Sociological Review* 48 (1983), 735–754.

———. *Freedom Summer.* New York: Oxford University Press, 1988.

McCarthy, John D., and Mayer N. Zald. "Resource Mobilization and Social Movements: A Partial Theory." *American Journal of Sociology* 82 (1977), 1112–1141.

McConahay, J. B., and J. C. Hough, Jr. "Symbolic Racism." *Journal of Social Issues* 32 (1976), 23–45.

Macpherson, C. B. *The Political Theory of Possessive Individualism: Hobbes to Locke.* London: Oxford University Press, 1962.

McQueen, William Robert James. "Community Groups in the Eastern Santa Monica Mountains: With Special Reference to the Beverly Glen Residents Association." M.A. thesis, Dept. of Geography, University of California at Los Angeles, 1979.

Maliban, Michael (ed.). *Parties, Interest Groups and Campaign Finance Laws.* Washington, D.C.: American Enterprise Institute, 1980.

Mannheim, Karl. *Ideology and Utopia: An Introduction to the Sociology of Knowledge.* Trans. Louis Wirth and Edward Shils. New York: Harcourt, Brace, and World, 1936.

Markus, Gregory B. "Political Attitudes during an Election Year: A Report on the 1980 NES Panel Study." *American Political Science Review* 76 (1982), 538–560.

Merton, Robert K., Marjorie Fiske, and Patricia L. Kendall. *The Focused Interview: A Manual of Problems and Procedures.* Glencoe, Ill.: The Free Press, 1956.

Messinger, Sheldon L. "Organizational Transformation: A Case Study of a Declining Social Movement." *American Sociological Review* 20 (1955), 3–10.

Michels, Roberto. *Political Parties.* Glencoe, Ill.: Free Press, 1949.

Miller, Steven D. "Contemporary Racial Conflict: The Nature of White Opposition to Mandatory Busing." Ph.D. dissertation, Political Science Department, University of California at Los Angeles, 1981.

Miller, Zane L. *Suburb: Neighborhood and Community in Forest Park, Ohio, 1935–1976.* Knoxville, Tenn.: University of Tennessee Press, 1981.

Mills, C. Wright. *White Collar: The American Middle Classes.* New York: Oxford University Press, 1951.

Mills, C. Wright, and Melville J. Ulmer. "Small Business and Civic Welfare." In *The Structure of Community Power,* ed. Michael Aiken and Paul E. Mott. New York: Random House, 1970.

Molotch, Harvey. *Managed Integration: Dilemmas of Doing Good in the City.* Berkeley, Los Angeles, London: University of California Press, 1972.

———. "The City as a Growth Machine: Toward a Political Economy of Place." *American Journal of Sociology* 82 (1976), 309–332.

———. "Capital and Neighborhood in the United States." *Urban Affairs Quarterly* 14 (1979), 289–312.

Molotch, Harvey, and John Logan. "Tensions in the Growth Machine: Overcoming Resistance to Value-Free Development." *Social Problems* 31 (1984), 483–499.

Mullins, Willard. "On the Concept of Ideology in Political Science." *American Political Science Review* 66 (1972), 498–510.

O'Connor, James. *The Fiscal Crisis of the State.* New York: St. Martin's, 1973.

Oakland, William H. "Proposition 13—Genesis and Consequences." *National Tax Journal* 32 (1979), 387–409.

Oberschall, Anthony. *Social Conflict and Social Movements.* Englewood Cliffs, N.J.: Prentice-Hall, 1973.

———. "Loosely Structured Collective Conflict: A Theory and an Application." In *Research in Social Movements, Conflict and Change* 3 (Greenwich, Conn.: JAI Press, 1980), 45–68.

Olson, Mancur, Jr. *The Logic of Collective Action: Public Goods and the Theory of Groups.* Cambridge: Harvard University Press, 1965.

Orfield, Gary. *Must We Bus? Segregated Schools and National Policy.* Washington, D.C.: Brookings Institution, 1978.

Orloff, Ann Shola, and Theda Skocpol. "Why Not Equal Protection? Explaining the Politics of Public Social Spending in Britain, 1900–1911, and the United States, 1880s–1920." *American Sociological Review* 49 (1984), 726–750.

Paige, Jeffrey M. "Political Orientation and Riot Participation." *American Sociological Review* 36 (1971), 810–820.

Paul, Diane. *The Politics of the Property Tax.* Lexington, Mass.: D. C. Heath, 1975.

Perlman, Janice. "Grassrooting the System." *Social Policy* 7 (1976), 4–20.

Peterson, Paul E. *City Limits.* Chicago: University of Chicago Press, 1981.

Phillips, Kevin. *Post-Conservative America.* New York: Random House, 1982.

Piven, Frances Fox, and Richard A. Cloward. *The New Class War: Reagan's Attack on the Welfare State and Its Consequences.* New York: Pantheon, 1982.

Polanyi Karl. *The Great Transformation.* Boston: Beacon Press, 1944.

Polsby, Nelson W. *Community Power and Political Theory.* New Haven: Yale University Press, 1963.

Popper, Frank. *The Politics of Land Use Reform.* Madison, Wis.: University of Wisconsin Press, 1981.

Public Opinion. "Opinion Roundup." Vol. 1 (1978), 33.

Przeworski, Adam. "Proletariat into a Class: The Process of Class Formation from Karl Kautsky's *The Class Struggle* to Recent Controversies." *Politics and Society* 7 (1977), 343–401.

———. *Capitalism and Social Democracy.* Cambridge: Cambridge University Press, 1985.

Rabushka, Alvin. "Tax and Spending Limits." In *The United States in the 1980s,* ed. Peter Duignan and Alvin Rabushka. Stanford, Calif.: Hoover Institution, 1980.

Rabushka, Alvin, and Pauline Ryan. *The Tax Revolt.* Stanford, Calif.: Hoover Institution, 1982.

Ranney, Austin. "The Year of the Referendum." *Public Opinion* 1 (1978), 26–27.
———. "The Year of the Referendum." *Public Opinion* 5 (1982), 12–13.
Reagan, Ronald. *Ronald Reagan's Weekly Radio Addresses.* Vol. 1, *The First Term.* Wilmington, Del.: Scholarly Resources, 1987.
Rex, John, and Robert Moore. *Race, Community, and Conflict.* London: Oxford University Press, 1967.
Roberts, Paul Craig. *The Supply Side Revolution: An Insider's Account of Policymaking in Washington.* Cambridge, Mass.: Harvard University Press, 1984.
Rogin, Michael. *The Intellectuals and McCarthy: The Radical Specter.* Cambridge: MIT Press, 1967.
Rossiter, Clinton. *Conservatism in America.* New York: Alfred Knopf, 1955.
Salzman, Ed. "Dear Landlord: You Have a Friend in Howard Jarvis." *New West* (February 27, 1978), 68.
Samuelson, Robert J. "Economic Report: Middle-Class Media Myth." *National Journal* 15 (1983), 2673–2678.
Saunders, Peter. *Social Theory and the Urban Question.* London: Hutchinson, 1981.
Schattschneider, E. E. *The Semi-Sovereign People: A Realist's View of Democracy in America.* New York: Holt, Rinehart, and Winston, 1960.
Schiesl, Martin. *The Politics of Efficiency: Municipal Administration and Reform in America, 1880–1920.* Berkeley, Los Angeles, London: University of California Press, 1977.
Schwartz, Barry (ed.). *The Changing Face of the Suburbs.* Chicago: University of Chicago Press, 1976.
Schwartz, Michael. *Radical Protest and Social Structure: The Southern Farmers Alliance and Cotton Tenancy, 1880–1890.* New York: Academic Press, 1976.
Sclar, Elliott, Ted Behr, Raymond Torto, and Maralyn Edid. "Taxes, Taxpayers and Social Change: The Political Economy of the State Sector." *Review of Radical Political Economics* 6 (1974), 134–153.
Scott, James. *The Moral Economy of the Peasant.* New Haven, Conn.: Yale University Press, 1976.
Scott, William B. *In the Pursuit of Happiness: American Conceptions of Property from the Seventeenth to the Twentieth Century.* Bloomington, Ind.: Indiana University Press, 1977.
Sears, David O., and Jack Citrin. *Tax Revolt: Something for Nothing in California.* Cambridge: Harvard University Press, 1982.
Sears, David O., Carl P. Hensler, and Leslie K. Speer. "Whites' Opposition to 'Busing': Self-Interest or Symbolic Politics." *American Political Science Review* 73 (1979), 369–384.
Selznick, Philip. "Foundations of the Theory of Organization." *American Sociological Review* 13 (1948), 25–35.
———. *TVA and the Grass Roots.* New York: Harper and Row, 1965.
Sethi, Parkash S. *Advocacy Advertising and the Large Corporation.* Lexington, Mass.: Lexington Books, 1977.
Silk, Leonard, and David Vogel. *Ethics and Profits: The Crisis of Confidence in American Business.* New York: Simon and Schuster, 1976.

Simon, William. *A Time for Truth.* New York: Reader's Digest Press, 1978.

Stein, Robert M., Kieth E. Hamm, and Patricia K. Freeman. "An Analysis of Support for Tax Limitation Referenda." *Public Choice* 40 (1983), 187–194.

Steinberg, Bruce. "The Mass Market Is Splitting Apart." *Fortune* (November 28, 1983), 76–81.

Stinchombe, Arthur L., and D. Garth Taylor. *On Democracy and School Integration.* New York: Plenum, 1980.

Stockman, David A. *The Triumph of Politics: How the Reagan Revolution Failed.* New York: Harper and Row, 1986.

Suttles, Gerald. *The Social Construction of Communities.* Chicago: University of Chicago Press, 1972.

Thompson, Edward P. *The Making of the English Working Class.* New York: Vintage Books, 1963.

Thompson, Paul. *The Voice of the Past: Oral History.* New York: Oxford University Press, 1978.

Tilly, Charles. *From Mobilization to Revolution.* Reading, Mass.: Addison-Wesley, 1978.

———. *The Contentious French.* Cambridge: Harvard University Press, 1986.

Tipps, Dean C. "California's Great Property Tax Revolt: The Origins and Impact of Proposition 13." Manuscript.

Touraine, Alain. *The Voice and the Eye: An Analysis of Social Movements.* Cambridge: Cambridge University Press, 1981.

Turner, Ralph. "Needed Research in Collective Behavior." *Sociology and Social Research* 42 (1958), 461–465.

———. "The Public Perception of Protest." *American Sociological Review* 34 (1969), 815–831.

Turner, Ralph H., and Lewis M. Killian. *Collective Behavior,* 2d ed. Englewood Cliffs, N.J.: Prentice-Hall, 1972.

U.S. Bureau of the Census. *U.S. Census of the Population, 1950.* Vol. 3. *Census Tract Statistics.* Chap. 28. "Los Angeles, California and Adjacent Area: Selected Population and Housing Characteristics." Washington, D.C.: Government Printing Office, 1952.

———. *U.S. Census of Population and Housing, 1960. Census Tracts. Los Angeles–Long Beach, California Standard Metropolitan Statistical Area.* Washington, D.C.: Government Printing Office, 1962.

———. *1970 Census of Population and Housing. Census Tracts. Los Angeles–Long Beach, California Standard Metropolitan Statistical Area.* Washington, D.C.: Government Printing Office, 1972.

———. *1980 Census of Population. Detailed Population Characteristics, United States Summary.* Sect. A, vol. 1, pt. 1. Washington, D.C.: Government Printing Office, 1982.

———. *1980 Census of Population and Housing. Census Tracts. Boston, Mass. Standard Metropolitan Statistical Area.* Washington, D. C.: Government Printing Office, 1983.

———. *1980 Census of Population and Housing. Census Tracts. Los Angeles–*

Long Beach, California Standard Metropolitan Statistical Area. Washington, D.C.: Government Printing Office, 1983.

——. *County and City Data Book.* Washington, D.C.: Government Printing Office, 1983.

U.S. Congress, Joint Economic Committee. "Fairness and the Reagan Tax Cuts." Washington, D.C.: Government Printing Office, 1984.

Useem, Bert. "Solidarity Model, Breakdown Model, and the Boston Anti-Busing Movement." *American Sociological Review* 45 (1980), 357–369.

Useem, Michael. *The Inner Circle: Large Corporations and the Rise of Business Political Activity in the U.S. and the U.K.* New York: Oxford University Press, 1984.

Veblen, Thorstein. *The Theory of the Leisure Class: An Economic Study of Institutions.* New York: A.M. Kelley, 1899. Boston: Houghton Mifflin, 1973.

Vidich, Arthur J., and Joseph Bensman. *Small Town in Mass Society: Class, Power, and Religion in a Rural Community.* Garden City, N.Y.: Doubleday, 1960.

Vogel, David. "The Power of Business in America: A Re-appraisal." *British Journal of Political Science* 13 (1982), 19–43.

Walton, John. "A Systematic Survey of Community Power Research." In *The Structure of Community Power,* ed. Michael Aiken and Paul E. Mott. New York: Random House, 1970.

Warren, Donald I. *The Radical Center: Middle Americans and the Politics of Alienation.* Notre Dame, Ind.: University of Notre Dame Press, 1976.

Weatherford, M. Stephen. "Popular Participation and Representation in the Urban Environment: The School Desegregation Issue in Los Angeles." *ERIC Reports* ED166267 (1978).

Weber, Max. *From Max Weber: Essays in Sociology.* Trans. Hans Gerth and C. Wright Mills. New York: Oxford University Press, 1958.

Weinstein, James. *The Corporate Ideal in the Liberal State, 1900–1918.* Boston: Beacon Press, 1968.

Wellman, David. *Portraits of White Racism.* Cambridge: Cambridge University Press, 1977.

Whitaker and Baxter (Public Relations and Campaign Management). "A Report, General Election, November 5, 1968." San Francisco: Whitaker and Baxter, 1968.

Wiley, Norbert. "America's Unique Class Politics: The Interplay of the Labor, Credit, and Commodity Markets." *American Sociological Review* 32 (1967), 529–541.

Williams, Oliver P., Harold Herman, Charles Liebman, and Thomas Dye. *Suburban Differences and Metropolitan Policies.* Philadelphia: University of Pennsylvania Press, 1965.

Williams, P. M., and S. J. Reilly. "The 1980 U.S. Election and After." *Political Studies* 30 (1982), 371–392.

Wilson, James Q. *The Amateur Democrat: Club Politics in Three Cities.* Chicago: University of Chicago Press, 1962.

Wirt, Frederick M., Benjamin Walter, Francine F. Rabinovitz, and Deborah R.

Hensler. *On the City's Rim: Politics and Policy in Suburbia.* Lexington, Mass.: D. C. Heath, 1972.

Wirthlin, Richard B. "The Republican Strategy and Its Electoral Consequences." In *Party Coalitions in the 1980s,* ed. Seymour Martin Lipset. San Francisco: Institute for Contemporary Studies, 1981.

Wolfinger, Raymond and Fred I. Greenstein. "The Repeal of Fair Housing in California: An Analysis of Referendum Voting." *American Political Science Review* 52 (1968), 753–769.

Wood, Robert C. *Suburbia: Its People and Their Politics.* Boston: Houghton Mifflin, 1958.

Wright, James D. *The Dissent of the Governed: Alienation and Democracy in America.* New York: Academic Press, 1976.

Yankelovich, Daniel, and Larry Kaagan. "One Year Later: What It Is and What It Isn't." *Social Policy* (May/June 1979), 19–23.

Yates, Douglas. *Neighborhood Democracy.* Lexington, Mass.: D. C. Heath, 1973.

Zald, Mayer N., and Roberta Ash. "Social Movement Organizations, Growth, Decay and Change." *Social Forces* 44 (1966), 327–341.

Zald, Mayer N., and Patricia Denton. "From Evangelism to General Service: On the Transformation of the YMCA." *Administrative Science Quarterly* 8 (1963), 214–234.

Newspapers, Newsletters, Magazines, and Other Popular Serial Publications

Alhambra Post-Advocate, Calif.
The Apartment Owner
Arcadia Tribune, Calif.
Boston Globe
Boston Herald-American
Burbank Daily Review, Calif.
CBS News/*New York Times* Poll
The California Poll, Field Institute, San Francisco
California Real Estate, formerly *California Real Estate Magazine*
Cal-Tax News, newsletter of the California Taxpayers' Association
Chicago Sun-Times
Chicago Tribune
Daily Evening Item, Lynn, Mass.
Dollars and Sense, published by the National Taxpayers Union, Washington, D.C.
Fortune
Glendale News Press, Calif.
The Harris Survey, Tribune Media Services, Inc., Orlando, Fla.
Kansas City Times, Mo.
Long Beach Independent Press-Telegram, Calif.
Los Angeles Mirror News
Los Angeles Times

Los Angeles Times Poll
Nation's Business
New York Times
Pacific Business, California Chamber of Commerce
Palos Verdes Peninsula News, Calif.
Pasadena Star News, Calif.
Pomona Progress Bulletin, Calif.
Public Opinion
Real Estate Today
The Register, Santa Ana, Calif.
San Gabriel Valley Tribune, Calif.
San Pedro News Pilot, Calif.
Santa Monica Evening Outlook, Calif.
Taxachusetts, newsletter of Citizens for Limited Taxation, Mass.
Taxpayer's Watchdog, newsletter published by Don Schauer and later by an
    organization in Van Nuys, Calif., Taxpayer's Watchdog
Time
Torrance Daily Breeze, Calif.
Valley News, Calif. (formerly *Valley News and Green Sheet, The News, Daily
    News,* and *Van Nuys Daily News*)
Washington Star, Washington, D.C.
Washington Times, Washington, D.C.

Index

Designer: U.C. Press Staff
Compositor: Huron Valley Graphics
Text: 10/12 Times Roman
Display: Helvetica
Printer: Haddon Craftsmen
Binder: Haddon Craftsmen